SCi.

11x/11.08/9/11

D0699922

4155

The Southwest Center Series

Ignaz Pfefferkorn, *Sonora: A Description of the Province*

Carl Lumholtz, *New Trails in Mexico*

Buford Pickens, *The Missions of Northern Sonora: A 1935 Field Documentation*

Gary Paul Nabhan, editor, *Counting Sheep: Twenty Ways of Seeing Desert Bighorn*

COUNTING SHEEP

Twenty Ways of
Seeing Desert Bighorn

Edited by GARY PAUL NABHAN

The University of Arizona Press   Tucson & London

The University of Arizona Press
Copyright © 1993
Gary Paul Nabhan
All Rights Reserved

⊛ This book is printed on acid-free, archival-quality paper.
Manufactured in the United States of America

98   97   96   95   94   93   6   5   4   3   2   1

Library of Congress Cataloging-in-Publication Data

Counting sheep : twenty ways of seeing desert bighorn / edited by Gary
  Paul Nabhan.
     p.   cm.—(The Southwest Center series)
    ISBN 0-8165-1385-6 (cl : acid-free).—
    ISBN 0-8165-1398-8 (pb : acid-free)
    1. Bighorn sheep.   2. Bighorn sheep hunting.   3. Bighorn sheep—
Folklore.   1. Nabhan, Gary Paul.   11. Series.
  QL737.U53C685   1993   93-12477
  599.73'58—dc20   CIP

British Cataloguing-in-Publication Data
A catalogue record for this book is available from the British Library.

To six people who have known this desert terrain far better than I ever will: the late O'odham elder José Juan Orosco, a former O'odham resident of Quitobaquito; his recently deceased grandson, Juan Joe Cipriano; their Hia C-eḍ O'odham kinsman Candelaria Orosco; and three Anglos who have taught me just as much about desert life: Bill Broyles, my guide; Caroline Wilson, my ranger sweetheart; and Julian Hayden, our mentor.

CONTENTS

ACKNOWLEDGMENTS

This anthology grew out of a bighorn sheep writing archival project sponsored by the Southwest Center of the University of Arizona. With the support of Joe Wilder and his staff, I was able to archive historic field notes and published essays on Sonoran and Arizona bighorn sheep, as well as to commission new essays by contemporary writers. I am grateful for Joe Wilder's unfailing commitment to promoting interdisciplinary exchanges on Southwestern cultural and natural history. In addition, I have been encouraged and assisted in tracking down materials by Greg McNamee, Amadeo Rea, Ann Zwinger, Bill Broyles, Chris Szuter, Richard Nelson, Ginger Harmon, Neil Carmony, David Brown, Anita Alvarez de Williams, and Eric Mellink. Contributions by Hilah and Norman Simmons, Gayle Jandrey, Gordon Fritz, Amadeo Rea, Ottomar Van Norden, Alfred North, Ben Tinker, and Jack O'Connor are also included in the archival project. David Hancocks, the Arizona–Sonora Desert Museum director, kindly offered me a writer-in-residence position and personal encouragement to complete this project. Finally, I'm grateful to Chris Szuter, Mindy Conner, Stephen Cox, Marie Webner, and Alan Schroder for their care with the manuscript, and Paul Mirocha, Helga Teiwes, and Omega Clay for assistance with graphics.

INTRODUCTION:
Diversity in Desert Wildlife Writing

This book is more than a collection of essays about the bighorn sheep that
live in the desert along the U.S.-Mexico border. It is an attempt to broaden
what the natural history essay can be, for many of the following offerings
build upon but diverge from the narrative journal style and didactic tone
of the early twentieth-century scientist-explorers who searched exotic
lands for wildlife and wisdom. It is also a challenge to our imaginations to
consider what other lives are like—not just those of the creatures referred
to as *Ovis canadensis*,[1] popularly called the desert bighorn or *borrego
cimarrón*—but wild lives wherever they are beyond the human domain.
At the same time this anthology celebrates the diversity of cultural responses to this one animal species in its Sonoran Desert habitat within
two hundred miles of the Colorado River delta.

Most of these responses, however, run counter to the common view of
the "stinking hot desert" as a barren place where humans and other large
mammals such as bighorns lead an impoverished existence, barely eking
out a living. It is our lack of knowledge and imagination, not an absence
of plant foods or animals skilled in finding them, that makes us call such
habitats *deserts*, a term that comes from the Latin *desertus*, meaning "an
abandoned, forsaken wasteland." Dismissing a place as "mere desert" is
like dismissing all other living creatures on this planet as "beasts." Such
labels provide no insight into their true nature; they simply hide what we
don't understand.

"There's a modern myth," wildlife biologist Harley Shaw told a gathering of nature writers recently,[2] ". . . that we know something about animals and how they live. We don't." This concession is particularly humbling because it came from a fine field zoologist at the zenith of his career. The "we" in Harley's statement refers to people like himself who have devoted their careers to understanding a few charismatic species such as bighorn sheep, mountain lions, turkeys, or deer. Yet it might as well refer to all of us, for if we have had the good fortune to know even one other species well—moth, toad, coyote, raven, or Gila monster—how many other vertebrates and invertebrates have we hardly studied, let alone lived with and fully respected? And how much time do we have left to get to know them before they are gone?

We live in an era when wildlife populations are being extirpated through habitat fragmentation, land degradation, and overhunting. As a species, *Ovis canadensis* is not globally endangered, and some studies suggest that the desert bighorn numbers are no longer decreasing in the United States. Nonetheless, local desert sheep populations face a variety of pressures unprecedented in scope, particularly in Mexico. And despite tremendous efforts to protect, reintroduce, and promote wild sheep, there has been "no noteworthy recovery" anywhere, according to eminent wildlife biologist Valerius Geist.[3] "Protection of sheep has been locally in force in the United States since the turn of the century," Geist has observed, "yet only exceptionally have sheep spread from the restricted areas to which they were confined." Why?

Sheep tend to harbor in small patches of rocky but forage-rich habitats, only sporadically crossing the unsuitable stretches of open flats between them.[4] The locations of all suitable patches within the territory of one genetic lineage are culturally transmitted by older ewes to the young ones they lead. Over the centuries it has proved more adaptive for them to maintain a strong fidelity to these places, imprinting their young on familiar ground rather than wasting much time exploring or colonizing areas where they might be at risk over the long run. During the last century, however, as individual habitat patches have become more like relict islands of wildness within a sea of human perturbations, physical barriers have curtailed the chance outmigrations that formerly led to sporadic genetic intermixing of herds or successful colonizations.

Today, many desert bighorn populations are up against the wall; or, as essayist David Quammen has quipped, "It's we who've got nature surrounded. The object-to-ground relations are reversed. Wild landscapes survive only as enclaves in a matrix of human dominion." Quammen fears that pampered, protected animals within these enclaves may become little more than "biological knickknacks, meaningless in their disconnection from context."[5] These concerns are echoed in wildlife biologist Paul Krausman's contribution to this book.

We know that the current rate at which genes, populations, and species are being lost is unprecedented in human history, but what of the concomitant loss of ecological and cultural *context*? We hardly know when we are losing genes or herds for good, let alone the *why, what,* and *where* questions that go with these losses. Too few of us have stepped far enough for long enough beyond the world dominated by human artifice to glimpse the essential contexts of the lives of species wilder than our own.

Before the end of the twentieth century a minimum of twenty-five thousand species—twenty-five thousand distinctive ways of responding to this world—will have been lost without our knowing much of what their lives were like.[6] Thousands more will be "rescued from extinction" and locked away in zoos, greenhouses, and test tubes "until favorable conditions return," if we ever learn what those favorable ecological conditions really were. This book collects memories of what those contexts were and are, and where they may continue to exist; it is an antidote against isolated knowledge.

Our gathered voices also attempt to stave off "the extinction of experience," a term conservation writer Robert Michael Pyle coined for the loss of visceral contact with the *other*—that is, all life beyond our own.[7] What shapes will human dreams take when we have lost touch, when we have lost even the memory of sheep and other big game that have sparked our visions, metaphors, and legends for millennia? If human ecologist Paul Shepard is correct, the loss of biological diversity in our lives stunts and distorts our capacity for thought, speech, vision, and psychological health.[8]

Although most people today neither count nor dream of wild sheep, the naturalists who do may be important to our society, for they do not suffer the stunting and distortion of thought unconnected to the natural order that is the psychological infirmity of our times. Ironically, the very people who have spent the most time tracking and observing bighorn sheep have not been encouraged to tell others about what their senses absorbed and what their hearts felt. For example, most Mexican and Indian inhabitants of isolated mountain ranges where bighorn sheep abound hold their knowledge within their oral traditions; today, those once-verdant traditions appear to be withering from the electronic heat of television, radio, and video.

Field scientists today may spend as much time stalking sheep as hunters and their guides did in yesteryear. They have new tools, new theories, and, sometimes, fascinating new insights into the same bighorn populations that have fascinated human minds for as long as the two species have been in contact with one another. Under the pressure to "publish or perish," the game managers and university-based vertebrate zoologists who know sheep best often have to boil their stories down to "factoids"—technical details devoid of much living context but printable amidst the dreadful prose that dominates most scientific journals. These technical reports may tell us about the quantifiable parts of sheep's diet, behavior, or movement, but where reductionist science still reigns, speaking of the whole is strictly taboo. We seldom ask our finest field scientists what motivates them, what puzzles or gives them pleasure in their work with other organisms; we seldom know whether these same organisms find their way into scientists' dreams.

Peter Steinhart recently complained that "our civilization moves from the experience of wildlife to the measurable to the ownable, and science is the best at this."[9] The animal itself may have dropped out of sight by the time the wildlife technician has his hard-won refereed journal article in hand.

Fortunately, a number of scientific observers of wild sheep have bucked this system and speak or write about bighorn with grace, among them George Schaller, Valerius Geist, Joan Scott, Paul Krausman, Harley Shaw, and David Brown. Scientifically astute sportsmen such as Charles Sheldon, William Hornaday, and Kermit Roosevelt offered lucid and illuminating observations of desert bighorn, yet their writings are sometimes scorned by today's animal rights and anti-hunting activists. Nonetheless, it is hard to deny the contributions these Boone and Crockett Club hunters have made to both the early conservation movement and the historical development of nature writing.[10] Desert literature would be far poorer fare if it lacked what a Charles Sheldon or an Aldo Leopold brought to the table.

Still, the fact remains that the names Charles Sheldon and Aldo Leopold are no more household words in the Southwest than are Gale Monson or Eric Mellink. The so-called popular science writing of our times reaches a relatively small audience of American and Mexican readers, perhaps only two orders of magnitude greater than that reached by the scientists who write exclusively for technical journals. The typical resident of desert bighorn country is no more likely to learn about sheep through the writing of naturalists and scientists than his predecessors were half a century ago.

More likely, the average Arizonan, Sonoran, or Baja Californian recognizes the *borrego cimarrón* only through the contrivances of made-for-television nature films and close-up photos of captive animals published in tourist promotion magazines. The desert bighorn has become an icon of wildness through schmaltzy Southwestern paintings, postcards, and wood carvings made by and sold to people who may never see the animal in the flesh—except, perhaps, in a zoo. Today, more than 58 percent of the *rural* children in the desert borderlands claim that they see more animals through electronic media than through direct experience in their natural habitats.[11] I think it fair to say that their views of mountain sheep and their furry kin are likely to be more distorted now than ever before.[12]

While filmmakers and videographers may err on the side of sound bytes and cameo shots of wildlife, the writers whose words fill pages of nature magazines and natural history books too often fail to offer their audiences fresh perspectives on the richness and complexity of all the worlds larger and smaller than the humanized landscape. Not long ago, acclaimed American novelist Joyce Carol Oates teased her nature-writing colleagues about the redundant themes and styles found within outdoor adventure, science, and wildlife literature: "Nature inspires a painfully limited set of responses in 'nature writers' . . . REVERENCE, AWE, PIETY, MYSTICAL ONE-NESS."[13] If Oates is correct, it is because many nature writers have not taken enough risks with their essays and have not shown how varied our responses to wildlife and habitats can be. Perhaps practitioners of the genre have used formulas, plucked their readers' heartstrings the same way too many times. We need to express that variety of responses, for our capacity to be alert to movement in the larger world is exactly what can keep us from a certain doom.

Naturalists, I insist, can be the antibodies of our society; they can reduce our susceptibility to the ills and indulgences of our own culture and species and help us recognize the *other* in the world. They keep our tendencies toward ethnocentrism and anthropocentrism from becoming all-consuming. Without them, our society would become incapable of reading the signs that we have irreparably damaged our life-support system.

Counting Sheep is a culturing of the natural antibodies needed for survival. It gently refutes Oates's joco-serious claim that nature elicits a limited range of responses and that all nature writers sound the same. Ultimately, it celebrates the diversity of desert beings as well as the diversity of voices within and around us: masculine and feminine; Anglo, Hispanic, Kiliwa, Paipai, Cucapá, Quechan, Chemehuevi, and O'odham.

This also a test, an experiment. Put a number of nature writers in the same unrelenting stretch of Sonoran Desert, between the Sierra Juárez in Baja California and Pusch Ridge above Tucson, from the volcanic Pinacate shield on the south to scenic Gila Bend on the north. Tell them to focus their attention on just one animal—wild sheep—and have them write about it. Write about bighorns, regardless of whether it is the animal in the flesh or in the form of droppings, tracks, and broken-open barrel cactus. Write from makeshift blinds, where sensory deprivation and heat exhaustion are bound to set in quickly during June. Or write from behind a gun barrel. Write down a fragment from a Kiliwa Indian origin story and use a sheep bone burned in an ancient campfire as a writing instrument. Write while walking across the Cabeza Prieta at night, or while flying over it trying to radio-collar the elusive horned rascals. Write from within a bombing range, without permission, counting jets as well as sheep. Write what the editors of the *Journal of Wildlife Management* won't accept because it is too specific, too political, too poetic, too sensual, or too rich and complex.

Instead of a limited set of responses, this one species living in a small patch of desert will elicit a panoply of insights too diverse to summarize here. The stinking hot desert experience will boil out of these nature writers any superficial similarities to one another. It will distill each individual's distinctive response to the world, to wildness. It will expose each person's raw nerve endings, the peculiar wiring of each. Ultimately, each of us has a distinctive visceral response to nature because each of us embodies a different package of DNA and is shaped by the various environments through which he or she has roamed.

Our goal is simply to demonstrate that historic and contemporary nature writers can delight all of us by the varied ways in which they practice their craft. There are many approaches to combining the two cultures of humanistic art and technical science into a seamless view of culture and nature interacting—humans and sheep encountering one another. The result may take the form of beautifully detailed notes from a scientist who has fallen into "the naturalist's trance" that sociobiologist E. O. Wilson so aptly described.[14] Or it may sound like a story shaped by a novelist, an ethnographic sketch roughed out by an anthropologist, or a quirky feature forged by a gonzo journalist. The writers whose essays are included here have been trained in zoology, botany, cultural anthropology, American history, linguistics, Western literature, geology, arid lands geography, art history, and ethnobiology.

In another sense, this collection of essays is more than a mere hybrid of C. B. Snow's *two* cultures of techno-oriented sciences and the human-oriented arts; it is on the verge of being fully *multicultural:* Hispanic, Kiliwa, O'odham, and Cucapá views are being added to a genre historically and presently dominated by male Anglo-Americans. Terry Tempest Williams and Ann Haymond Zwinger provide strong contrast to the male voices; compare, for example, the essays of Zwinger and Charles Bowden, both derived from sheep counts in the same week, just a few miles away from one another.

There are crumblings and fractures in the notions that nature can be objectively known by what was assumed to be a value-free science, that a well-trained scholar could write an objective history of human interactions with bighorn sheep that would make a collection such as this obsolete. Such an ethnocentric view of science has given rise to a Western scientific monoculture that is driving into extinction other, equally valid, ways of knowing the natural world. Instead, it may be preferable to acknowledge and celebrate each cultural filter that gives us a different perspective on "what nature is." We can only try to plumb the depth and diversity of human responses to a charismatic animal in its desert home, an environment to which individuals have gone for centuries to seek spiritual inspiration as much as or more than caloric sustenance.

The allowance of such pluralism in views of nature reflects a major paradigm shift in environmentalist literature and philosophy. We can no longer seek to preserve biological diversity unless we respect the myriad cultural approaches that may all make important contributions toward this end. Nearly a decade ago, ethnographic literature underwent a similar paradigm shift, after acknowledging its own crisis in representing other cultures. Ethnographers realized that most anthropological writing said more about the cultural biases of the observer than it did about the lives of the cultural communities and individuals being observed. In a parallel way, nature writers have come to agree with anthropologists George Marcus and Michael Fischer that they have not always been able "to ask the right questions, let alone provide the answers, about the variety of local responses to the operation of global systems. . . . Older dominant frameworks are not so much denied—there being nothing so grand to replace them—as suspended. Ours is once again a period rich in experimentation and risk-taking."[15]

I hope that readers will be able to sense this increasing tendency toward risk taking as they follow the trajectory in the literature about desert bighorns from the turn of the century to the present. At the same time, all of us wish to pay our respects and debts to earlier nature writers who shaped our tradition, however much in flux that tradition is at present. We use the Anglo-American nature-writing genre as our point of departure for parts unknown, but we hope to stand on the shoulders, not in the faces, of those who went before us. If we affect our contemporaries as much as or more than the Roosevelts and Sheldons and Hornadays affected theirs, then those of us known as contemporary nature writers will be all the more gratified.

This anthology is organized, first, to remember the ancient traditions that preceded this Anglo-American genre; then to honor some early practitioners of the classic English nature-writing tradition. Following these glimpses at historic interactions with bighorn sheep, the essays demonstrate the range of responses one can take to counting sheep (most often, in blinds near water holes). Finally, the remaining essays place bighorns in the context of the larger world, a landscape forever changed. Our desire, ultimately, is to change the way you, the reader, imagine your relationship to bighorn sheep and to other wild organisms, wherever they may be.

Gary Paul Nabhan

NOTES

1. For a modern treatment of bighorn biology, including subspecific taxonomy, see G. Monson and L. Summer, eds., *The Desert Bighorn Sheep: Its Life History, Ecology and Management* (Tucson: University of Arizona Press, 1980). Except for Eric Mellink's essay, we will be exclusively discussing *Ovis canadensis mexicana*.

2. The quotes from Harley Shaw and Peter Steinhart are from "Writing Ecology in Different Genres," a panel discussion at a writers' retreat I organized in February 1992 through Arizona State University's Creative Writing Program. Many of the topics elaborated in this introduction are addressed in abbreviated form in my summary of the issues discussed at that retreat, "Representing the Lives of Plants and Animals," *Wild Earth* (Spring 1992): 2–3.

3. Valerius Geist discusses the limited successes of sheep recovery efforts in *Mountain Sheep: A Study in Behavior and Evolution* (Chicago: University of Chicago Press, 1971). This view of bighorns' tight allegiance to place has not been challenged so much as put into a broader perspective by V. C. Bleich, J. D. Wehausen, and S. A. Holl, in "Desert-dwelling Mountain Sheep: Conservation Implications of a Naturally Fragmented Distribution," *Conservation Biology* 4 (December 1990): 383–94; see also H. E. McCutchen, "Desert Bighorn Zoogeography and Adaptation in Relation to Historic Land Use," *Wildlife Society Bulletin* 9 (1981): 171–79.

4. David Ehrenfeld, a leading conservation biologist, discusses the implication of Geist's conclusions in an essay titled "Changing the Way We Farm," first published in *Orion* and recently included in a collection of Ehrenfeld's essays, *Beginning Again: People and Nature in the New Millennium* (New York: Oxford University Press, 1993).

5. David Quammen discusses endangered species locked up in refuges in his essay "A Future as Big as Indonesia," *Left Bank* 2 (Summer 1992): 54–60.

6. Two-time Pulitzer Prize winner Edward O. Wilson discusses current

rates of extinction in *The Diversity of Life* (Cambridge, Mass.: The Belknap Press of Harvard University Press, 1992).

7. Robert Michael Pyle's essay, "Intimate Relations and the Extinction of Experience," is also featured in the special "Extinctions" issue of *Left Bank* 2 (Summer 1992): 61–69.

8. On animals and human psychological health, see Paul Shepard, *Thinking Animals: Animals and the Development of Human Intelligence* (New York: Viking, 1978), and Shepard, *Nature and Madness* (San Francisco: Sierra Club Books, 1982).

9. Steinhart is quoted from comments made during a February 1992 panel discussion (see n. 2 above); see also his "Dreaming Elands," in *The Norton Book of Nature Writing,* ed. R. Finch and J. Elder, 811–16 (New York: W. W. Norton, 1990).

10. For a history of Boone and Crockett Club conservationists see J. F. Reiger, *American Sportsmen and the Origins of Conservation* (Norman: University of Oklahoma Press, 1986).

11. The survey of fifty-two rural desert children is discussed by G. P. Nabhan and S. St. Antoine in "The Loss of Floral and Faunal Story, the Extinction of Experience: Ethnobiological Perspectives on Biophilia," in *Testing the Biophilia Hypothesis,* ed. S. Kellert, B. Dean, and E. O. Wilson (Washington, D.C.: Island Press, 1993).

12. On the distortions of wildlife in the media, see Peter Steinhart's essay "Electronic Intimacies," *Audubon* (1991): 10–13.

13. Joyce Carol Oates wrote "Against Nature" for *Antaeus;* it is included in *On Nature: Nature, Landscape, and Natural History,* ed. D. Halpern, 36–43 (San Francisco: North Point Press, 1987).

14. The naturalist's trance is described in E. O. Wilson, *Biophilia* (Cambridge, Mass.: Harvard University Press, 1984).

15. George Marcus and Michael M. J. Fischer are quoted from their chapter "A Crisis of Representation in the Human Sciences," from their book *Anthropology as Cultural Critique: An Experimental Moment in the Human Sciences* (Chicago: University of Chicago Press, 1986): 7–16.

Remembering Traditions

Being Glimpses at Cultural Connections with Wild Sheep
That Predate the Arrival of Europeans in the Desert

A clay figurine of a bighorn sculpted by Salvador Magaña of Tecate, Baja California Norte, 1991. (Purchased by Anita Alvarez de Williams from the artist; in possession of Gary Paul Nabhan; photograph courtesy of the Arizona State Museum, University of Arizona, Helga Teiwes, photographer)

O'odham Bighorn Sheep Songs

Danny Lopez is a Tohono O'odham teacher, poet, singer, and folklorist who has been involved in the expression of O'odham traditions through a variety of communications media: oral performance, the written word, radio, video, and television. A native of Ge Oidag (Big Fields) village, Mr. Lopez has been both a classroom instructor and a curriculum materials specialist in bilingual cultural education for communities on the Tohono O'odham Reservation. Yet his work does not stop when the school bell rings, for he has also been involved in assisting the Wa:k Desert Indian Dancers, a youth group that performs traditional O'odham dances and songs; in serving as a master of ceremonies for the Waila Festival, an annual celebration of chicken-scratch music at the Arizona Historical Society; and in announcing on "Desert Voices," a weekend radio program on KUAT-AM that is presented in both English and O'odham.

Although Danny has recorded folk stories and sung traditional songs of the O'odham for years, his involvement in composing songs, poems, and stories has flourished since the early 1980s. Around that time, songs began to come to him in the traditional way—through dreams—and two of the resulting mountain songs are included in *When It Rains/Mat Hekid O Ju* (Tucson: Sun Tracks/University of Arizona Press, 1982), a volume of Papago and Pima poetry edited by Ofelia Zepeda. Danny shared these songs and others in a performance at the University of Arizona in 1992 as part of the highly acclaimed Poetics and Politics series of Native American writers.

With respect to written contributions, Lopez was the project director and writer for *Tohono O'odham: History of the Desert People* (Salt Lake City: University of Utah Printing Services, 1985), a tribal history compilation supported by the National Endowment for the Humanities. This primer—which is intended for O'odham readers themselves—draws on oral and documentary histories as well as information from traditional calendar sticks, a mnemonic device for recalling key climatic, social, and political events for each past year. Lopez also recorded O'odham folklore about ocotillo for a beautiful poster exhibit designed by Paul Mirocha, *Singing Down Roots: Plant Folklore of the Desert Southwest* (Tucson: University of Arizona, Office of Arid Lands Studies, 1991). Other readers have learned of his life through an inspiring essay called "Danny," written by his longtime friend Bernard Fontana and included in *Of Earth and Little Rain* (Northland Press, 1981; reprint, University of Arizona Press, 1990), which Fontana wrote in a collaboration with John Schaefer.

The contribution presented here reminds us that oral traditions remain alive and well in many rural communities, where stories and songs of notable places, hunting trips, pilgrimages, floods, and droughts continue to enrich daily exchanges between neighbors. The songs and commentary Danny selected are derived from his own creative efforts and from the reminiscences of his mother-in-law, Frances Manuel, and his mother, Clara Lopez. They demonstrate that the richness of O'odham oral tradition extends well beyond the creation stories, coyote parables, and ceremonial orations that have already been recorded in various forms. It is clear that O'odham traditions retain considerable knowledge about the desert and its creatures on both sides of the U.S.-Mexico border.

Introductory Remarks by Frances Manuel,
as Told to Danny Lopez

There was a man who was my grandfather. He was a half brother to my real grandfather. His name was Gewṣp Wonomim,[1] and he was my *wosk*.[2]

I remember him as a very old man. My "ka:k,"[3] or grandmother, would sometimes tell me, "Take some food to your other grandparents."

4

I would go to their home and give them the food. Gewṣp Wonomim was a very, very old man.

He used to be a hunter; he used to hunt with the bow and arrow. I heard that a long time ago he went to hunt at Babad.[4] Some place up there he shot a mountain sheep and it fell over a cliff. The cliff was very steep and difficult to climb down. He could not go down there to get the mountain sheep, so he left without getting it.

The next year, he went to hunt up there again. I guess he climbed a different way, and he went to the place where he thought the mountain sheep fell down. Somehow he found the place. He saw the bones, and his arrow was stuck in the bones. He saw that the ground was greasy from the fat of the mountain sheep.

I guess later on he dreamt about this song. This song is about that place that is in the dark mountain shadow. It tells about the animal fat and how it spreads on the ground when the sun is hot.

Gewṣp Wonomim was a song dreamer, and he had songs about many things.

Bighorn Song of Gewṣp Wonomim

Babad nowan kukuk abo cukam kakakoli wipisim-he
Kun heg yeda k-am wa:ki, gi:gi k-abo yaki meheda
S-abai kukun abo gi:gi wakumai na wewece-he
Yahaneke yane ṣ-abo yakimehe-da

Frog Mountain cliff bottom, the dark shadow remains
I walk into the mountain shadow, the mountain sheep's fat begins to run
There the rotting fat lies, oozing
The warm fat begins to run down

As remembered by Frances Manuel
San Pedro village
January 17, 1993

Introductory Remarks by Danny Lopez

This song did not come overnight; it took me a while. I had to focus in
on the bighorn and look a lot at the mountain (Giho Du'ag, behind Big
Fields). The English is a loose translation. I have taped the song so that
the O'odham kids can hear it in the future.

Bighorn Song of Danny Lopez

Ceşoñ, ceşoñ, ceşoñ, ceşoñ
Ga hu Giho Nowan t-abai ce:şañ-me
Taşai yoidam tatai ceşañ-me-he
Gan hu Giho Nowan naman yoi-me c an ki:hi-me

Mountain sheep, mountain sheep
Up Burden Basket Mountain you climb
All day long you climb the rocks
From rock to rock you jump
On top of Burden Basket Mountain you wander
Burden Basket is your mountain

Danny Lopez
Big Fields village
January 18, 1993

NOTES

 1. "Gewş" means "to place a rock on top of something so it will not
blow away." "Whomim" means "hat." This was the name of the hunter
and song dreamer.

 2. "Wosk" is the term for a paternal grandfather.

 3. "Ka:k" is the term for a paternal grandmother.

 4. Babad Du'ag means Frog Mountain. This mountain is now called
Mount Lemmon.

When the Spring of Animal Dreams Run Dry...

My interest in the relationship between desert bighorn sheep and cultures of the prehistoric and historic Southwest was kindled by discussions in the mid-1970s with two ethnozoologists, Amadeo Rea and Gordon Fritz, whose research had uncovered an extremely curious relationship between large ungulates and the O'odham communities of early historic times. Fritz in particular believed that the large piles of sheep horns that had been found historically near O'odham villages near the Gila River indicate "a gap" in that area's settlement following a late prehistoric collapse of the Hohokam villages. When the Akimel O'odham (River Pima) resettled that area, his theory suggests, they quickly decimated the sheep populations that had multiplied in the temporary absence of human predation.

Fritz was one of many who believed that after the Hohokam collapse, a different people took control of the Gila, Salt, and Santa Cruz river valleys—the Pima Indians, who are there today. This issue of the Hohokam-Pima continuum remains hotly debated between and among archaeologists, historians, and repatriation activists—and will not be settled here. However, I soon realized that scientists still hadn't learned much more from O'odham elders regarding their knowledge of sheep. A few years after my discussions with Rea and Fritz, my interest in sheep was rekindled by an O'odham friend. Hia C-eḍ O'odham (Sand Papago) program assistant Juan Joe Cipriano invited me to submit to his office the locations of hunting and gathering sites used by the O'odham beyond their reservations, in preparation of future land claims cases. Since it was

7

still possible to learn from O'odham elders who lived off-reservation where certain sheep-hunting and plant pit-roasting sites were situated, I began to comb historic references for place-names to correlate with their extant knowledge. Along with a young Pima scholar, Culver Cassa, and two ethnobiologists, Frances Fellows and Wendy Hodgson, I began to interview elderly O'odham about their remembrances of places that they once frequented for bighorn and other food resources. This information was summarized on behalf of the Hia C-eḍ O'odham Program before the Tohono O'odham Tribal Council in 1989, and parts of it have been published with O'odham activists Mike Flores and Fernando Valentin in the *Cultural Survival Quarterly* (Spring 1990).

Although I remain ignorant of the spiritual relationship between the O'odham and bighorn sheep, this essay establishes that a unique ecological relationship existed between the historic O'odham and bighorn herds resident in their territory, a relationship that lasted hundreds if not thousands of years. It is my hope that this legacy will be taken into account in future discussions of the O'odham people's access to public lands in the United States. This essay was inspired by the work of my good friend Richard Nelson, whose essay "The Embrace of Names" (*Northern Lights,* Summer 1992) recounts his efforts to use place-names for hunting and gathering sites as a means to legally establish Inupiaq and Koyukon people's tenure on their historic homelands.

Where could I go to find ancient bonds between cultures and creatures, connections somehow firmer and stronger than the fragile web entwining the aspects of my own individual life? After two decades of following the "environmental movement," I had come to doubt that any single generation's feeling for wildlife is enough—enough to save species, to keep their archetypes alive in our minds—if there is not enough cultural continuity to extend such concerns into future generations. This doubt had sent me out searching for cultural connections with animals that reached back before "wildlife conservation" became a distinct profession, a concern separate from simply living well with others in the world. It was then that

I began to stumble upon desert Indians who shared a peculiar tradition about bighorn sheep; they began to teach me something I could not learn from zoology texts, computerized data banks, or game management agency files.

Here, and nowhere else in the world, people ritually cremated the bones of their largest prey: bighorn sheep, pronghorn antelope, and other large game. Here, in some of the driest reaches of the Sonoran Desert, hunters stacked sheep horns higher than the treetops and kept the bones of freshly killed animals beyond their village boundaries. It was as if the spirit of wildness had to be kept outside the confines of domestic life to keep either from becoming endangered.

Suddenly I glimpsed an underground aquifer of uncharted waters. Despite my training as a biologist, I was unsure that I could fathom another, more ancient, way of seeing, dreaming about, and hunting the wild sheep known as *cimarrón* in the desert borderlands between the United States and Mexico. Nevertheless, I began to recognize a sensibility among my O'odham Indian neighbors that had none of the superficial zeal of born-again wildlife protectionists. For an untold number of generations, bighorns had embodied *wildness* for O'odham dwellers of the Sonoran Desert, and that is what made me look into these waters: the chance of glimpsing how an oral tradition expressed relationship with *wildness*, the likes of which we may never know in the same way again. Although I could never be immersed in their cultural way of seeing and dreaming bighorns—just as I could never see the world as a bighorn sees it—I could at least recognize the existence of a world beyond my vision. As I tried to peer beneath the surface, however, I was just as likely to see my own reflection—my cultural biases—as I was to glimpse the lives within that other realm.

"Ṣa: p u-wua?" I asked, peeking around a wall of dried organ-pipe cactus ribs and cracking mud. I had heard someone working around the corner, in the dooryard garden of cactus, aloes, and canna lilies. It was a young woman, O'odham Indian and Mexican by descent, washing clothes over a scrubbing board perched on wooden legs.

"Estoy lavando la ropa, pues," the young woman responded, drying her hands and holding one out to me for a brief, limp handshake. She understood some of the Piman language and was amused that I was using it. Still, she would not speak it herself, at least not beyond her familiars.

"No ki: Don Lu:siano?"

"Si, Luciano está en la casa. Pásale, señor."

"S-ape. Muchas gracias."

We did not go into the house, but rather through the yard to the porch. It was actually a *ramada,* or brush-covered shade structure, which extended the living area out from the enclosed rooms. There, Luciano Noriega sat in a chair, looking out over the desert, drinking his coffee. He and I spoke awhile in a mixture of Spanish and O'odham, catching up. We had known each other for about eleven years.

Our conversation wandered on familiar paths. At one point, however, as we discussed the animals that had been drinking at the lagoon a few hundred feet away, I asked him if the *cimarrón* (sheep) ever come in during the dry months. Before Luciano could answer, one of his nephews working in the yard cut in: "There are perhaps some in the mountains nearby, but if the cimarrón ever came down across the road, they would either be run over or shot before they arrived here."

Luciano was silent for a moment longer, whistling quietly to himself. Then, in a barely audible voice, the old man added, half smiling, half grimacing, "They're far from us now."

After that the conversation trailed away, so my friends and I ambled over to take a look at the *laguna* of Quitovac. What I gazed at was only a ghost of what I had first seen at this spring-fed lagoon fourteen years ago, but still, the specter is a sight worth beholding. Quitovac sits in the midst of the hellaciously hot desert plain, the only perennial body of water for twenty-five miles in any direction. Located where artesian flows well up along a fault line, Quitovac has served as magnet for wildlife and human cultures for thousands of years.

Together with other biologists from the United States and Mexico, I had spent years tallying up the number of species found among its wildflowers and its feathered and furred creatures.[1] We had surprised the scientific community by confirming that despite centuries of human "disturbance," Quitovac stands as one of the most biologically diverse localities anywhere in the deserts of North America. It has faced eight thousand summers of hot weather, mineralized waters, and long spans of drought, but still it flourishes with an abundance of plants and animals. Bighorn and other large game may have come to its springs less frequently after the arrival of humans and, later, livestock and firearms, but the life at Quitovac has remained rich.

However, a mess of well-meaning Mexican government programs arrived in the 1980s to "develop and improve" the local economy. Quitovac was suddenly shorn clean of four hundred acres of ancient cactus and ironwood forest, cut short as a hairy kid arriving for duty in boot camp. Bulldozers and graders demolished the old houses on the mesa overlooking the lagoon. By *old* houses, I mean some that had been standing since last century, and all were made from limestone slabs containing bones of now-extinct creatures which had lived and died in the marshland there during the Ice Age. I walked among bulldozed windrows of limestone rubble like so many graves in a military cemetery.

A D-10 caterpillar had even started to rip out all the tules and bushes in and around the lagoon. Someone had the notion that if the pond was deepened, it could hold some big fish, so they drained the pond down to the slow trickle of seven tiny springs. But before they could dredge out all the marshy growth to make way for exotic fish transplants, the D-10 bogged down. The bulldozer nearly buried itself, another giant body stuck in the muck of the Quitovac lagoon.

The following year, when the masked dancers of a summertime ceremony came around to bless all the homes in the village—to offer them good harvests and rains but to protect them from floods—a dancer paused near the edge of the empty lagoon and inspected the rubble. He hesitated, then showered blessings on the ruins, giving them their last rites.

But the economic development never materialized; the equipment needed to turn the acres of bulldozed cactus forest into irrigated alfalfa did not arrive. The Quitovac locals who had acquiesced to the government's grand scheme found their agricultural acreage reduced, not increased. Fortunately, they did not end up pumping away all the artesian flows that had served their ancestors at the oasis for centuries. Luciano could still gravity-feed water into his traditional field, but it now stood next to four hundred acres of scarred land and tumbleweeds too exposed for wild sheep to venture across, even when potable water beckoned to them on the other side.

It struck me as ironic that economic "development" had clearly diminished the local capacity for growth—plant, human, or otherwise. The oldest ways of farming in the desert were being ravaged by the same forces that were breaking our oldest bonds with wild creatures. Why were both wildness and ancient culture so vulnerable?

I shook my head sadly as we walked around the degraded lagoon. With every step, one of us would notice where lime-laden bone fragments had surfaced from the earth, reminders that a rich Pleistocene megafauna must have congregated in the marshlands here for tens of thousands of years. Teeth, ribs, and jaws of extinct fauna often appear in the Quitovac ditches, exposed wherever there has been water movement or a little digging.

It is no surprise that these fossils have fueled the imaginations of the O'odham—that these bones have become familiars in their dreams. They have often told the story of the Ne:big, an enormous creature that emerged from the lagoon,[2] to their children, and to visitors as well, several of whom have recorded the story on paper. The Ne:big's breath was a strong, wild wind, and when it inhaled, the Ne:big created a vacuum. People from a long way off would be sucked into its mouth and swallowed. Although the heart of the animal was slashed and its mouth was finally closed, old-timers still wonder during thunderstorms if the Ne:big is making the lightning strike.

I recalled the time nearly a decade ago when Luciano surprised me by showing me the remains of the Ne:big, which he had sequestered in a place where mischievous kids and casual visitors were unlikely to find them. He unwrapped a protective cloth and showed me the stuff from which legends are made. If I were a paleontologist, I might have examined those bones to discern what species they represented. But I had no professional inclination toward such a pursuit. They could have been from an animal unknown to Western science; they could just as easily been from Ice Age mammoths or last century's bighorn sheep. All I was sure of was that they were sacred and belonged with the O'odham, where I hoped they would stay.

As I listened to Luciano that day in 1981, I was not so impressed by the bones themselves as by the flesh that Luciano's story wrapped around them. For, as he talked in his softspoken Spanish spiced with O'odham, the mythic animal came alive. He was restoring animal stories to their central place in what it means to be human. He was letting some creatures run wild again in our dreams.

Now, long after my first view of the fossils, I had been walking around one of the springs, one of the places where skeletal fragments of mythic monsters well up out of the underlying aquifer. I took a quick side glance at the spot where the bubbles emerged from the limey mud. I couldn't bring myself to gaze directly at this *nacimiento del agua,* this birthing ground of water. It would be too much like watching a stranger in the throes of spouting forth a delicate new life. I had to turn aside.

I could not get it out of my head that even the smallest spring in the desert is something divinely precious. These springwaters are brewed with the tusks, horns, and bones of ancient wild animals. When I drink from them, or winnow out a few bone fragments from their mud, I am constantly reconnected to an animal past. Or at least that connection is constant as long as the artesian water flows. A center-pivot irrigation system cannot spray out animal dreams.

Fifty miles due west of Quitovac, center-pivot sprinklers and bighorn poachers have had brief careers near the edge of the Pinacate volcanic shield. From Pinacate and Carnegie peaks, wild sheep could have seen the spray of water rise into the air and evaporate before hitting the talclike soils in the valley below. It is the Rio Sonoyta valley, and the twin *ejido* (public land) collectives where poachers and pivoters enter the Pinacate Protected Zone are called Ejido Nayarit and Ejido El Pinacate. There, for a period that lasted barely four years, the Mexican government grubstaked the farmers in their attempts to grow 120 acres of alfalfa and ryegrass to feed 370 calves. If well nourished over the winter, the calves could have been sent off to feedlots for the final fattening—and a good price. It looked pretty good on paper.

At present, it does not look pretty at all. The Rio Sonoyta valley grows more tumbleweeds than salable goods, and the only signs of cows are the dried pies they left behind. Some of the farmers, with their fields fallowed, have turned to guiding bighorn poachers into the Pinacate, but the law has caught up with their hunting just as "real world" economics caught up with their farming.

When the federal discount on electrical pumps short-circuited, the ejidos could no longer afford to keep a diesel pump running at the pace required to irrigate the ryegrass on demand. Although they irrigated as little as twice a month during the winter, they had to keep the sprinklers on a nonstop cycle during the hotter part of the year. The movable fountain would take a day and a half to make a complete loop around the acreage, then would begin again.

But something had been left out of the circle. The "experts" had not factored in the heat, the wind, the blowing sand—the very kinds of wildness you cannot spray, blade, bulldoze, or breed out of a desert. Regardless of how much irrigation water spewed out of an eight-inch pipe protruding from the ground, the crops looked awfully stressed. The aerial sprinkling of this forage—in the midst of black lava cinder plains and shining dunes—no doubt faced the most aggravated rates of evaporation of any farmland in North America. Send a blistering wind across barren rock and sand for twenty-five miles, have it hit a wicklike patch of irrigated grass or beans, and you have what meteorologists call "the clothesline effect." With about three-fifths of an inch of water being lost per hour from each square inch of leaf surface during much of the warm season, moisture loss from the Pinacate forage patch likely exceeded all values ever reported in the literature from mainstream agricultural areas.[3]

I once visited the Pinacate with the Argentine ecologist Exequial Escurra, now director of a Mexican environmental protection program and always a master at making quick calculations on napkins.[4] "Hijo de la *!?!?*," Exequial exclaimed, borrowing a curse from his Mexican colleagues and smacking his forehead with his hand. I looked at the numbers at the bottom of the napkin. For the ejidatarios, a one-pound steak from Pinacate beeves cost 2,500 to 3,500 gallons of pumped groundwater to produce.

A desert-dwelling ram is lucky if even once during his lifetime he finds a *tinaja* (water catchment) in the bedrock holding a full 2,500 gallons of water! Desert bighorn have been known to endure droughts in areas where no surface water is discernible, but the ejidatarios, after mainlining groundwater for several years, couldn't break their addiction overnight. After a few years of astronomical pumping costs, the collective decided to dismantle the pipes of its center-pivot system; they sit, slowly being buried by sand, like so many bones left out in the sun to dry.

Most of the ejidatarios packed up and left before they were reduced to mere bones themselves.

I have seen animal bones in the Pinacate that were not bleached by the sun but scorched by fire. They had been exposed to high temperatures in a white-hot blaze of specially selected ironwood trunks. Perhaps leaking grease had scorched some of them, for a few of the vertebrae were blackened on one end. The rest looked ghostly white, cemented together by the lime that had leached from the bones themselves. These are called *calcined* bones, and heaps of them abound on the Pinacate lava shield, adjacent dunes, and nearby Cabeza Prieta range. They are most frequently found at old campsites close to tinajas that bighorn hunters have used for as long as this land has been inhabited. And yet, these skeletons are heaped up apart from the multipurpose hearths and roasting pits found at the same campsites. It is as if someone turned away from the feast and moved over to another spot to burn the leftovers from the main course.

Blanched or charred portions of sheep, pronghorn, white-tailed deer, and mule deer skeletons have been found together in the same heaps. (All are considered kinds of deer in O'odham folk taxonomy.) Not far from Tinaja del Cuervo in the Pinacate, one mound of cremated bones approaches the size of a shrine. In fact, it *is* a shrine.

Julian Hayden first heard of such cremations years ago when he was working with Milton Wetherill at the Anasazi cliff dwelling of Kiet Siel.[5] Wetherill had once labored down on the Mexican border, at Rancho de la Osa on the edge of Papaguería. There, he had been told of Indians far to the west who "had the curious custom of cremating the bones of animals killed for food." Such a practice was not known for any Native American culture at that time.

That casual comment somehow lodged itself deep within Hayden's head, to surface again when he began to see calcined bone piles for himself in the Pinacate twenty-five years later. Was this an ancient but obsolete occurrence, Hayden wondered, or a practice that had somehow persisted into modern times?

Few people have known the Pinacate even half as well as Hayden, but one of them, Ronald Ives, gave him a clue. While visiting the Quitobaquito oasis on the Mexican border, Ives noticed that José Juan Orosco, an O'odham elder—medicine man, hunter, and venerable survivor of the Pinacate band of Sand People—was tossing bones into the campfire, bones removed from a recently butchered and eaten bighorn. Ives asked him why he was doing that.

"Sheep bones are burned by the old ones. . . . It's to quiet the spirits of the dead animals," he answered. "It's so they will not alarm the sheep still living in the area," he added, watching the bones heat up over the ironwood coal and the smoke rise away from the fire.[6]

Ives had stumbled upon the ancient connection, still alive in one man's practice.

José Juan Orosco died and was buried at Quitobaquito in 1945, but a great-grandson kept up the family connections to that place. Until his death in 1991, Juan Joe Cipriano lived over at Ge Wo'o—the Big Water Hole. Occasionally, he drove around the Ajo Mountains to Quitobaquito to collect medicinal plants, a tradition of gathering that was permitted only if Juan Joe first touched base with the U.S. Park Service, because that oasis is now part of Organ Pipe Cactus National Monument.

I first met Juan Joe when he tracked me down in Papago Park, on the rough edge of Phoenix. We talked over a heap of Mexican food and became friends. We saw each other now and then, at his home or down at the oasis. I felt comfortable that first day asking him to teach me about bighorn hunting, but I tried to avoid asking Juan Joe anything about cremations—my interest was not archaeology or theology but biology. Just to be clear, I posed one question to guide us away from any potentially sensitive matters.

"Anything special about hunting bighorn? If there is any tradition that is best kept secret, I'll understand . . ."

"No," Juan Joe answered matter-of-factly. "Nothing special I remember." I breathed a sigh of relief. "Well," he continued, "I guess they were hunted in special places. Like the *cecpo*—what do you call them, tinajas? Or sometimes the people would look for them in caves."

The idea of particular places for stalking bighorns was in synch with what hunting guide turned game warden Ben Tinker observed in the Pinacate on his visits there between 1919 and 1926. He had come upon O'odham families who slept in volcanic caves while tracking bighorn sheep around the craters of the Pinacate. Tinker claimed that "bands of mountain sheep descended into their depths by narrow trails. The hunters sent their squaws down to drive the sheep up while they blocked the trails' entrance and killed the frightened sheep with spears, arrows, and ironwood clubs."[7]

I asked Juan Joe if he himself ever sees this animal that his people call *ceṣoñ*.

"They stay up in the mountains now, seems like even more than before."

"Before?"

"I haven't seen them lately. Of course, being on kidney dialysis three times a week, I don't get up into the mountains much at all. But when I was growing up at Darby Well, I would see them. When I was a boy, they would come down from the Ajo Mountains sometimes."

"Are they still hunted in the traditional way?"

"Not much hunting nowadays. Except when they go to get deer for the *keihina*, a traditional dance. If they can't get deer, they hunt javelina for it."

"Do they still butcher and divide the game according to custom?"

"When an animal is killed, the hunters still give parts of it to relatives and neighbors. You can eat it right away or make jerky out of it. You know, bighorn tastes different than cow. Then, in the old days, I guess they used the bones to make tools, or maybe bows or arrows."

"Did they use the horns, the *a'ag*, for anything?" I wondered.

Juan Joe paused and thought for a moment. "Sometimes when they would bring back the a'ag, they would hang them up, outside, over a ramada. Sometimes they had to use them to help bring the rains."

I didn't know what he meant. He tried to explain.

"Well, José Juan, maybe he was the last one to know how to do this. It was after a long time with no rains. Nothing else they had done did any good. So he went to this hill near where we were living." (José Juan was said to divide his time between Quitobaquito Springs and an *ak-ciñ* flood-water field in the present-day Cabeza Prieta Wildlife Refuge. I wondered if he was at the very hill where historian Bernard Fontana found calcined sheep bones years ago.)[8]

"What did he do?" I asked.

"Well, he poured water into the sheep horns that he had turned upside down. He did some kind of dance, singing. Then he spilled the water from the horns onto the ground."

"Because the rains hadn't come for a long time?"

"José Juan was the last I ever heard of who knew how to do this."

It saddened me to think of José Juan's passing, but not long after the conversation about the old man, Juan Joe followed him. Juan Joe Cipriano died of medical complications related to kidney failure and his longer suffering from diabetes. I felt as though he would be the last O'odham I would ever speak with who had glimpsed this bighorn tradition.

José Juan may have been the last O'odham who knew how to perform that particular rite, but remnants of other old customs are still practiced by Tohono O'odham bighorn hunters. I came across a man who practiced some of these customs himself, long after I had given up thinking that I would find anyone who knew them as anything but distant memory. I was driving out of Why, Arizona, one morning at dawn when a stocky man in a baseball cap popped up out of the weeds on the side of the road and stuck out his thumb. I pulled over, and he came running up to the car. Panting, he got in.

"My car broke down between here and Gila Bend last night. I got Esker there in Ajo to go and get it with his tow truck. Meantime, while he's fixing it, I gotta get home. So I tried to get a ride last night but nobody came around. So I just slept over there away from the road a ways."

I glanced at him. Other than a little grass chaff sticking to his shirt and jeans, you could hardly tell he had been out all night. No blanket, sleeping bag, or heavy clothes. This guy must be hardy if he can camp impromptu at the end of winter without voicing complaints, I thought.

"Where you going?"

"Over there, on the other side of those hills," and he nodded toward the northeast side of the Ajo Mountains, on the reservation. "You know, just before the last rains, I saw a herd of sheep over in those hills. They had been coming down from the Ajo Mountains, I guess."

"So they still come down into the desert on that side? They don't stay up high all the time?"

"No, they come down to the hills. Yeah, I got me a ram."

"You did?"

"A bull ram. He was a big one. You know, they find little cubbies, wherever they go in the rocks, but when they see something they don't know, they come out to be sure what they're seeing." He turned to me, adding, "Do you understand? He had to be sure about what he was seeing, so that gave me plenty of time to get in a good position."

"Oh, maybe he was the one that is like a sentry in the army . . ." The man looked to be over fifty; maybe he had done some time in military service. "You know, that ram could have been their lookout."

"Yeah, I think so. They do that. So I shot him and then had to get some friends to help me haul him out, because I couldn't get my pickup that close to those hills. We butchered him out there."

"When you do the butchering, do you take everything back to the village with you?"

"No, you have to leave those ram horns out, away from the houses for three or four weeks. Then, after that, you can claim them as your own. Even then, you have to put them up high on the ramada, I guess, so that the spirits can bless them there."

We were approaching his turnoff, where I was going the other way. "*Sap cugik api*? What's your name? I didn't even ask you who you are and where you come from."

"They call me Woodpecker. Just ask down this road, they all know where I live. Looks like you have to go someplace now, but come around sometime if you're interested in hunting. There are a lot of things you have to do if you are a hunter. Like there is this one kind of deer. After you kill it, you aren't allowed to touch it. Then it's up to the medicine man, not you. So I have to know things like that. Anyway, if you hunt, maybe we can talk sometime. Take it easy."

He hopped out and started walking down the road. I took it easy until I got to the reservation's edge. There, I noticed a barn owl caught in a barbwire fence, leg muscles shredded, unable to fly. Out of the corner of my eye I saw a coyote running in for the kill. I drove on toward the Gila River, but my mind was not easy all the rest of that day.

"The horns of the mountain sheep were never brought home by hunters," Akimel O'odham chief Antonio Azul told Frank Russell at the beginning of the century, when Russell spent many months working among the Piman settlements along the Gila River.[9] "Each man had a place set apart where he deposited them in order that they might exert no evil influence upon the winds or rains."

The more southerly O'odham also associate violent winds with large game animals, just as they do with the Ne:big. One man told me matter-of-factly, "Yes, when you kill a *ceşoñ* or a *koji* [javelina], it brings winds. Not whirlwinds, like the *sivuloki*, but regular winds."

The association between wind and sheep has persisted among the Akimel O'odham even though they seldom hunt sheep anymore. When I first climbed the Sierra Estrella with zoologist Amadeo Rea in 1975, sheep were still marginally present there, but only one traditional sheep hunter remained among the Piman villages at the base of the sierra. Nevertheless, elderly Pimas cautioned Amadeo that the hide and horns of the *ceṣoñ* "must be kept in a safe, respected place, as an insult would result in either violent wind or rain."

That safe place—like the ones where Luciano harbored the bones of the Ne:big—could be either somewhere in the house or in an undisturbed place outside. On occasion, the bones would be brought forth for special uses. The late Joseph Giff told Amadeo of one such time when a bighorn hide was enlisted by the Pimas for its power. "Old Tasquinth had a hide. Don't think he killed it. He was never a hunter."[10]

Giff continued relating Tasquinth's experience: "Someone needed to winnow their thrashed wheat but there was no wind at all, and he was waiting. Was afraid the rain would come and ruin the grain. . . . [So this man], he went to Tasquinth, who took out the hide and asked him which way he wanted the wind to blow from." Joe explained, "We wouldn't want the chaff to blow on our house."

"Tasquinth took the hide in that direction and tapped it gently. He said, 'This man wants some wind. Will you give him some wind from this direction?'"

Joe stopped for a moment, remembering the wind. "It came." Then he turned to Amadeo and added, "No one has hides anymore."

Today, the mountain ranges within walking distance of the Pima villages hold few sheep, and those that occasionally descend from the heights are met by myriad treacheries: barbwire fences, superhighways, irrigated fields, and retirement subdivisions. Three centuries ago, when Captain Juan Mateo Manje made his second visit to the Akimel O'odham along the Gila, there were enough sheep within reach that the entire human population of Tusonimoo village was out hunting them and gathering mescal.[11] The village name itself, Ceṣoñ Mo'o in modern O'odham, means "bighorn sheep heads."

Two years earlier, Manje had learned that the village was named "for its grand accumulation of horns of wild sheep in the shape of a hill; and for their abundance there, enough to provide for sustenance; and additionally, because the hill itself towers high above the roofs of their low-lying houses. It seems that it consists of more than one hundred thousand horns."

That number is astonishing, for it exceeds by an order of magnitude the highest estimate of sheep living in Arizona in any given year. Although some scholars doubt Manje's estimate, his journals show him to be a consistently accurate measurer of mileage and village population sizes. Even if one assumes that the pile had accumulated over decades or even centuries, the sight of so many horns of an elusive animal, all concentrated in one place, would be no less awesome.

The cimarrón must have nourished the historic O'odham to a degree impossible to imagine occurring today anywhere within the range of desert bighorn. Of course, sheep habitat then was not the ragtag fragments of former range that it is today. O'odham land uses did not alter cimarrón country on anywhere near the scale that modern farming, ranching, and urban sprawl have affected it.

The hundred thousand horn cores stacked at Tusonimoo were not the only piles within Pimería Alta. In 1774, Juan Bautista de Anza encountered an O'odham camp near the present-day Cabeza Prieta Tanks, where such a pile persisted until the early 1960s, when it was burned by a white man. Anza claimed that O'odham hunters had been very careful to preserve the horns of the cesoin. They carried them intact to a place near the tinajas, where they were piled "to prevent the Air from leaving the place." Other horns, since vandalized, were in a rock shelter not far from the water holes.[12]

Additional piles are known from the Tohono O'odham Reservation, where cowboys on roundup sporadically stumble upon them and wonder about their origins. In 1960, Gerald Duncan encountered mounds while monitoring the impact of bighorn hunting on and to the west of the "Sells" reservation: "Mounds of desert bighorn horns seen in the vicinity of waterholes attest to the fact that these Indians were very active in killing sheep for food and other uses. These mounds of horns have been seen in the vicinity of the tanks in the Cabeza Prieta, Tule and Granite Mountains. . . . The horns were placed in this particular manner as part of a ritual."[13]

Whether or not Duncan had firsthand knowledge of bighorn rituals, he clearly established that the horn piles that Anza and Manje saw were not isolated occurrences: find an ancient water hole and look for calcined bighorn bones within a few hundred yards of it. Some of these places are the same spots where the O'odham historically hunted, as indicated by arrowheads made of broken glass and awls of cut iron nails found with the heaps of bone. But how far back in time do such traditions reach? How deep is the bighorn connection?

Fastimes. Water World. These do not sound like places you would go to learn about bighorns and human antiquity in the desert. They are, in fact, places where the Bureau of Reclamation has constructed aqueducts that carry water from the distant Colorado River to help farmers who have already squandered the aquifers beneath their farms. During their efforts to keep the desert blooming and nearby cities booming, the bureau is obligated to let archaeologists survey, and in some cases excavate, cultural materials that might be obliterated by federal works. Folks like William Gillespie and Christine Rose Szuter sort bones from these salvages, identify them, and figure out how people butchered the beasts. They also interpret the value of animals to earlier cultures, in exercises Szuter calls "the whys and how-comes of zooarchaeology."

Among the animal bones from Hohokam homes that migrate onto a zooarchaeologist's desk, bighorn, pronghorn, and deer appear now and then. At Water World, twenty big mandibles were found on floors and in pits near cremations. Fastimes yielded another seventeen mandibles. The deer antlers and sheep horn cores found at these Hohokam sites are racks that trophy hunters would give their eyeteeth for, exceeding in size the largest recorded modern specimens from the state.[14]

Szuter, an old friend of mine, is particularly curious about the condition and placement of bighorn, pronghorn, and deer remains salvaged from Hohokam sites. Nearly half the bones show signs of having been burnt, a proportion far higher than that of charred rabbit bones. In addition bighorn were much more likely to have their bones reworked into tools and ornaments than were rabbits or birds.

Sheep remains have been discovered in special wall niches or in corners of pit houses with other objects of ceremonial import: decorated pottery from Chihuahua, large cardium shells from the Sea of Cortez, rectangular pumice stones from Lord knows where.

"The bones of bighorn sheep are just burnt most of the time," Chris explained. "But some are grouped with bones of pronghorn or deer. It seems that the hunters were taking special care with bighorn cranial elements, keeping them in pit houses that are somehow different from all the other pit houses in the village. I've wondered if they were hanging up the horns for ceremonies . . . or safekeeping them to use later, to attract living animals as part of the hunt."[15]

Like most careful scientists, Chris notices when her comments start to slide over into speculation. She cautioned herself, and me. "Of course, not *all* bighorn bones are found in special places. Sometimes there is a scatter of fragments. I've probably looked at reports from all Hohokam sites where animals have been found, and big game animals have not even been recovered from the majority of them."

I reminded her of the words she wrote several years before, when she said that among the Hohokam, "exploitation of artiodactyls, from the hunt through the disposal of bones, is imbued with ritual."

"Chris," I asked, "do you still sense that the use of bighorn by the Hohokam was wrapped in ritual connections?"

"Yes. Yes. I would stick by that."

"How long does that go back?"

"Perhaps into the Pioneer Period." That's the period of Hohokam cultural emergence in southern Arizona that extended up to A.D. 800. It may have begun not long after the birth of Jesus in Bethlehem, in a desert half the world away. But Chris has also found that Hohokam animal remains from the Pioneer Period look more like those of the earlier Archaic, and less like those of the later Classic and Colonial periods of Hohokam civilization.

I thought this over. Subsistence during those earlier times depended more on gleaning wild desert resources and less on the weeds and animal visitors to the irrigated fields surrounding big Hohokam villages. In this regard their lifestyle was more like that of the wayfaring bands out beyond the Hohokam frontier, in the Pinacate and Cabeza Prieta. Not surprising: that's where the bighorn sheep rites may have persisted the longest.

Julian Hayden reckons that sheep cremations began as early as the first Amargosan Period during Archaic times, perhaps three thousand years ago. He sees a relationship between the "bighorn sheep cult" of the Hohokams and the stockpiling of horns by the historic O'odham, but he has never been too sure about how long this deep connection between desert bighorn and people lasted. The last big heaps of cremated sheep bones he has come across are those at Sunset Camp, abandoned by 1851.

Camps abandoned, wells gone dry, tinajas drained or spoiled by livestock. Sheep populations corraled into smaller and smaller areas, where they are more vulnerable to birth defects rising out of shallow gene pools, or to decimation by exotic diseases. And seasonally migratory bands of desert people being corraled as well, told to stay put on reservations or being enslaved to cotton farmers. What is being lost is not merely water under the bridge; it is not simply a chunk of desert nature. This is not, necessarily, only the waning of native culture.

No, what is being lost is a certain capacity for a long, deep relationship between wild animals and cultural traditions.

Desert bighorns, although no longer abundant, are not truly endangered as a subspecies. O'odham culture, although it has suffered innumerable insults since the arrival of Europeans in the Sonoran Desert, has not reached a vanishing point. As Daniel Janzen has observed, "What escapes the eye . . . is a much more insidious kind of extinction: the extinction of ecological interactions."

I am concerned about active engagement between a people and another species—the ability of a collective imagination to run wild beyond the confines of its own settlements and constructs. I am wondering about a native artist's propensity to dream of sheep and to take the image wired inside him toward some outward expression—pottery design, petroglyph, dance. Yes, I am even talking about sheep sensing some familiar people waiting near the water hole or crater rim—the same recognition of risk they might feel if their range overlapped with that of a puma or a wolf.

I am worried that wild sheep may slip out of sight, then mind, then dreams—not only among desert people but among all people. I am worried that if we do not have their nature before us as a standard of what wildness can be, we ourselves will be more easily domesticated to the point of no return.

The O'odham language still has embedded in it this notion of wildness as the prototype of health. Their term for a wild animal is *doajkam,* "one who is untamed, unbroken." Their terms for health are *doa,* "to be healthy, well"; and *doaj,* "to heal, cure, or recover"; for one filled with wholeness and life: *doakam,* as in *S-doakam 'o 'uuv,* "It smells of being alive."

I have smelled that fragrance, seen the movement of *something that is alive,* no more than two hundred yards from where I live in Organ Pipe Cactus National Monument: a young ram rushing over a volcanic ridge. I have seen mountain sheep climbing what looked like a sheer cliff face above Hohokam ruins near New River, Arizona. I have waited days for them to come to tinajas in the Cabeza Prieta, and I was once close enough to feel the tension in their haunches owing to my presence. I have waited other times to no avail, learning to respect the fact that their wildness determines that they will behave in ways oblivious to my mind's predictions.

But all my searchings for sheep, all their momentary appearances in my dreams, are like so many brief showers in a desert land where the aquifer has already been mined. The showers are refreshing, and they will help desert life today, replenishing what is at the surface. The deeper problem—the depletion of fossil groundwater set down during the Ice Age but unlikely to regain its former levels over the next hundred human lifetimes—is not even temporarily relieved. You and I—or dozens of well-meaning Bighorn Sheep Council volunteers, wildlife photographers, or New Age wilderness worshipers—may offer our meager gestures of respect toward the cimarrón, but these do not guarantee that a critical mass of our cultural descendants will follow with similar gestures. We are losing a deep cultural connection to wild sheep, and to wildness itself. Both will need more than our appreciation if we are ever to bring them back.

NOTES

1. G. P. Nabhan et al., "Papago Influences on Habitat and Biotic Diversity: Quitovac Oasis Ethnoecology," *Journal of Ethnobiology* 2 (Fall 1982): 124–43.

2. R. L. Ives, "The Monster of Quitovac," *Masterkey* 15 (1941): 196–98; and D. Saxton and L. Saxton, *O'othham Hoho'ok A'agatha: Legend and Lore of the Papago and Pima Indians* (Tucson: University of Arizona Press, 1973), 305.

3. C. H. M. Van Bavel et al., "Transpiration by Sudangrass as an Externally Controlled Process," *Science* 141 (1963): 269–70.

4. Dr. Exequial Escurra, personal communication in the Sierra Pinacate, 1983, and in Ciudad Victoria, Tamaulipas, 1989.

5. J. Hayden, "Food Cremation Animals of the Sierra Pinacate, Sonora," *Kiva* 50 (1985): 237–48.

6. J. Hayden et al., "On Sheep Cremations and Massacres," in this volume.

7. B. Tinker, *Mexican Wilderness and Wildlife* (Austin: University of Texas Press, 1978), 38.

8. B. Fontana, *An Archaeological Survey of the Cabeza Prieta Game Range* (Tucson: University of Arizona/Arizona State Museum, 1965).

9. F. Russell, *The Pima Indians* (Tucson: University of Arizona Press, 1975).

10. Joseph Giff, quoted in A. Rea, "Pima Indian Animal Foods" (Unpublished manuscript, University of Arizona, Department of Ecology and Evolutionary Biology, 1976).

11. Juan Mateo Manje, quoted in E. J. Burrus, *Kino and Manje, Explorers of Sonora and Arizona, Their Vision of the Future: A Study of Their Expeditions and Plans* (Rome: Jesuit Historical Institute, 1971), 348.

12. Regarding de Anza's comments, see H. E. Bolton, *Anza's California Expeditions* (Berkeley: University of California Press, 1930), 2:30; and Fontana, *Archaeological Survey.*

13. G. Duncan, "Human Encroachment on Desert Bighorn Habitat," *Transactions of the Desert Bighorn Sheep Council* (1960): 35; see also D. E. Brown, "The Status of Desert Bighorn Sheep on the Papago Indian Reservation," *Transactions of the Desert Bighorn Sheep Council* (1972): 30–35.

14. See discussions of faunal analyses by Gillespie, Szuter, and others in C. R. Szuter, *Hunting by Prehistoric Horticulturists in the American Southwest* (New York: Garland, 1991).

15. Personal communication from Szuter, University of Arizona, summer 1991.

On Sheep Cremations and Massacres

Julian Hayden is the foremost cultural historian and field archaeologist for the region covered by this anthology, but he is more than that. For the last several decades he has served as mentor and guide to the Sierra Pinacate for several of the authors whose works are included here, and to numerous others, inspiring them to consider a view of desert history much larger and richer than that which they might have come to on their own. It is clear to all who have spent time with him that he not only loves the desert but also knows it well from firsthand experience, extensive interviewing, and reading. His worldview is based on careful observations of archaeology, geology, cultural ritual, and individual human behavior. He forces others to know "what is in the field" before they elaborate heady but superficial theories about cultural origins and dispersals in the Sonoran Desert.

Born in Montana in 1911 and raised in Riverside, California, Julian was well versed in the fields of archaeology and geology while still quite young, thanks to his Harvard-trained father, Irwin Hayden, and family friends such as M. R. Harrington. He first came to Arizona in 1929, and by 1934 he had begun to make contributions to the archaeology of the Sonoran Desert. His work carried him from caves in Nevada and along the California coast to Kiet Siel, Snaketown, Pueblo Grande, University Ruins near Tucson, Ventana Cave, and, finally, to the Sierra Pinacate—a six-hundred-square-mile region that has consumed his interests for more than four decades. His pioneering and often controversial archaeological analyses have appeared in *American Antiquity, Kiva,* and other technical journals. He received the Arizona Archaeology Council's Award for Public-Spirited Archaeology in 1987 and was honored by Friends of Pronatura in 1992.

His reputation as an archaeologist has perhaps overshadowed his talent as a folklorist, cultural historian, and storyteller. Nevertheless, his transcription of the Pima creation epic and his firsthand account of the Viigita ceremony—both recorded before World War II—contain detail and color perhaps no longer found among all extant O'odham versions of these traditions. His nontechnical writings have not gone unnoticed, however; they have engendered nearly a cult following among aficionados of the Sierra Pinacate. "Talking with Animals: Pinacate Reminiscences" was first published in 1986 in the now-defunct *City* magazine, and then again in 1987 in the *Journal of the Southwest*, and it has been read numerous times around campfires in the Pinacate. Some of his fans erroneously assume that Hayden's attempts at nontechnical writing emerged rather late in his career. Quite the contrary; by 1942 he was writing of his adventures with O'odham scholar Juan Xavier and ethnographer Gwyneth Harrington while traveling among the Seri Indians (in *Arizona Highways*), and he contributed two fine essays to Marc and Marnie Gaede's *Camera, Spade, and Pen* (University of Arizona Press, 1980).

The following excerpt of a longer interview addresses many of the issues dealt with by Hayden in more detail in a 1985 article in *Kiva,* "Food Animal Cremations of the Sierra Pinacate, Sonora, Mexico." In that article he provided the first substantive description of a ritual cremation tradition unique to the region. Here, we catch both aspects of this man's unique talent: precise field scientist and great oral storyteller. In this anthology Hayden is our bridge between the great oral historians of the Pinacate— José Juan, Alberto Celaya, Jeff Milton, Pete Brady, and Tom Childs—and its new literati, including Charles Bowden and William Hartmann.

Gary Nabhan is interviewing Julian Hayden, assisted by Bill Broyles, who is also taping Hayden as part of a larger biographical project. Also present are ethnographer Anita Williams and ranger-interpreter Caroline Wilson.

We sit at Julian's kitchen table, in the house where he has lived since the 1940s, surrounded by his pet lizards, night-blooming cereus, mesquites, and memories.

Williams   Julian, do you want some hot tea to get you through this? [laughing].

Hayden   It won't do anything good [looking pained, shaking his head]. No thanks . . . it wouldn't help, even if *you* made it [chuckling].

Nabhan   Julian, we are interested in two stories that you have told in different ways over the years. Maybe if you can connect those two stories in a new way, all our questions might be worth your time. One is the story of bighorn sheep cremations. How long did it take you to put them into the context you see them in today? The second story is that of the relationship between the historic horn piles in Papaguería and the prehistoric sheep cremations. Are they related? How do you see them elucidating the presumed Hohokam-O'odham continuum, if such a continuum existed? In other words, were sheep cremated and horns piled up by the same people prehistorically and historically?

Hayden   Well, let's begin this way. When I first went into Pinacate with Paul Ezell in 1958, why, I noticed, and so did he, these heaps of burned bone. We speculated on them a little but didn't think all that much about them at first. But as I began to work down there more, I found them everywhere, usually at some distance from water holes. Then I remembered Milton Wetherill, because many years before, perhaps twenty-five years before, he had told me about cremations of game by Mexican Indians. Somehow the image of cremations hung up in a crevice of my brain, and so I revived it. I asked Don Alberto Celaya of Sonoyta about this practice, and he wasn't impressed that I was onto anything new. He said, as I recall, "Why, yes." But the geographer Ronald Ives is the one who really settled it when he told me about talking with Juan Orosco. Was that his name?

Nabhan   José Juan Orosco? The O'odham resident of Quitobaquito, mentioned by Lumholtz, Ives, and others? Yes.

Hayden   Yes. José Juan Orosco, the old man whom Ives knew in the
1930s. José Juan told Ives about burning these bones after
game had been eaten. After they had cooked the animal and
had eaten it, they took some of the bones and cremated them.
Put them in a hot fire until they cooked down, burnt way down.
That ritual pacified the spirits of the dead so that they wouldn't
interfere with hunting. That made a lot of sense. I've heard
that among Papago too [those who call themselves Tohono
O'odham and Hia C-eḍ O'odham today].

So I got to wondering about the identity of the bones. I collected some of them and I took them over to Vance Haynes, and
he took them to Don Gray. He was a bone man. He did a very
thorough analysis of the content of several of these piles of
charred bones. I had sampled many of them, scores of charred
bone fragments by that time. Gray went through most of them
to identify species, and George Lammers identified others.
Most of the bones were from sites that no longer exist as a
result of cattle trampling, winds, and those great *tormentas*
that we've had over the years. Hurricane Katrina, you know,
and others like her, did tremendous damage; important stuff
washed away.

Well, anyhow, I was collecting all the information I could
on everything, with the help of various specialists. In addition
to the bones, well, I was interested in Amargosans, because I
had it in my head that Ventana Cave, after the Altithermal,
was occupied by the Amargosan culture. There wasn't any
doubt in my mind. Emil Haury wanted to make them Cochise
culture, but they were all the same as far as I was concerned. I
had seen a linkage in Pinacate, with the cultural remains on
desert pavements and in other extremely arid sites.

I got to wondering about these bones, how old they were. So
I analyzed two of them that had been found side by side, with
a trail running between them, nearly identical piles. They had
roughly the same composition, including both sheep and either
antelope or whitetail; that was it. Deer—yes. I had them dated
here at the University of Arizona radiocarbon dating lab, but
they wouldn't charge me in advance because they thought that

they wouldn't get a date that would be satisfactory. As the story goes, one of the dates ran around the present time, and the other ran fifty years in the future! [We all chuckle.] Contamination from the Russians' atomic bomb in 1956. So that killed that!

So then I started looking for potsherds and whatever else I could find to date them by association. I did find good, datable material at Papago Tanks and in its tributary arroyo. I found the same mix of bones—big game and jackrabbits—at Sunset Camp, which was a camp way down in the Pinacate's southwest corner where the lava and the dunes come together. Below Chivos Tank. You've never been there?

Nabhan   No, not within a few miles, at least.

Hayden   Oh, you've got to go someday. It apparently was abandoned, perhaps as late as 1851, when the yellow fever came and the Papago left and went north. But there are dug-out windbreaks on top of this arc of lava. There are a number of bone heaps in the area, and they're the ones that contain jackrabbit and fox and badger, as well as bighorn sheep. Which makes me guess that possibly from around 1700 or so, sheep became a little scarce.

Nabhan   Now, how about the ranges of the large ungulates. Do you have any sense if they changed through time? Was there a time when the cremations were exclusively for bighorn or another large ungulate, while at other times this cremation custom was extended to all animals that they hunted? Or is it too hard to tell?

Hayden   Well, you have the dating problem again. The ones that were a half a mile or so from Chivos Tank at an extinct water hole there were on a flat that was densely occupied from 750 A.D. to 1100 or so by Pinacateño O'odham in a cultural continuum. For dates, I'm going by the pottery chronologies that have been worked out. But there were animal cremations right in the village there. And one of these contained Yuman red-on-buff pottery sherds that were trade items.

We know that the cremations at Sunset Camp lasted up until historic times because I've found European-introduced materials. I don't see any reason to doubt that they were still cremating animals at the time of abandonment. We have glass arrowheads and an old harmonica and God knows what mixed in with the cremations found here and there. It all ties in with what José Juan told Ronald Ives. And yet, other than the brief comments by Wetherill and Ives, I can't find anything about any other indigenous tradition of cremating the bones of animals which provided food.

Nabhan   There are no other ritual cremations anywhere in North America?

Hayden   Not that I have found in my limited research, no.

Nabhan   That seems curious in the sense that other native peoples were diligently working to mediate the spirits of the game that they hunted. Yet the situation in the Pinacate really points to a unique relationship between these people and . . .

Hayden   And the bighorn.

Nabhan   So the calcined bone piles are unique for all of North America? They occur in a very limited area?

Hayden   Yes, a very limited area. Other archaeologists occasionally report burned bones, but not the ritually placed heaps. Elsewhere, burnt bones were just scattered over the terrain or around the campfire.

Williams   Just casual burning but not big ceremonial heaps?

Hayden   That's right. Perhaps the tradition north of the Pinacate was more casual. I once noticed Juan Xavier, an O'odham man who camped with a friend at Ventana Cave when I worked there. They had a *ramada* [shelter] down below the cave. They ate a javelina and deer and so forth, but nearly always threw at least the ribs into the fire, which calcined the bones. But then they threw them away. It seemed so perfectly natural, to strip the meat off and just toss the bones into the fire. I think that's what the situation was in the Cabeza Prieta historically. I have no knowledge of bone heaps in the Cabeza.

Nabhan   So the cremation heaps occur from the Sonoyta River on the north, down toward the Sea of Cortez coast?

Hayden	Yes, I would say so. I don't know how far toward the coast it goes.
Nabhan	Bill, have you seen anything in Cabeza Prieta Wildlife Refuge like what you've seen with Julian in Pinacate?
Broyles	I would have to confirm what Julian says about the bone heaps. There are a number of places that have calcined bones of wild animals in the Cabeza Prieta. But they're not in heaps. They're not in piles. They're not as distinct as the piles of sheep horns, for instance.
Nabhan	Is there any direct connection between the sheep horn piles recorded historically and the cremations that you know of? We know from De Anza and two or three other historic accounts that there were the huge piles of horns in southern Arizona during Jesuit times. I am curious about whether you have ever visited any of the horn piles.
Hayden	Only at Cabeza Prieta Tanks, where I saw that one with Norm Simmons. The pile which somebody had burned. There were sheep horns piled in the mountain by the tanks. I've seen them a number of places. I had a photograph of one. And I've seen horns and skulls at other water holes. But from the state of weathering, it was probably Sand Papago, well within the continuum from prehistoric to contemporary peoples. Certainly they were piled up in the last couple of hundred years.
Nabhan	The interesting thing to me about the horn piles is the concurrence with these accounts from Antonio Azul, the historic Pima leader, that his people would not bring a bighorn carcass back into their camp, for it would cause *tormentas* and storms.
Hayden	They would only butcher it outside the village.
Broyles	Julian, the places you say these bones have been found are places where sheep still live. For instance, there are still sheep down low in the lava west of the Ives Flow. And, of course, at the other *tinajas* [water catchments] you are talking about, you can always find sheep signs, scat, beds, and tracks.
Nabhan	What do you all think of the comment often found in technical sheep literature that bighorn were everywhere prehistorically,

even in the valleys and plains. They were not limited to the mountains where we find them today.

Hayden   I've heard that story and read it. I suspect there is something to it, but I don't know.

Nabhan   Bill, do you have anything to say about that?

Broyles   Well, some of the sheep experts say that the sheep are basically a prairie or flatland animal to begin with. It was human encroachment, pressure from settlers, that pushed it up in the hills. I've heard this.

Hayden   That's what I've heard, too.

Broyles   Well, another thing is that with bighorn sheep, they will frequently range miles out from the mountains when the seasonal vegetation production is good. And then you have the question that biologists are asking today: How far do sheep migrate between mountain ranges? They have to eat on the way, obviously.

Nabhan   Several zoologists from Southern California have just done a real nice map of all the sheep migration routes between the small mountain ranges, west of the Colorado River. Bleich, Wehausen, and Hull just published a paper in *Conservation Biology* saying that they think that migrations occur an order of magnitude more frequently than suspected in the past. Each range's population is not an isolated gene pool. Bighorn are getting back and forth, visiting and exchanging genes, or whatever they do at parties. Each little population that we normally think of as an island is getting some gene flow into it, some washing of new blood into it. That makes sense.

Hayden   Sure it does.

Nabhan   Have you seen sheep in relatively the same abundance in your thirty-some years over the Pinacate?

Hayden   I've only seen sheep once in Pinacate. Bill Robinson and I were sitting on a flow that comes down toward Phillips Butte from Sykes Crater. We were camped there for a time. While sitting there, we looked up and saw a ewe with a yearling ram coming down, crossing over, headed for the water hole. They obviously hadn't drunk for a number of days, for they were abso-

34

lute skin and bone. You couldn't see how they could even walk. They were dirty, you know, and tattered. They didn't pay any attention to us; they were headed for water. Fairly close. They are the only sheep I've seen. And I've only seen three or four deer. Never seen javelina. Heard them, but I've never seen them.

Nabhan   Were there many Anglo hunters going into the Pinacate when you first started to go in? Have you seen evidence of much sheep hunting over the years, legal or otherwise?

Hayden   Yes. I did not see this myself, but Don Alberto Celaya told me that in 1945 or 1946 a lieutenant colonel from Davis-Monthan Air Force Base went over to the Pinacate, hired a guide, who took him to the rim of Crater Elegante. The colonel sat there and shot at twenty-six sheep and dropped them all. He left them there, too. Celaya and others, Quiroz and Grijalva, knew about it. They all knew about it. They were outraged, of course.

And now and then, of course, in what they called the Gunnery Range during the war, they used to go down there and poach sheep and antelope. That's to be expected from the military. And that's about all I know about that. . . . Except for my friend Lew Walker's tale about a ranch on the far side of the Baja California. Walker, you know, walked all over Baja California. . . . He was coming north after a disaster of some sort when he fell in on the west coast at a bay where there was a ranch. This ranch was at the foot of an arroyo, a steep arroyo, and had been there for two hundred years. The ranching family had never moved out of there. They were all interbred by the time Walker showed up. But they had sustainably harvested one band of sheep for two centuries without diminishing its numbers. The band lived up in the rocks above them. And they had never told anybody about it. The only reason we know about it now was that some American sportsmen came down in a boat, got the family's males so drunk that some of the ranch boys showed them where the sheep were. The Americans proceeded to shoot them all. So now the ranchers have no meat.

Nabhan   Well, there is Western history collapsed into a three-minute story.

Hayden   Bill, you look like you've heard that story. Where did you hear it?

Broyles   From you.

Hayden   Then it must be true! [Laughter from all.]

Translated by MAURICIO MIXCO

 # Kiliwa Mountain Sheep Traditions

Mauricio J. Mixco has worked, on and off, for the last three decades to analyze the grammar and interpret the oral traditions of the Kiliwa Indians of Baja California. He has also faithfully rendered Kiliwa oral texts into English. Not since Perevil Meigs undertook field ethnographic research among the Kiliwas in the 1930s has any scholar devoted so much attention to these people and their culture, which are sometimes overlooked or dismissed as "extinct." Mixco has collected and translated directly from the Kiliwa language some of the same myth fragments originally told to Meigs in Spanish. Born in El Salvador and raised in the San Francisco Bay area, Professor Mixco obtained both his B.A. and Ph.D. degrees in linguistics at the University of California at Berkeley. Mixco's monographic *Kiliwa Texts* was published as University of Utah Press Anthropological Paper no. 107 in 1983. This publication demonstrates both a linguist's care for technical accuracy in translation and a mythologist's fascination with primordial themes in folk literature.

The stories presented here from *Kiliwa Texts* are the only extant versions of what were presumably longer myths that required several nights to tell. However, they do provide us with an indication of the richness of the oral literature among indigenous Yuman peoples of the Baja Peninsula, of whom the Kiliwas were only one. The Kiliwa culture is the sole surviving member of its own branch of the Yuman family of languages. The Kiliwas seem to have had strong ties with groups to the south, such as the now extinct Cochimí, as well as with the Kumeyaay and Cucapá peoples to the north.

Whenever I look up at the night sky, in whatever season, I don't look for the Big Dipper or Polaris. The first thing I look for is Orion, and really, only that part we call the sword, which the Yuman-speaking peoples of the Colorado River region—including the Kiliwas of Baja California—call *?muw,* the Three Mountain Sheep.

For hunting peoples all over the world, the constellation Orion is associated with the element water—heavenly and terrestrial. Water, in the form of images of the sea, abounds in the following Kiliwa stories. It is no mere coincidence that these stars are also the harbinger of the hunting season around the globe, hence the theme of hunting in the following stories.

The narratives from the Kiliwa oral tradition reveal the mythic origins of the link between hunting, the stars, and the sea. They are also a reminder of the sacred code of the desert hunter, which prescribes selfless sharing, especially with the very young and the very old. Failure to abide by these strictures may have dire consequences, as these myth fragments from a past now lost to us demonstrate.

The Kiliwa homeland in Baja California Norte is an area rich in natural resources, both on the land and in the sea. The native peoples exploited both the usually foggy Pacific and the sunnier Gulf shores in the winter, hunted and gathered in the hills and mountains in the spring and fall, and lived in the cooler highlands during the hot desert summer. Often referred to as warlike, the Kiliwas were merely determined to preserve their freedom at all costs. In the 1840s they participated in an attack on the Santa Catarina mission that brought to an end the brief period of Spanish colonization in the mountainous interior of the northern peninsula. Here the Kiliwas have remained into the present, when greater pressures are at work to transform their lives. In the face of many trials, the few remaining Kiliwas have maintained a keen sense of humor and have lost none of their aboriginal thirst for freedom.

The Creation of the Giant Sea Bass and the Mountain Sheep

Earth-person created things. There was no land anywhere. Then he came out from under this land. Three men came out also. They sat in a circle (where they were sitting was round). With them there, he sat and he sat. He was creating things. He created the seas. He took the spirit which lay thrust in his breast. He spat four times repeatedly toward the four sacred directions: South, North, West, and East. He created the seas. He planted a creosote bush there and sat creating under it. The sun he created, the moon, the heavens, the stars. He created the seas. By the second or third day they were coursing along. Blue-green water stretched out everywhere. The miniature seas were spreading over the earth. He created mountains and placed them in the four holy places: South, North, West, East. He created a mountain sheep, and he created a giant sea bass. Having created the sea bass, he lay the fish on the mountain; it didn't budge. Having created the mountain sheep, he stood it in the water; it didn't budge either. And then the companions asked, "How is he creating? How is he doing it?" The three who were sitting with him asked this. "He did it this way: He created the sheep and stuck it there in the water; it didn't budge!" "That's not the way!" they said. "Take the mountain sheep and stand it on the mountain! Take the sea bass and lay it in the water!" He took the sea bass and laid it in the water! . . . When the fish was placed in the water, it plunged yonder into the sea. He created the mountain sheep and stood it on the mountain. The sheep leapt up over the mountain crests and away!

Mountain Sheep Constellation

The-Being-Hereabout really relished sheep marrow. The-Being-Hereabout sired The-Creature-Who-Sits-in-the-Earth. The latter went about killing sheep. He usually brought it home. He'd bring the marrow home for his father. The father always ate it. So it happened, over and over. But after a while, the son brought some home for himself. He thought, "I wonder what it tastes like?" He tasted some. Yummy! It was absolutely delicious! He ate it all up. He made blood-sausage and pit-roasted the innards. He brought it all on his back. When he arrived, the old man sat down with great difficulty. He groped about, seeking the marrow. There was none! He scrubbed his hands with earth. He sat down there at a distance. "I brought deer-blood sausage there, I brought pit-roasted head. Why isn't he eating any?" thought the son. But the father didn't offer to answer the son's question. In fact, the father angrily took his leave. He went off to who knows where. Thus it stood; he was angry. The son gave chase but to no avail. He came home. He again went hunting for mountain sheep. He hunted to the south; he didn't kill a one. At the Pacific Coast, the sheep eluded him. He hunted again, heading north; there was nothing at all. The sheep did not come. He headed west; again it was the same. The next morning he did the same. Eastward he headed; he saw the sheep crossing Mountain-Sheep Mountain [San Felipe Desert]. The sheep went off in that direction. They ran along the very crest of the peaks. Three yearling rams were racing along. He headed them off at this place, the Ascension; he ambushed them. He shot the young ram that ran in the middle.

The arrow entered under the right foreleg and was driven up to the feathering. The arrowhead splintered and flaked off. And so they are still traveling. They were hurtled across the Gulf of California from which they rise as the Mountain Sheep constellation, Orion's belt; the sword is the splintered arrow.

Sheep Constellation and the Sea

The god, The-Being-Hereabout, was awakened by his daughter-in-law who was there with him. Her husband was lying there, for his father had put him to sleep. The father strode around the room, his staff in hand, singing. When he left off singing, he angrily headed far, far away to the south, through the door and away. He came to a distant land. There he was about to smoke; he set his pipe down on the ground and sat cleaning it with a little stick. He stabbed the stick into the ground, saying, "At some future time a person of mortal flesh shall name this place. Dirty-Mountain-in-the-North [Cerro Capirota, a volcanic cone near Mexicali] it will be called." He took off and came to a distant land called Gray Earth; he turned back, at that very spot. He was coming along here; he came to Santa Catarina. When he arrived, he sat down and had a smoke. He finished his tobacco. He knocked the tobacco out of his pipe, spilling it out. Right then he created tobacco: "Sprouting-Tongues-of-Tobacco this place shall be called," he thought. He continued on his way, leaning over the edge of San Rafael Canyon; "Hey!" he thought. "It sounds like water roaring somewhere!" He thought it sounded like weeping as he stood there. He gazed to the south sky. The sound went away to the north, so he looked at the north sky. He was all turned around by the song. Huh! He heard more singing; he went to see what was making the sound. So it was a river! He crossed it; leaving it behind, he left immediately. In a distant place called Willow Creek, leaning over the stream, he saw some stars in the water. Huh! He had arrived at the sea. And there his body suffered a horrid transformation! He took up an incantation; he was still chanting when his son caught up with him. The son leapt at him to grab him, but to no avail. He plunged into the sea emerging nearby. He looked like some sort of crow black seashell. Simply terrifying! He cast a curse at his son. He dove farther out, emerging farther yet. His face had turned completely black, so he didn't look human any more.

He cast a curse at his son, who stood there. There, among the breakers, his head protruded. Then he really looked like some sort of mountain, bristling with a pine forest. He cast another curse at his son. He dove farther out saying, "Formerly my name was The-Being-Hereabout; not now; I am called Ancient-One-of-the-Extended-Kelp," he said. He drifted off, saying, "I'm going to the Spirit-House-Under-the-Shadow-of-the-Distant-Land-in-the-Western-Sea!"

Painted Caves and Sacred Sheep: *Bighorn Ethnohistory in Baja California*

Anita Alvarez de Williams is an art historian, ethnographer, museum educator, photographer, and ethnobotanist based in Mexicali, Baja California Norte. Over the last three decades she worked with the Cucapá (Cocopah) of the Colorado River delta through archival and field studies of their subsistence ecology, oral history, and material culture. Her *Travelers Among the Cucapá* (Dawson's Book Shop, 1975) brings together the early journal accounts of the riverine culture of the Cucapá, which has since been largely disrupted by dams and irrigation systems on the Colorado River. While working with the Regional Museum of Baja California in Mexicali, she developed major exhibits on the prehistoric and extant peoples of the peninsula and wrote *Primeros Pobladores de Baja California* (Talleres Gráficos, B.C.N., 1975) celebrating the original people of the peninsula. She is currently working on an updated, expanded edition of this book for an English-speaking audience.

Anita Williams's personal reflections are interwoven with a wealth of oral literature about bighorn sheep derived from monographs of anthropologists who have worked on both sides of the U.S.-Mexico border. She demonstrates great respect and care in using this source material but also highlights the beautiful story lines hidden within such works. Williams somehow places this material in a context in which it can once again be appreciated as part of living cultures. Bilingual and multicultural herself, Anita Williams helps us step beyond the presumption that any single culture knows all there is worth knowing about bighorn sheep. Instead, we

42

glimpse the many insights which Cucapá, Chemehuevi, Yavapai, Kiliwa, and Yuman cultures have contributed to bighorn ethnozoology.

The Cucapá, Kiliwa, Quechan (Yuma), Maricopa, Yavapai, and Mohave are all culture groups within the Yuman language family, which includes the peoples of the lower Colorado River and Gila watersheds, extending into southern Arizona, Nevada, California, and well into Baja California Norte. Also mentioned in this essay are the Chemehuevi, migratory desert Indians of southeastern California related to the Southern Paiute, of another language group, the Numic branch of Uto-Aztecan.

Startled by sudden movement in the bushes just by me, I looked up in time to see a white rump disappear into the greenery. Sounds of small stones scattering, rhythmic hoofbeats of running animals. I glanced over at the sandy gravel and saw hoofprints and fresh scat . . . mountain sheep! Heart beating fast and camera ready, I watched the greenery shimmer as the concealed animals zigzagged away from me. The sound of their running faded into desert quiet.

Two of them eventually emerged at the far end of the valley and raced up a pale brown rocky hill that matched their color almost exactly. They paused, and one looked back. I released the shutter once before they disappeared over the rim. Too far away for a good photo, but at least I had a graven image of that memorable moment. I had long wanted to see wild sheep in their habitat. Having just read Gale Monson and Lowell Sumner's *The Desert Bighorn*[1] and two books on tracking, I was confident about what I had seen.

As we leisurely crunched along the rustic roads carved into California's Picacho Park, my husband, Charlie, and I filled our eyes with the volcanic wilderness.[2] Rounding a high curve, we stopped to photograph. Below us lay the small valley, much of it lush with mesquite and palo verde or thickly textured with desert bushes and grasses. After driving down to the sands and gravels of the dry streambed we stopped again for more photographing. As we usually do, Charlie headed one way and I went another. A bright green palo verde backed by a red hill attracted my attention, and

I started toward that. Then, distracted by a white splash of desert prim-rose, I turned aside to photograph the flowers. That was exactly when my heretofore unseen animal neighbors took flight. Later, a park ranger confirmed that bighorn sheep are sometimes sighted in the Picachos.

Earlier that same day, driving out through the farmlands east of Calex-ico, we had seen something unfamiliar ahead of us on the old highway. We slowed down and stopped. We soon found ourselves surrounded by a herd of domestic sheep being moved by competent Basque shepherds from one pasture to another across the road. As they swarmed around us, a heaving woolly sea of gray sheep, we sat still, listening to their anxious bleats and the soft thuds of their hooves on the pavement. We breathed the dust they stirred into the air. I looked into the faces and eyes of the sheep as they hurried by. They seemed nervous, worried.

Suddenly they were gone, and we continued on our way out of the farmland and through the desert to Picacho State Park. Later I would remember the sounds and appearance of the huddled domestic sheep as they were herded along the road as a counterpoint to the gravel-scattering dash and freedom of the wild creatures on the hillside.

When I got home, still thrilled, I wrote to my daughters and to my friend and desert mentor Julian Hayden about seeing the domestic and wild sheep. I sent the film off to be developed.

When my slides came back I could hardly wait to get them home and onto the light box. I spread them all out, flipped on the light, and quickly located the one of the mountain sheep. My heart almost stopped. I ran for the magnifying glass and looked again. They weren't mountain sheep. They were deer.

I found my book of field sign and looked up mule deer, and then moun-tain sheep. Both have whitish rumps. Their prints in gravelly terrain could be similar. Reading further, I found that Monson and Sumner conceded that bighorn sheep and deer droppings cannot be consistently distin-guished.[3] And as for the sighting? Well, I had already decided they were mountain sheep, so that's what I saw. I turned the light box off. I was mortified.

The original people of this desert land would not have made such a mis-take. These Yuman-Hokan speakers knew mountain sheep too well, and not from reading about them. Generations of concentrated and precise sightings had familiarized the native folk with the sheep's coloring, texture, and shape, as well as their way of moving—individually or in herds, and against different landscapes. They were familiar with the sounds mountain sheep make, and no doubt even knew their scent. Not only could they distinguish bighorn sheep tracks from those of other animals, but they learned to recognize sign left by individuals in varied terrain. Sign literacy was essential to folk dependent on animals for food and tools.

Long ago, native people carved small images of bighorn sheep into the darkly patinated faces of basalt cliffs in desert canyons, old watercourses worn into the eastern slopes of the Sierra de Juárez and the Sierra San Pedro Mártir. Mountain sheep still live in those canyons, still come to streams and water holes to drink beneath their ancient portraits, keeping themselves discretely hidden from humankind.

We went to such a Baja California canyon in 1989 along with wildlife photographer Tupper Ansel Blake to look for bighorn sheep.[4] Following our guide, a game warden for sheep-hunting camps, we eventually headed south across an old dry lakebed, rooster tails of white alkaline dust marking our vehicle's progress. Then we turned west again and drove up through increasingly dense mesquite forest, into the mouth of El Diablito Canyon in the Sierra San Pedro Mártir.

We settled under the ironwood and mesquite trees near a seasonal sheep-hunting camp. Invited to the plywood cookhouse, we sat on benches at the oilcloth-covered table, drank coffee, and visited with the camp cooks, guides, and beaters. Most of them came from ranches and villages of the Central Baja California mountains. The camp was open for about a month, beginning in January. Hunters at that time paid twelve thousand dollars for the privilege of a ten-day opportunity to shoot a bighorn sheep. (With sheep hunting officially banned in northern Baja California, the going price in southern Baja California in 1991 was twenty thousand dollars.)

The hunter in residence was a slim, elegant gentleman dressed in khakis. He spoke Spanish with a French accent and was said to be highly placed in Mexican politics. His reasons for hunting mountain sheep were far removed from those of the ancient hunters of Baja California, but in some ways he shared their reverence for this animal. Back for his fourth year of hunting, the politician was after a trophy ram of certain specifications. One season he had trained his sights on twenty successive rams without shooting. Seeking a world's record, this hunter would not kill what was, to him, an undersized ram. So for several seasons he had paid his dues and put in his time, but had gone home without a kill.

We all dreamed of mountain sheep and were up the next morning in time to see the hunter's party leave. He was escorted by two pickups loaded with guides, carriers, and beaters; food; water; camping gear; and, of course, his guns. The impressive entourage, charged with excitement and anticipation, headed north toward a designated camping place beyond Diablo Canyon.

Tupper and his cameras had been assigned two *mochileros,* or carriers, who were to serve that day as beaters. Our writer friend Peter Steinhart took off with them in our vehicle shortly after the hunter had gone, heading east toward another small range of mountains. Local ghosts of the ancient hunters probably had plenty of comments regarding these two different sets of mountain sheep hunters who had no interest in the animal's edibility.

Madeleine Blake, Charlie, and I accompanied the camp cooks and caretaker on an excursion to a waterfall near Diablo Canyon. Starting from an open area among cardón and senita cactus, we took the trail toward the mouth of the canyon, up past an old cave that showed signs of long habitation, perhaps by the original hunters of the canyon. We angled down past a weathered corral where we encountered the largest mesquite tree any of us had ever seen—surely several hundred years old—then worked our way down into the boulder-strewn mouth of the canyon. Following the stream, we threaded our way up through grasses and water-worn stones. Our guides pointed out sheep scat and hoofprints as well as signs of deer.

We came to a perpetual shower. Someone had diverted stream water up and over a high boulder through a plastic pipe, from which a cut plastic milk bottle hung. The bottle caught and sprayed the running water. The day was hot enough that we set our cameras aside and took turns standing under the shower, refreshing ourselves, clothes and all, before proceeding.

As we advanced, the smooth stone walls up the canyon became higher and narrower. Long, sleek *tinajas* (water basins) in pale stone reflected the sky. Then we came to a series of small musical cascades and, at last, to the dark pool fed by the waterfall. Steep, smoothly sculpted white stone walls

almost surrounded us and impeded further progress. An old cable hanging down the slippery stone wall at the far side of the pool provided the
only access. The young cook grabbed it and then pulled herself up hand
over hand, climbing crablike, diagonally upward toward the waterfall.
She moved as easily as if she were walking across the street. Charlie and
I decided that was as far as we wanted to go. We watched as Madeleine
tried, failed, and then bravely tried again, until she got herself up and over
the fall.

She returned with an enthusiastic description of the upper canyon, and
we all headed back downstream. As we neared the mouth of the canyon
Madeleine stopped and said, "Are those recent?" We looked to where she
was pointing and saw that she had discovered a set of petroglyphs carved
into the desert varnish high on the north canyon wall. On closer inspec-
tion we found mountain sheep among the figures portrayed.

So we returned to camp triumphant. We had found mountain sheep—
not the ordinary walking-around kind but their ancient portraits. We felt
as though the ancient hunters had smiled upon us.

Tupper and Peter returned to camp in an altogether different mood.
They had followed the beaters up and down dry hills, and up again, but
the closest they got to any sheep was when they sighted a pair three ridges
away. The beaters chased the sheep but were unable to get behind them to
direct them toward Tupper. The ancient hunters had done him no favors.

That night the desert night wind came roaring down through Diablito
Canyon "like witches fighting," as Peter remarked the next morning. Not
fortuitous weather for photographing mountain sheep, or anything else,
so we decided to leave. We said farewell to our guides and found that,
despite the modest sums we were able to pay for their services, we had
made friends. As we were breaking camp I found a whitened sheep skull
and leaned it up against a dark, weathered mesquite trunk. No one had
the heart to photograph it.

Later, we heard that after several days the hunter and his entourage
had succeeded in finding and taking a sheep with a horn span of record
size, a prized trophy. Even better news came that Tupper, working in a
different area under very different circumstances, had succeeded in getting
excellent photographs of bighorn sheep.

Life-size paintings in red and black of mountain sheep and other animals liven the walls of great rock shelters further down the peninsula in steep palm canyons that cut through the Sierras de San Borja, San Juan, San Francisco, and Guadalupe. I have seen the great red-and-black *borregos* painted in profile, their great curving horns depicted frontally. Sometimes one horn is painted black and the other red. The mountain sheep's hooves are shown as pointed feet, often including the dewclaws.

The ancient rock art of Baja California also reveals a prehistoric hunting weapon: the *atlatl,* or spear thrower, depicted with double or single fingerholds. By the seventeenth century the native people were hunting with bows and arrows instead of the atlatl.

Years ago I rode a mule and walked steep trails to visit a few of the thousand painted sites in the central peninsula and marveled at the red-and-black images of human or mythical beings standing tall with upraised arms. Vigorously painted deer, antelope, rabbits, mountain sheep, and other creatures race across, around, and beyond the painted people, fairly bursting out of the caves that contain them. I could almost hear the animals panting through their open mouths as they ran.

Yet Harry Crosby, author of the essential book on this rock art,[5] insists that these are not pieces of meat on the hoof but creatures with spirits. He sees a bond between artist and animal. Padre Luis Sales wrote in the 1800s of one old peninsular "Guama" who spoke of himself as Lord of Water. Another was known as Lord of Seeds, and yet another as Lord of Animals. In at least two sites, El Cacarizo and La Palma, painted figures wearing bighorn headdresses have been identified by rock art expert Ron Smith as mountain sheep shamans. These shamans reach out and touch the mountain sheep in the paintings. Smith sees the contact between man and animal as metaphoric of communication between humans and other creatures on a mythical level, perhaps as a dream experience. In the Cacarizo painting, not only does the shaman touch the mountain sheep, but a curved symbol is shown coming out of the mountain sheep's mouth toward the shaman, as if the sheep were telling him something. Campbell Grant affirms that the paintings were part of ritual hunt propitiation. Tom Hoskinson observes further that this sometimes included ritual transformation of man into creature.

The painted caves I have seen look down on the streams and water holes where *Ovis canadensis cremnobates* still come for sustenance. There are no easy exits to those canyons. Under the guidance of their animal shaman, painted red-and-black hunters could have swooped down on their prey from those caves. Their beaters—helpers with upraised arms— could have run from the caves to herd the animals toward waiting atlatls or bows and arrows. But missionary Miguel del Barco wrote in the 1700s that mountain sheep sometimes escaped the native hunters. In describing the *borrego cimarrón*, Barco says:[6]

> This animal is always in the mountains and it is told of him that, when he is pursued by Indian hunters and finds himself in a tight spot, the sheep approaches the edge of a precipice and jumps off, taking care to land squarely on his head so that his thick horns can absorb the impact of the fall. Once down, he gets up and runs away, having frustrated the hunters, who look at him from the heights without venturing them-selves to attempt a similar trick. In truth, the horns are so strong and so well made that it appears that Nature's Author gave them to the beasts so that they could elude their pursuers in the aforementioned manner. It is also reasonable to assume that He gave their entire head such a constitution that they should suffer no ill effects from such a hard blow.

Another Baja California missionary, Jesuit Jakob Baegert, gives a similar description of leaping mountain sheep landing on their horns.[7]

This seemed preposterous to me until I read that far to the north the Southeastern Yavapai also mentioned this curious bit of lore. The Yavapai liken themselves to mountain sheep in their ability to cover rugged ground. They admire the sheep's ability to negotiate jumps impossible to human beings. A Yavapai informant told E. W. Gifford[8] that his father and uncle had tried to corner a male sheep at the edge of a forty- or fifty-foot precipice with talus below. Before either could discharge his arrow, the sheep jumped off the precipice, landing on its horns in the talus. Front feet braced, it then slid down to the bottom of the slope and trotted away.

Barco wrote that in the southern peninsular Monqui language the mountain sheep was called *tayé*. He believed these creatures to be un-known in the Old World or in New Spain, saying: "This is an animal about the size of a year-old calf, very much like the calf in appearance, though its head resembles that of a deer. The horns are extremely stout, and like those of a ram, although more twisted and less open than the

49

latter's. The feet are large, round and cleft like those of the oxen, the skin like a deer's except of shorter hair and somewhat spotted. It has a small tail and good tasting meat and is a real delicacy."

Mountain sheep were also relished and respected by the Kiliwa people of the Sierra San Pedro Mártir in northern Baja California. I learned from linguist Mauricio Mixco about a Kiliwa version of the creator's naming the bighorn: "The mountain sheep he named, Forehead-Carved-(of)-Mountain-Cliff."[9] Mixco also made me aware of the Kiliwa myth fragment that tells of the creation of the giant sea bass and the mountain sheep, which is presented elsewhere in this volume by Mixco himself. But the Kiliwa creation myth fragment that intrigues me the most involves a cooperative effort involving mountain sheep and mole. Their job is to hold up the newly created sky, as Emiliano Uchurte told Peveril Meigs:[10]

> Metipa thought he would make the sky. And he did not know how he was going to make the sky. Then he thought, and removed the skin from his body. Then he made four mountain sheep and four mountains. Then he put one hill here . . . to the south. Then he put another hill here, north. And then another here, west. And then another here, to the east. The names of these mountains are Amatjuilul Wey Keméy, south mountain shaman; T'kniámkas'kal Wey Keméy, west; Metái Wey Keméy, north; Ne'k's'pám Wey Keméy, east.
>
> The four shaman mountains were placed in the spaces between the four seas. And Metipa thought that with his skin he would be able to make the sky, resting it on the mountains. But no, it sagged, being very fresh and not stiff enough. Then he put a mountain sheep on each mountain (the hills were still close together). The two horns of each sheep were of different colors. The horns of one sheep were dark brown and blue; of another, yellow and tan; of another, glittering and gray; and of the remaining one, red and white. . . . Then he tried to rest the skin on the mountain sheep, but no, it sagged, because it was very fresh. Then he made a mole . . . the mole went under the hide and patted above his head with his hands (you know the big flat hands he has), pushing up the hide all around and making the sky. At last it no longer sagged. The sky remained.

Margarito Duarte, who lives in the Kiliwa/Paipai mountain community of San Isidoro, still knows how to hunt with bow and arrow. I asked him to make a set for our regional museum sixteen years ago. When his children teased him about making something so old-fashioned, he took the bow and arrows and left. A couple of hours later he came back with dinner, earning the respect of the younger generation.

My Cucapá friends, however, have only a memory of using bows and arrows to hunt mountain sheep, *Mu lyayák,* that live in the Sierra Cucapá and in the canyons of the Sierra de Juárez to the west. Although most beliefs and customs concerning mountain sheep seem to have been forgotten by these river people, old Pascuala told me that once there were a lot of mountain sheep in the Sierra Cucapá.[11] She said they looked very pretty jumping from stone to stone until they reached the highest. Then they would remain up there, just looking around. Pascuala said that mountain sheep were funny, that they slept in circles "just like people." "If one of them coughed," she chuckled, "all of them would cough."

What has been lost from the oral history of my Cucapá friends was fortunately recorded by Yuman-speaking people of the Gila River in their work with anthropologist Leslie Spier.[12] These Yuman speakers also referred to Orion's belt as the mountain sheep constellation. They considered mountain sheep to be sacred and hunted them carefully, observing continence, speaking softly, and not mentioning their name at all since the night, cousin to the sheep, might tell. Spier writes that these people hunted mountain sheep in the spring, when the palo verde was in bloom, in the Gila Bend Mountains. Their hunts were shrouded in secrecy; the hunters didn't even tell their families when they were leaving. After hushed prayers, as many as five or six men would travel quietly, timing their arrival at the hunting place for midday. Then they would sit quietly and smoke until dawn the next day, talking softly and telling hunting stories about all kinds of fat animals, but never about mountain sheep.

The hunt began at sunrise and continued until noon. Even one sheep was considered a sufficient kill. If the first day's hunt was unsuccessful, the hunters returned home, believing that one of their party had in some way frightened the sheep.

When a sheep was killed, hunters approached the animal carefully, according to Spier, and avoided mentioning any part of the animal; otherwise rain might pour down. The man who skinned the sheep worked slowly and meticulously, pausing to smoke four times with his friends as he removed the hide. When they were finished, the hunters left the carcass resting on the hide while they moved away and spoke of happy things and smoked four cigarettes.

After the animal had been butchered and divided among the hunters, they lifted the meat up slowly, carefully. Any offensive act could cause a thunderstorm. The horns, treated respectfully, were not carried home.

Spier describes the hunters placing the meat on their horses and proceeding slowly homeward. When they neared home, the hunters cautiously lowered the meat from the horses and divided it amongst friends and relatives. The meat was placed gently in the cooking pot, and even those tending the fire took care to put sticks in slowly. Whoever received the meat expressed gratitude in order to avoid extreme bad weather, and everyone ate slowly to avoid choking. Even the sheepskin had to be handled carefully.

To my mind, one of the most remarkable cultural connections with bighorns is the mountain sheep songs of the Chemehuevi, used to define their territory on the Colorado River northwest of the Gila River Yumans.

Carobeth Laird learned that only those Chemehuevis who inherited a mountain sheep song could ritually sing it and claim the hunting ranges defined by that song.[13] This system of landownership continued into the closing decades of the nineteenth century. In the Chemehuevi tradition, "How does that song go?" meant "What was the route it travels?" Each mountain sheep song described an ordered map of Chemehuevi territory, including the name and recognizable allusion or description of each landmark and watering place therein.

Native American people defined space both materially and metaphysically through song. Laird writes that along with the character and "feel" of the land the song conveyed compassion for the animal hunted and a sense of the relationship between the hunter and the hunted. A man was sacredly and inevitably one with his song, his land or mountain, and the animal he pursued.

Women too could own and sing these songs, says Laird, but because they did not personally know the land traversed, they could not lead the singing. If the mountain sheep song had to be shortened, for instance, a woman wouldn't know the shortcuts from one place to another.

When all the owners of a song had died off, someone else who knew the song could claim it. Such was the case of the mountain sheep shaman described by Laird who laid claim to all game in the Providence and Granite mountains, which had formerly been covered by different songs. He lived most of his life alone between the two ranges, using the water from a spring to irrigate his small field. He was said to have used shamanistic powers to protect his game from all other hunters.

One of the last mountain sheep people to own the Whipple Mountain range, according to Laird, was Manaviso Otsi (Thorn Baby). His descendant, Pagiinampa (Fish Foot), whose English name was Pete Chile, lived well into this century and remembered his people's version of the mountain sheep song, which also described the hunter's gear and how it moved in response to the swift and rhythmic movements of his body.

This description appears in a song fragment remembered by Chemehuevi leader George Laird. He tells of the hunter's canteen as he runs and leaps in pursuit of his prey:

My mountain canteen
Will go swinging like a pendulum
Swing like a pendulum
My mountain canteen
Will go bouncing up and down
Will go bouncing up and down
My mountain canteen.

The canteen carried by the hunter was made of the round gut of the mountain sheep, which was cleaned and put away to dry when the animal was butchered. When needed for a hunt, the gut was soaked till soft, filled with water, and its mouth tied tightly with a buckskin thong. The hunter never abandoned this canteen, for it served as both a water container and an emergency food ration. In time of hunger it could be boiled and eaten.

Another song fragment remembered by George Laird tells of the single white sheep found in each flock. These were not killed; to do so would bring ill fortune:

That unseen white lamb will go along crying
That unseen white lamb will go along crying . . .

Chemehuevi hunters of mountain sheep customarily ambushed their prey, sometimes as it was driven past a designated point by other people. Not only the meat but also the skin, sinews, and bones of the mountain sheep were put to good use. Even the dewclaws were used. A hunter might give them to his woman to sew on her garments, to make a soft clicking noise in rhythm with her walking or dancing.

Mountain sheep figure in many of the Chemehuevi myths recorded by Laird. In one, Red-tailed Hawk hunts them and puts their eyes into the empty eye sockets of his wives; in another Bat and Coyote feast on mountain sheep, and Bat says, "I could not see anything because my eyes are so weak. I heard mountain sheep running and playing and fighting all around me. I heard the sound of their hoofs striking against the fallen timbers in the canyons and on the mountainsides." In yet another myth, Coyote has his torn loin replaced by a mountain sheep loin given him by Wolf.

Deer, Mountain Sheep, and Chuckwalla find their habitats in another myth fragment recorded by Laird. As they travel together from north to south, Deer decides to remain in the foothills. When the other two reach the foot of the rocky desert mountains, Chuckwalla complains of the cold, so Mountain Sheep cracks a rock with his horns and tells Chuckwalla to live there. When asked by Chuckwalla what he is going to do, Mountain Sheep replies that he is going to live in the mountains.

Like the Kiliwas and the Yuman-speaking people, the Chemehuevis saw mountain sheep in Orion's belt.

Although not believed to have been a person or shaman in mythic times, as were other animals, the mountain sheep was a beneficent familiar to the Chemehuevis, "never malignant like the carnivores," writes Laird. Chemehuevi shamans repeatedly dreamed a nonterritorial mountain sheep song in which the spirit animal and its song instructed the shaman in the arts of healing.

I read that and remember that ancient painting in central Baja California in which the shamanic figure reaches out and touches the "speaking" mountain sheep, a communion with a powerful spirit creature. A glimmering of that idea shines across the centuries, opening a window to my predecessors in this land, allowing me to share their respect for the bighorn.

NOTES

1. The starting point for desert bighorn study is Gale Monson and Lowell Sumner's *The Desert Bighorn: Its Life History, Ecology, and Management* (Tucson: University of Arizona Press, 1980). In particular, the chapter by Campbell Grant, "The Desert Bighorn and Aboriginal Man,"

pp. 7–39, provides an excellent summary of archaeological evidence of human-bighorn interactions.

2. Charles B. Williams, my husband, is an accomplished photographer. Picacho Park is in southeastern California on the Colorado River.

3. Among the three field guides is T. Brown, Jr., and B. Morgan, *Tom Brown's Field Guide to Nature Observation and Tracking* (New York: Berkeley Books, 1983).

4. Wildlife photographer Tupper Ansel Blake is working with designer Madeleine Graham (his wife), writer Peter Steinhart, Kelly Cash of The Nature Conservancy, and me on the Smithsonian-SITES Two Eagles/Dos Aguilas exhibition on the ecology of the Mexican-American border. A Blake and Steinhart book, *Two Eagles/Dos Aquilas,* will follow.

5. I keep a running bibliography on the rock art of Baja California; as of September 1991 it is up to sixteen pages. Two excellent books on the subject are Campbell Grant's *Rock Art of Baja California* (Los Angeles: Dawson's Book Shop, 1974); and Harry Crosby's *The Cave Paintings of Baja California—The Great Murals of an Unknown People* (Los Angeles: A Copley Book, 1975). Campbell Grant also wrote about the atlatl in "The Spear Thrower from 15,000 Years Ago to the Present," *Pacific Coast Archaeological Society Quarterly* 15, no. 1; and "The Bighorn Sheep— Pre-eminent Motif in the Rock Art of Western North America," in *American Indian Rock Art,* vols. 7 and 8, ed. F. G. Bock (El Toro, Calif.: American Rock Art Research Association, 1982). Ron Smith discusses rock art in "Rock Art of the Sierra de San Francisco: An Interpretive Analysis," in *Rock Art Papers,* vol. 2, ed. Ken Hedges, San Diego Museum of Man Papers no. 18 (San Diego, 1985).

6. Other accounts by missionaries that provide interesting information on Baja California are Luis Sales's *Noticias de la Provincia de California 1794* ... (Madrid: José Porrua, 1960); and Miguel del Barco's *Historia Natural y Cronica de la Antigua California,* ed. M. L. Portilla (Mexico City: UNAM, 1973); an English translation is *The Natural History of Baja California,* trans. F. Tiscareno (Los Angeles: Dawson's Book Shop, 1980).

7. J. J. Baegert, *Observations in Lower California,* trans. M. Brandenburg and C. L. Baumann (Berkeley and Los Angeles: University of California Press, 1952).

8. Ethnographer E. W. Gifford wrote *The Southeastern Yavapai,* Uni-

versity of California Publications in American Archaeology and Ethnology 29, no. 3 (Berkeley, 1932).

9. See Mauricio Mixco's splendid *Kiliwa Texts—When I Have Donned My Crest of Stars,* University of Utah Anthropological Papers 107 (Salt Lake City: University of Utah, 1983).

10. P. Meigs, *The Kiliwa,* Ibero Americana 15, no. 3 (Berkeley: University of California Press, 1936).

11. Pascuala Dominguez is in her seventies and lives on the Hardy River near her Cucapá relatives. See the general account of Cucapá subsistence in A. Alvarez de Williams, "The Cocopa," *Handbook of North American Indians,* 10:99–112 (Washington, D.C.: Smithsonian Institution Press, 1983); see also William Kelly's *Cocopa Ethnography,* Anthropological Papers of the University of Arizona (Tucson: University of Arizona Press, 1977).

12. The native people of Baja California are Yuman speakers and therefore related to the Yuman Tribes of the Gila River; see Leslie Spier, *Yuman Tribes of the Gila River* (New York: Cooper Square Publishers, 1970).

13. Although the Chemehuevis were not in Baja California, and not Yuman, mountain sheep figured in their rituals and traditional songs; see Carobeth Laird's *The Chemehuevis* (Banning, Calif.: Malki Museum Press, 1976), which underscores the importance this kind of song could have had in other cultures.

⟡ The Sporting Life

Being Adventures with Scientist-Explorers Intent on Bagging
Trophies and Discovering Something Novel About the Land

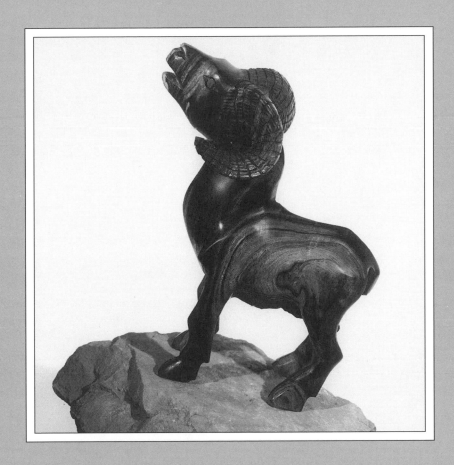

An ironwood figurine of a desert bighorn by Francisco Gonzales of El Gulfo de Santa Clara, Sonora. (In possession of Gary Paul Nabhan; photograph courtesy of the Arizona State Museum, University of Arizona, Helga Teiwes, photographer)

Diversions in Picturesque Game-Lands: *The Wildest Corner of Mexico*

William Temple Hornaday's legacy embodies the best and the worst of what can occur when a scientific adventure writer popularizes a place and its wildlife. This 1908 essay first appeared in *Scribner's* magazine as a prelude to Hornaday's *Camp-Fires on Desert and Lava* (Charles Scribner's Sons, 1908; reissued by Arno Press, 1967), which opened the door of the Gran Desierto to science, tourism, and sport hunting. Although a stream of Anglo and Mexican travelers had hurried through this country for nearly half a century, and *Outing* magazine had already run Charles Slade's sheep-hunting adventures from lower California five years earlier, Hornaday's writings ignited interest in the western Sonoran Desert like nothing before or since.

"Diversions in Picturesque Game-Lands" appears to be an early, condensed draft of *Camp-Fires on Desert and Lava*, which was released at the height of Hornaday's popularity as a naturalist, sportsman, and conservationist. As the first director of the New York Zoological Garden, Hornaday was a frequent speaker on the Eastern lecture circuit. His own articles on hunting in Asian jungles and the Canadian Rockies did much to portray him as the kind of scientific adventurer recently satirized by the Indiana Jones films and Tim Caudill's essays for *Outside* magazine.

By 1907, when Hornaday joined the staff ecologists of Carnegie Institution's Desert Botanical Laboratory for this adventure, he was working hard to strengthen his ties with other legitimate scientific conservationists. In fact, he had professional reasons to downplay the obvious pleasure he still gained from big-game hunting, and during the trip he dismissed local guide Rube Daniels for shooting at everything that moved in front of them on the trail. There is a curious tension in this essay which is driven by Hornaday's psychological transition from hunter–wildlife enthusiast to conservationist–ecosystem appreciator. He had hopes that this expedition would solidify his reputation in conservation.

Unfortunately, Hornaday's game plan backfired. Within five years after these works were published, the Pinacate and Cabeza Prieta were being overhunted by his fans, who sought the same adventures that their hero had described. Shaken by reports of bighorn and pronghorn depletion in the Pinacate, Hornaday felt compelled to stem the tide. He raised enough money for the New York Zoological Society to hire Ben Tinker to serve the Mexican government as its first game warden in the frontier region. Laughably, Tinker was given responsibility for controlling game hunting from the Sierra Madre Occidental, through the Gran Desierto, clear to Baja California. Tinker's attempts at using Hornaday's "guilt money" in Mexico are recorded in his own slim volume, *Mexican Wilderness and Wildlife* (University of Texas Press, 1978) and were briefly discussed by Hornaday in "Saving the Big Game of Mexico" (*Nature Magazine*, 1924). Hornaday himself, scarred by the damage other hunters had done, gradually alienated many of his earlier sportsmen colleagues by stridently advocating "scientific wildlife conservation" not based on hunters' desires and demands. Yet he remained at heart an adventurer-philosopher, and bona fide zoologists drew less and less inspiration from his work. His biography, *Thirty Years War for Wild Life: Gains and Losses in the Thankless Task* (Charles Scribner's Sons, 1931), was largely forgotten soon after Aldo Leopold's *Game Management* (Oxford University Press, 1933) appeared two years later.

Nevertheless, Hornaday's boldness and irascibility are refreshing, or at least amusing, in retrospect. Hornaday's ethnocentric bias would hardly be considered appropriate today. His childlike wonder over the desert flora keeps his penchant for pompousness in check most of the time, and his spicy dialogues and yarns remain charming to this day.

It is worth remembering that this expedition—of the many he took over his lifetime—was enlightening to Hornaday like no other: "That trip of ours was like a visit to the moon, or to Mars. . . . It was the first time in my life wherein I achieved surroundings in the plant world in which there was not even one old acquaintance."

The desire to kill big game for sport in a region that is totally uninteresting and devoid of the picturesque, implies a genuine blood-lust that is fairly deplorable. There are men who can hunt the white goat in the Rocky Mountains and see nothing but the goat; and after the goat has been killed, the beautiful mountains are nothing.

On the other hand, there are men who think that killing great numbers of giraffes, rhinoceroses, zebras and hartebeests, waterboks, gnu, and gazelles on the flat and uninteresting plains of East Africa is very great sport.

To sportsmen who keenly enjoy the picturesque aspects of Nature, it is occasionally possible to become so fascinated by scenery and plant life that even the finding of big game becomes a secondary consideration. I am sure that had Dr. MacDougal, Mr. Phillips, and I been obliged to choose once for all between photographing the Pinacate region and the hunting of mountain sheep therein, we would unhesitatingly have chosen the picture records of that wonderland.

In the great lava field, and around it, the handiwork of Nature was weird and unearthly, beyond compare. That trip of ours was like a visit to the moon, or to Mars. To me there was not a shrub, tree, water-hole, valley, peak, nor even a blade of grass that was of a familiar type, save the few species of desert trees and cacti that we met on the way down the desert from Tucson, and found repeated on the lava. It was the first time in my life wherein I achieved surroundings in the plant world in which there was not even one old acquaintance. Even the prickly pear of New York and Montana was totally absent, and in its place were various species of *Opuntia* that I never before had seen.

The penetration of that lava-and-dead-volcano district cost us many a long mile of desert travel. There was a time wherein it seemed as if we never would make an end of circling to the left around grim and black old

Pinacate, at a radius of fifteen miles from its summit. At last, however, we did achieve the Tule Tank, seven miles into the lava field and eight miles from the summit of the Mystery. We were a long way from any tules, but with a good supply of delicious water in the lava-bound basin, and enough galleta grass for our horses, we cared naught for names. It was from that camp that we went to the summit.

I must pause here long enough to explain that we were bent on the exploration of an unmapped, undescribed, and unknown region in the north-western corner of Old Mexico. It is the angle that is formed by the north-eastern shore of the Gulf of California and the International Boundary. The trip was planned and led by Dr. D. T. MacDougal, Director of the Desert Botanical Laboratory at Tucson, and for companions in arms we had Mr. John M. Phillips, of Pittsburgh (and "Camp-Fires in the Canadian Rockies"), and Mr. Godfrey Sykes, of Dr. MacDougal's official staff. At Sonoyta, Mexico, we were joined by Mr. Jefferson D. Milton, U.S. Inspector of Immigration, who entered with keen and intelligent interest into the various objects of the expedition.

Primarily it was a geographical exploration, with Mr. Sykes as civil engineer and geographer, and after that it was a botanical-zoological-big-game reconnaissance. With a record of more than two hundred years for the little oasis of Sonoyta, the Pinacate region, fifty miles westward thereof, had remained a complete mystery; and the longer the Doctor sought detailed information at Tucson, the less he found out.

As we had suspected, we found that the reasons for the Mystery of Pinacate were water and grass. In dry years the water-holes are dry, the grass is burned up by the fierce heat, and the place is completely inaccessible, save to the Papago Indians. In any desert region the distance to which a horse can go and return, carrying water for himself and his leader, is not great. Most fortunately for us, the year 1907 was for that region "a rainy year," and we found enough water and grass so that we had no real trouble whatever. True, our horses and mules came out looking gaunt and thin, and feeling "used up"; but rest and plenty of food soon put them to rights again. We had a grand outfit—large enough to do everything required, but also small enough to be perfectly mobile.

When we struck the eastern edge of the great lava fields, at the point where the Sonoyta River also strikes it and turns southward to avoid it, we semicircled northwestwardly along its border. We kept on circling, until finally we discovered MacDougal Pass, the great crater at the south end of it, and came abruptly against a lava barrier so impassable that the wagons had to be abandoned. By pack train we went on to the Papago Tanks, found for us by Messrs. Milton and Daniels, and there we camped for a week.

It is a pity that those weird Papago Tanks—then well filled with delicious water—do not command the summit of Pinacate and the shore of the Gulf; for if they did, they would form an ideal base. But, even though they are too far north for that, they form the key to a really grand situation. Four miles west of them is the end of MacDougal Pass, the group of gray-granite mountains that last week were formally named in my honor, the grand crater that so astonished us all, and the edge of the sand hills of the Gulf shore. Four miles north of the tanks there descend four more deep craters—one of them very deep—surrounded by various peaks of red lava that once were parts of active volcanoes.

The whole region down to the sand hills is *lava,* and nothing else! Its total diameter is about thirty miles, and from its centre rises, like a black pyramid, the group of highest peaks that is called Pinacate—after a big black beetle of the desert that always stands on its head when it is disturbed. The name is pronounced Pe-na-cat'ty. The central group of peaks is surrounded by a plain, which everywhere rises toward the centre. Mr. Sykes says that according to his best count, he estimates that the district, as a whole, contains at least five hundred laval peaks and cones and deep craters, each of which represents what once was an active volcano.

It is painfully impossible to set forth within the limits of a dozen pages an adequate statement of even one-tenth of the interesting features of that weird region; and the utmost that I can do is mechanically to pick out a few scenes, and briefly throw them upon the screen. The natural features, and the works of Nature *in progress before our eyes,* so far surpassed in interest our mountain-sheep hunting that the latter seems in comparison quite trivial. The sheep, however, are to the zoologist and sportsman extremely interesting products, for they represent the great genus *Ovis* at one of its jumping-off places in America.

Crater hunting is most exciting sport. It beats mountain-sheep hunting literally "out of sight"! Mr. Sykes cared not a rap for hunting sheep with any other weapon than a camera, but as a crater-hunter he was great. His thrilling successes made our sheep episodes look like child's play. Each success was to him as the discovery of a new species is to a zoologist. And the way he went down to the bottom of every crater that he found, and measured it, and mapped it, and possessed himself of it for all time, actually filled the souls of the rest of us with unspeakable envy—as well as admiration. Now I would not have climbed down to the bottom of that "Deep," since named Sykes, Crater, 750 feet and three hundred risks of a broken neck—"not for *no* money!"

As a spectacle, I am inclined to think the Grand Crater, close beside my mountains—the one that we afterward named MacDougal Crater—surpasses the Sykes Crater; and the cameras fully support this view. With four plates in a row the cameras got the former, but in the presence of the Sykes Crater they all bogged down completely. Even Dr. MacDougal's panorama fails utterly to convey an adequate conception of the reality. The camera that can go down 750 feet, at an angle of seventy degrees, and also catch the rim, has not yet been invented.

As a fair example of crater-hunting, take the rosy dawn of the morning after we camped beside my mountains, in the extreme southern end of MacDougal Pass.

No sooner had the hunters of the party scattered for their several ways than Mr. Sykes suddenly appeared again, riding rapidly toward Dr. MacDougal, Mr. Phillips and me, waving and shouting:

"Come up this way," he cried. "*There's a huge crater,* just at the top of this ridge! *It's grand!*" And back he went again, as fast as his horse could go.

We quickly turned and followed the geographer up a brown slope covered with small lumps of lava, toward the crest of what seemed to be a perfectly innocent ridge. On reaching its summit, like a picture thrown upon a screen, an immense crater suddenly yawned at our feet! Its rim was almost a perfect circle, two miles in circumference, and its top was nearly level. Its diameter at the top was about three-fourths of a mile.

Far below, a floor almost as level as a lake spread across the abyss. Its surface was of clean yellow sand, but a dark area in the centre looked like moisture that had settled there during a recent rain. Evidently the sand which covered the floor had blown in from the nearby sand hills of the Gulf littoral.

And that crater floor was most strangely planted. It was actually fascinating to see, with such clearness of detail. Here Nature had gone about her work. Each item of the planting was so separate and distinct that with the aid of a moderately good glass one could have counted the individual plants, even from the rim. In places *the things were growing in rows,* radiating from the centre outward; and I particularly call upon the long lines of creosote bushes in the southern end of the crater to bear witness to the truth of what I say. I think this has been brought about by the wash of water from the steep sides of the crater flowing toward the central area.

The sandy floor was stippled all over with tiny creosote bushes, like dark-colored dots on pale-buff blotting paper, very far apart. This, evidently, is the most persistent and hardy Pioneer of the Sand. The mesquite had climbed down the walls of the crater, from every direction, and had marched about one-third of the distance out toward the centre. By and by, say in twenty-five years from now, they will meet in the centre. The eye easily picks them out by their greater height and larger mass than the creosote.

The oddest thing, however, was the invasion of the saguaro, or giant cactus. Its advance guard found it impossible to climb down the steep walls, but at the southeastern side of the crater they found a deep notch, and through that breach they were swarming in. About fifty of them had "made good" by getting down upon the crater floor, and they were marching forward in irregular open order, to capture the place. A few skirmishers had ventured out fully halfway to the centre, but the main body was back near the breach in the wall, as if to keep in touch with the one line of retreat. There was not one saguaro anywhere else (that I saw) on the crater floor. The invaders were just like so many soldiers in lightest fighting order—small, straight, and quite limbless.

Mr. Sykes lost not a moment in climbing down to the floor of the crater, taking its altitude, and measuring its diameter by pedometer. He reported it as being 400 feet in depth below the rim, 50 feet above sea level, and 1,200 feet in diameter on the bottom. As he paced across the floor, he looked like the terminal third of a pin, and it was with much difficulty that the unaided eye could pick him out. On the bottom he saw a jack rabbit, several doves, and a small rodent.

This crater was not so very deep, and its sloping walls were in many places quite practical for a good climber. There are many craters that are larger than this, and in comparison with such gigantic manifestations as Kilauea or Mauna Loa in Hawaii, this is a mere saucepan. For all that, however, as desert craters go, it is a big one, and the perfection of its modelling is thoroughly satisfactory. Excepting its floor, it was exactly as it was when the last ton of lava was thrown out, and the fire was permitted to go out because there was no more work for it to do. Unquestionably, on the western side of the crater, there is plenty of lava buried under the sands that have blown up from the Gulf; but at the present the only visible work of this crater, of any decided importance, is the lava field toward the east, which boiled out through the notch and ran toward Pinacate for two miles or more.

That crater was the leading sensation of the day. When the teams arrived opposite the point of view, the men leaped from the wagons and fled up the lava-covered slope to the sky-line, for a share of the wonder. At imminent risk to the safety of "Bill" and "Maude"—the leading mules of our stock company—the whole party of men and dogs strung itself along the rim, vainly striving to absorb into their systems an adequate impression of the wonderful scene. Early in the game three photographers got busy, but it took Dr. MacDougal's heavy artillery to do the subject justice. Of course, no camera could take in the entire crater, nor even the half of it, on one plate; so each of the real photographers made a three-section panorama. Their pictures are very good, especially when put together in a strip two feet long; but when an effort is made to reduce all that down to the length of a page illustration, the grandeur of it goes all to pieces, and the reduction is a tame spectacle.

It was while we were admiring the crater at the rate of twenty interjections per minute, and the two rapid-fire cameras were working their hardest, that we were startled by two thundering reports coming from the notch, just out of our sight, southward. As the roar of the shots rose on the still air, resounded through the crater, and undoubtedly travelled far beyond, we all looked at each other in astonishment.

"Who was that?"

"It must be Daniels and Charlie."

"They must have found some sheep in that notch!"

So they had. When Rube Daniels amused himself—quite contrary to the laws of the hunt—by "shootin' at some rocks over there," his shots raised five mountain sheep and also the largest disturbance that I ever saw in a hunting party. Incidentally they frightened the sheep quite out of that neighborhood, and nullified any otherwise fine hunt on the following day in the granite mountains that rose nearby.

Though we should all live a thousand years, I am sure that no member of our party ever could forget the Papago Tanks—so named because their tiny oasis once was a favorite halting place for the Indians of the Sonoyta Valley as they journeyed to and from the Gulf shore for supplies of salt. I expected a muddy pond in an alkaline arroyo, bad water, and many wigglers among those present. As usual in that blasted country, nearly all the items of my bill of expectations were wrong!

We found three glorious pools of clear, cold water, in deep basins of speckless basalt—or lava rock, to be strictly precise—walled in most carefully by immaculate natural masonry. The walls of the upper pool rose about thirty feet above the water, but for the larger pool one side had most humanely been left open to admit mountain sheep, antelopes, coyotes, tired horses, and thirsty dogs. The lava rock of the walls was of flinty hardness, dark bluish-brown in color, and it glistened like vitrified brick. The water in the horse's pool seemed abundant, but even during our short stay there we lowered it about eighteen inches. The supply could have been quite exhausted in six weeks. A bunch of thirsty range cattle could drink those pools stone dry in less than two weeks. The nearest water to the north is about twenty-five miles away, at the Represa Tank, and on the south the Tule Tank is about eighteen miles distant—if you know where to find it. If you don't know, it may possibly be as far as from you to the Styx.

I never before saw cameras break down, and go all to pieces, as they did in those Pinacate lava fields. All told, we had five machines, of all degrees of difficulty, but not one of them succeeded in making a long-distance picture of the worst of those lava fields that was a genuine success. It was the dull-brown monochrome, only very slightly flecked by the green of mesquite and palo verde, that defied all the attempts of lenses and boxes to dig out their details. If cameras could think and feel, and our five could know the extent to which they were baffled by the conditions existing there—including the fine sand in the atmosphere—they would become raving maniacs.

Excepting for the little oasis below the Papago Tanks—of about a square mile's area—the whole Pinacate lava district, say thirty miles in diameter, was absolute lava and volcanic ashes, and nothing more in the line of soils. In places there were wide plains, three or four miles in width and generally level, on which the lava was so fine that horses could march over it very easily. In years enough, when the process of laval disintegration has gone much farther, these plains will be covered with what will appear to be soil.

But there are miles upon miles of clean, fresh, naked lava, almost destitute of trees and shrubs, where the roughness is indescribable. There are places over which it is impossible to lead a horse. We saw great ridges of lava, like the pressure ridges of ice in the far North, upheaved, contorted, ragged beyond words, and so fresh and sharp it seems to have cooled only yesterday. Clinkers and cinders and slag, fresh from an iron-mill, are no more rugged and ragged than the lava on those ridges that seemingly lie there glowering and cursing the sky in impotent rage.

Over this awful desolation, Nature is bravely and persistently striving to throw a soft green mantle of plant life. The struggle is magnificent, no less. On lava as naked and inhospitable as the steel-clad deck of a man-of-war, in defiance of the terrors of fierce heat, absolute thirst, and blazing light, you will find the beautiful white brittle-bush (*Encelia farinosa*) gloriously growing as if all its wants were fully supplied. Each plant stands aloof and alone, its hemisphere of tender branches covered with a thick mantle of clean, white leaves. Ten feet away from it you may find a solitary giant cactus, shorn of its forty or fifty feet of stature, branchless, and by the awful dryness of its surroundings reduced to a club-shaped stem only eight or ten feet high. On the lava field they grow very far apart—miles, mostly—but they climb up Pinacate to an elevation of 2,500 feet or more, and are in evidence within two miles of the highest summit. Bigelow's abominable choya cactus is even more persistent, and wherever found its room is better than its company.

Like promises of better days to come, the beautiful palo verde ("green tree") and the ever-welcome mesquite bravely claim their place, at wide intervals in every arroyo or wherever any lava basin gathers water and holds it long enough to do good in this thirsty world. On the worst of the lava fields they are reduced to weak little bushes a yard high, but in the Papago Oasis, where water is held up for a time, they make trees fifteen feet high. The mesquite is the great wood-producer for the desert campfire.

The creosote bush successfully defies the sands and disintegrated granite of the desert plains, but it likes not the lava, and is hardly to be counted as a habitant of the volcanic district.

On the lava plains there grow picturesque clumps of the nigger-head cactus, a small pine-apple-like species related to the famous barrel cactus (*Echinocactus*), covered with a tangle of long, curved spines.

The four-footed animals that inhabit lavaland are by no means too numerous to mention—but far be it from me to offer an "exhaustive" list. [Here, with scientific names updated by the editor.] We saw the old-fashioned big-horn mountain sheep (*Ovis canadensis*), the prong-horned antelope (*Antilocapra americana*), the coyote (*Canis latrans*), the Arizona jack rabbit (*Lepus californicus*), the desert cottontail rabbit (*Sylvilagus audubonii*), and the white-throated pack-rat (*Neotoma albigula*). The desert kangaroo-rat, so common on the desert plains, especially in sandy situations, was quite absent from the lava, for obvious reasons. Its tiny paws were not fashioned for digging through lava. A flock of doves came to the Papago Tanks one evening at sunset and drank, and on the lava we saw a few Gambel's quail.

So far as I can remember, the above enumeration includes all the mammal species that we observed in the lava region, and it is my impression that our list of the four-footed habitants of the lava is not far from being complete.

After nearly a week at the Papago Tanks, we made up an extra-light pack-train, and made a long cast southward and southeastward to find the tank of water which a Papago Indian had described to us as the Tule Tank. "Tule" means "marsh." We found no marsh, but luckily for us we did find the tank, and a fair supply of galleta grass within three miles of it; so we blithely went into camp. We were then within striking distance of Pinacate Peak.

By the time we reached the Tule Tank, Mr. Phillips and Mr. Milton had each bagged two mountain sheep, but the Doctor and I had not yet scored; so, before climbing Pinacate, it seemed necessary for us to make good on *Ovis*, and get that feature of the trip out of the way. Mr. Phillips and I went hunting together, killed two big rams, and until the morrow left them lying where they fell. The next day we all climbed Pinacate. After that, Mr. Phillips, Jeff Milton, and I bivouacked on the mountain, with a lava-ravine bed to sleep in—or lie awake if we preferred—in order to get an extra early start on the morrow in skinning and otherwise preserving the two dead sheep that lay near us. This incident was quite unexpected, and we were none too well provided for bedding, but we fared very well. We had a grand camp fire; and with plenty of sheep liver, artistically roasted over a bed of glowing coals and well salted, we surely "made out."

Very soon after sunrise, we took the dun mule and a packsaddle, and foolishly *left our rifles at camp,* and laboriously picked our way over the rough lava northward around the foot of the red-lava mountain, nearly a mile, to where lay Mr. Phillips's splendid ram. We intended to skin the entire animal, and preserve it for the Carnegie Museum; but alas! the rascally coyotes of Pinacate had visited the remains, and left the body an unsightly wreck. The hindquarters had been completely devoured, and the skin of the body had been ruined past redemption.

The head, however, was untouched. Although Mr. Phillips had entertained no fear of coyotes, in deference to a long-standing principle of caution, when he dressed the carcass he had collected large chunks of lava, and with them completely covered the head. That was all that saved the trophy. Fortunately, my ram had not been visited by the marauders— possibly because of our close proximity to it throughout the night.

We cut off the head and placed it upon "Polly" the mule, for the return journey. Mr. Phillips elected to leave us there, and went off northward for a solitary scramble through the lava and a final return to camp by a new route. In five minutes the convulsed lava swallowed him up, and we saw him no more.

Mr. Milton and I started to hobble slowly back to our bivouac, and had picked our way over about half the distance when he asked me a question.

"Where did you say you were when you first sighted those two rams?"

I faced a quarter way round to the right, took my bearings, and finally said, "We were up on the crest of that ridge, behind the tallest mesquite bush which you see, yonder."

Jeff looked, and said, with a satisfied air, "Oh, yes, I see." And a moment later he added in the most matter-of-fact way imaginable—"*But why don't you shoot that big ram, over there?*"

By all the powers, there stood in full view on the crest of a lava ridge, and not more than two hundred yards to the left of the bush at which I had pointed, a splendid mountain ram—a "bunger," for fair! He posed on a high point, statuelike, head high up, squarely facing us, outlined against the sky, and staring at us with all-devouring curiosity. At that moment he was quite beyond fair rifle range; and we were without our rifles! What fools these mortals be!

I looked at him through my glass, and he stood as still as an iron dog. Not once did his gaze leave us, not once did he wink an eye nor move an ear; and, dear me! how grand he did look! It seemed as if he owned the lava field, and had caught us trespassing.

"What *fools* we were—not to bring a gun!" said Jeff, with an air of extreme irritation. I dare say it was the very first time in all his life that Jeff had found himself gunless in the presence of an enemy!

"Well, it doesn't matter," I said, "some other ram will serve my purpose quite as well."

"*I* believe he'll stay where he is until we can get our guns!" said Jeff hopefully. The wish was the father of the thought.

"Oh, impossible!" I said, "he *never* will wait that long! It's a long way yet to our camp; and he'll clear out in another minute."

"Well, now, he *may* not! Let's make a try for our guns, anyhow, and see if he won't wait. I'll tie this mule here, where his Nibs can see her, and we'll just quietly slip off after our shootin' irons. I wouldn't be one bit surprised if he'd wait!"

I thought that the effort was absolutely certain to come to naught, and that before we could get our guns and return with them, the ram would be a mile away. To follow him up would be out of the question—because of pressing duties ahead. But Jeff was so cheerful about making the effort that I could do no less than cheerfully join him, and take the chance. It was precisely like the occasion in the Hell Creek badlands when, to oblige old Max Sieber, who wished me to see where he "missed that big buck," I climbed after him to the top of a butte—and killed a fine mule deer, *in spite of myself!*

Milton's feet were almost as lame as mine were; but as fast as we were able we hobbled over the lava to our camp, caught up our rifles, and hiked back again.

"*He's there yet!*" said Milton, triumphantly, when we sailed up abreast of the yellow mule. "He'll wait for us!"

Then I began to feel an awakening of hope, and interest, and we applied ourselves seriously to the task of making a good stalk. An intervening mound of rough lava offered our only chance of an approach, and when finally we got it in line between ourselves and the ram, he was still there, gazing intently at the decoy mule.

The top of the mound was distant from the ram about 175 yards. Mr. Milton was on my left, and he deployed in his direction, while I made off to the right side of the hill. We must have been about a hundred feet apart. There was no such thing as signalling each other, and it was agreed that the first man to secure a fair chance should fire. Knowing the quickness of my good friend Jeff in getting into action with a gun, I let no great amount of grass grow under my feet after we separated.

Evidently I was first to reach a coign of vantage, for suddenly I found the living-picture ram standing full in my view, within fair rifle shot, squarely facing Mr. Milton's position, and with his side in perspective to me. Aiming quickly yet with good care at the exposed front of the left shoulder, I let go; and like a quick echo of my shot, Milton's rifle rang out.

Instantly the ram wheeled to the right, and—vanished, as if the lava had swallowed him up!

Jeff and I were almost dumbfounded with surprise. We expected a fall, a leap or at least a stagger—anything but swift and total disappearance.

"*Well!* What d'ye make o' that?" said Jeff, with a troubled air. "Can it be possible that *both* of us *missed him?*"

"It begins to look like it," I answered.

With the best speed that we could put forth, we hurried over to the crest of the ridge, where the ram had posed so long, and so beautifully, and with eager glances swept the view beyond it. Not a living thing was in sight. Jeff was more puzzled than before; but for once, reason came to my aid. I said, "Jeff, it is *impossible* for that ram to have run clean out of sight by this time. He must be somewhere near, either wounded or dead. Look for him lying down. He may jump up and run, any minute."

"We must trail him if we ever want to find him," said Jeff, gloomily.

"Trail nothing! I'm going to hustle off down yonder, the way he should have run, and see if I can't scare him up."

"Well, you go ahead; but I'll follow his trail. . . . See; here it goes!"

I figured that if wounded the ram would be certain to run downhill; so I ranged down and away, over the smoothest course I could find. In less than a hundred yards I turned a low corner of lava rock, and there, on a smooth spot, lay the ram—stone dead, without a struggle. He had been killed by a bullet that had entered close behind his left humerus, ranged diagonally through his vitals, and lodged so far back in his anatomy that my utmost efforts in dressing the carcass failed to locate it. He had also been hit by another bullet, but that shot was quite harmless.

Naturally, we were profoundly elated over our success; but I did not recover from the surprise of it for fully a month. Previous to that day, I thought that I had learned some things about mountain sheep; but my best efforts failed to read aright the mind of that ram. But for the insistence of my good friend Milton I never would have taken one step to fetch my rifle and stalk that animal; for I believed that the chances of his waiting for us were not more than one in a million.

And now, in the light of the final result, what shall we say of the mental processes of that animal? One man's opinion is as good as another's; and the Reader can judge quite as well as anyone. As for myself, I have two thoughts.

First, I think that ram never before had seen men; he did not know what we were, nor that we were dangerous, predatory animals. Next, his bump of curiosity was inordinately developed, and he was fairly fascinated by that Naples-yellow mule *with a big sheep head on her back*! I think he recognized the horns of a creature of his own kind, but the location of them—on the back of a strange mule—was to his simple mind an unmitigated staggerer. His efforts to solve the problem thus suddenly thrust upon him eventually cost him his life and gave me a trophy that will outlast its owner by half a century or more. The horns measured fifteen and one-eighth in circumference, by thirty-three inches in length, and their bigness was continued all the way from base to tip. The pelage of this sheep was thin, old, and poor. It seemed to be in a shedding period—out of all season for such a change.

With two men, three big sheep heads and two saddles of mountain mutton, our pack-mule and two saddle-horses were loaded down until the Plimsoll mark was buried out of sight. In order to get on, I was obliged to carry my last sheep head in my arms. At first I resolved to walk, and devote my horse to freighting the trophy; but Mr. Milton said severely,

"Oh, thunder! Get on to your horse, and make him carry you and the head, too. It won't hurt him a bit! Why, with my feet as lame as they are now, I wouldn't walk to that camp over this rough lava for all the mountain-sheep heads in Christendom!"

Even the ride to camp was tedious and tiresome. We arrived about noon, stiff and sore; and for my afternoon's rest and diversion I had to skin four sheep heads, the whole buck antelope which Charlie had brought in (most excellently protected) from our incoming trail, and prepare about fifty pounds of meat for drying. The only thing that sustained me, and really saved my life, was Mr. Sykes's account of stalking a fine mountain sheep ram that very morning on the north side of Pinacate. He said:

"It was on my way back from my work on the summit [his second trip], and while swinging around that north slope, quite near to the spot where I saw that bunch of sheep, I saw ahead of me a big ram. He was partly hidden by lava, but I saw his body quite plainly. He was lying down, resting himself, and I made up my mind to have him.

"When I first saw him he was about four hundred yards away, and the mountainside there was very bare and open. Well, I tied my horse, well out of sight, got down on my stomach, and wormed my way over the lava until I got within about a hundred yards of where I had marked down my sheep. I raised my head, and saw that he was still there. Finding that he was quiet, and evidently hadn't twigged me, I decided to work up closer; and I did. Lying as flat as I possibly could, I wormed my way up fifty yards farther, to make *real sure* of getting him. I was pretty well blown by that time, and the rough lava was mighty unpleasant to my hands; but I thought the ram was worth it.

"At last, when I had finished a real good stalk and was *quite* near enough, I got good and ready, slowly raised my head and my rifle, and was *just about to pull trigger,* when—I changed my mind, and didn't fire!"

"What! You *didn't fire?* And why not?"

"I saw that I didn't need to. The ram was already dead! *It was the headless body of the sheep that the Doctor shot yesterday!* . . . Then I came home."

The Sheep of the Desert

Kermit Roosevelt embodied the sportsman's ideals of the Boone and Crockett Club more purely, perhaps, than anyone, including his father, Teddy Roosevelt, who was one of the club's founders in 1887. The Boone and Crockett Club was more than a sporting society of the Eastern elite; it was the fomenting grounds of the twentieth-century conservation movement. Born two years after the club's founding, Kermit grew up in hunting camps and on outings with his father's naturalist friends, George Bird Grinnell, Gifford Pinchot, Albert Bierstadt, and John Burroughs among them.

Kermit Roosevelt was not even twenty-two when he wrote the first draft of this desert adventure for the January 1912 issue of *Scribner's,* but he was already an experienced hunter and quite familiar with various approaches to nature writing. Just a year before this trip on his own to the Mexican borderlands, Kermit spent a full year with his father in Africa, collecting big-game trophies for the U.S. National Museum. A few years before that, while the Roosevelts were still in the White House, Teddy had become embroiled in the "nature fakers" controversy that pitted John Burroughs against Ernest Thompson Seton and the Reverend Dr. William J. Long. The president had publicly congratulated Burroughs for his "warfare against the sham nature-writers—those whom you have called 'the yellow journalists of the woods.'" However, Roosevelt's use of the presidency as a platform for launching a literary battle angered many populists, including Mark Twain, who ridiculed Teddy as a pretentious weekend woodsman and game mutilator. Roosevelt and Burroughs were somewhat vindicated by the support of scientists who corroborated that Long and Seton had not merely interpreted facts about animal lives but had fabricated them to fit their moral parables. A teenager then, Kermit Roosevelt was no doubt admonished to "stick with observable facts" as a basis for anything that he might write about wildlife. Ralph Lutt's recent book *The Nature Fakers* (Fulcrum, 1990) documents how Roosevelt and Burroughs have shaped American natural history literature since the turn of the century and how "the root issues that underlay the nature fakers remain with us."

Kermit Roosevelt was also influenced by his father's challenge to "live the strenuous life." Who can but be amazed at a preppie from Harvard carrying a bighorn carcass on his shoulders, pestered by flies and bees, on a 120-degree August day in Yuma County, Arizona. His pleasant, humble demeanor seems hardly shaken by the physical hardships and cross-cultural communication lapses he suffered. Kermit's book *The Happy Hunting-Grounds* (Charles Scribner's Sons, 1920), from which this essay is excerpted, demonstrates his talents as a keen observer of flora and fauna and of humans under stress. His unflinching adherence to his sportsman's code of conduct, even under difficult conditions, shows that he had considerable stamina and ethical maturity even at an early age. Kermit Roosevelt's straightforward but modest style of writing still conveys the immediacy of a young man's visceral experience in an unfamiliar landscape.

I wished to hunt the mountain-sheep of the Mexican desert, hoping to be able to get a series needed by the National Museum.

At Yuma, on the Colorado River, in the extreme southwestern corner of Arizona, I gathered my outfit. Dr. Carl Lumholtz, the explorer, had recently been travelling and hunting in that part of Mexico. In addition to much valuable help as to outfitting, he told me how to get hold of a Mexican who had been with him and whom he had found trustworthy. The postmaster, Mr. Chandler, and Mr. Verdugo, a prominent business-man, had both been more than kind in helping in every possible way. Mr.

Charles Utting, clerk of the District Court, sometime Rough Rider, and inveterate prospector, was to start off with me for a short holiday from judicial duties. To him the desert was an open book, and from long experience he understood all the methods and needs of desert travel. Mr. Win Proebstel, ranchman and prospector, was also to start with us. He had shot mountain-sheep all the way from Alaska to Mexico, and was a mine of first-hand information as to their habits and seasons. I had engaged two Mexicans, Cipriano Dominguez and Eustacio Casares.

On the afternoon of the tenth of August we reached Wellton, a little station on the Southern Pacific, some forty miles east of Yuma. Win and his brother, Ike Proebstel, were ready with a wagon, which the latter was to drive to a water-hole some sixteen miles south, near some mining claims of Win's. August is the hottest month in the year in that country, a time when on the desert plains of Sonora the thermometer marks 140 degrees; so we decided to take advantage of a glorious full moon and make our first march by night. We loaded as much as we could of our outfit into the wagon, so as to save our riding and pack animals. We started at nine in the morning. The moon rode high. At first the desert stretched in unbroken monotony on all sides, to the dim and far-off mountains. In a couple of hours we came to the country of the saguaro, the giant cactus. All around us, their shafts forty or fifty feet high, with occasional branches set at grotesque angles to the trunk, then rose from the level floor of the desert, ghostly in the moonlight. The air seemed cool in comparison with the heat of the day, though the ground was still warm to the touch.

Shortly before one in the morning we reached Win's water-hole—tank, in the parlance of the country—and were soon stretched out on our blankets, fast asleep.

Next day we loaded our outfit on our two pack mules and struck out across the desert for the Tinajas Altas (High Tanks), which lay on the slopes of a distant range of mountains, about four miles from the Mexican border. For generations these tanks have been a well-known stepping-stone in crossing the desert. There are a series of them, worn out in the solid rock and extending up a cleft in the mountainside, which, in time of rain, becomes the course of a torrent. The usual camping-place is a small plateau, a couple of hundred yards from the lowest tank. This plateau lies in a gulch and is sheltered on either hand by its steep and barren sides. A few hundred feet from the entrance, on the desert and scattered about among the cactus, lie some 150 graves—the graves of men who have died of thirst; for this is a grim land, and death dogs the footsteps of those who cross it. Most of the dead men were Mexicans who had struggled across the deserts only to find the tanks dry. Each lay where he fell, until, sooner or later, some other traveller found him and scooped out for him a shallow grave, and on it laid a pile of rocks in the shape of a rude cross. Forty-six unfortunates perished here at one time of thirst. They were making their way across the deserts to the United States, and were in the last stages of exhaustion for lack of water when they reached these tanks. But a Mexican outlaw named Blanco reached the tanks ahead of them and bailed out the water, after carefully laying in a store for himself not far away. By this cache he waited until he felt sure that his victims were dead; he then returned to the tanks, gathered the possessions of the dead, and safely made his escape.

A couple of months previously a band of insurrectos had been camped by these tanks, and two newly made graves marked their contribution. The men had been killed in a brawl.

Utting told us of an adventure that took place here, a few years ago, which very nearly had a tragic termination. It was in the winter season and there was an American camped at the banks, when two Mexicans came there on their way to the Tule tanks, twenty-five miles away, near which they intended to do some prospecting. Forty-eight hours after they had left, one of them turned up riding their pack-mule and in a bad way for water. He said that they had found the Tule tanks dry, but had resolved to have one day's prospecting anyway; they had separated, but agreed at what time they were to meet. Although he waited for a long while after the agreed time, his companion never appeared, and he was forced to start back alone.

Twenty-four hours after the return of this Mexican, the American was awakened in the night by hearing strange sounds in the bed of the arroyo. When he went down to investigate them he found the lost Mexican; he was in a fearful condition, totally out of his head, and was vainly struggling to crawl up the bank of the arroyo, in order to make the last hundred yards across the plateau to the water-hole. He would never have reached it alone. By careful treatment the American brought him round and then listened to his story. He had lost himself when he went off prospecting, and when he finally got his bearings he was already in a very bad way for water. Those dwelling in cool, well-watered regions can hardly make themselves realize what thirst means in that burning desert. He knew that although there was no water in the Tule wells, there was some damp mud in the bottom, and he said that all he wished to do was to reach the wells and cool himself off in the mud before he died. A short distance from the tanks the trail he was following divided, one branch leading to the Tule wells and the other back to the Tinajas Altas, twenty-five miles away. The Mexican was so crazed that he took the wrong branch, and before he realized his mistake he had gone some way past Tule; he then decided that it was the hand of Providence that had led him past, and that he must try to make Tinajas Altas; a feat which he would have just missed accomplishing but for the American encamped there.

The morning after we reached the tanks, the Tinah'alta, as they are called colloquially, Win and I were up and off for the hunting-grounds by half past three; by sunup we were across the border, and hunted along the foot of the mountains, climbing across the out-jutting ridges. At about nine we reached the top of a ridge and began looking around. Win called to me that he saw some sheep. We didn't manage things very skillfully, and the sheep took fright, but as they stopped I shot at a fine ram, Win's rifle echoing my shot. We neither of us scored a hit, and missed several running shots. This missing was mere bad luck on Win's part, for he was a crack shot, and later in that day, when we were not together, he shot a ram, only part of which was visible, at a distance of 350 yards. As the sun grew hotter we hunted farther up on the mountains, but we saw no more sheep and returned to camp with Utting, who met us at a ravine near the border.

After we got back to camp, Win and I filled some canteens, threw our blankets on one of the pack-mules, took Dominguez, and rode back over the border to camp in the dry bed of an arroyo near where we had been hunting in the morning. We sent back the animals, arranging with Dominguez to return with them the following day. Next morning at a little after three we rolled out of our blankets, built a little fire of mesquite wood, and after a steaming cup of coffee and some cold frying-pan bread we shouldered our rifles and set out. At the end of several hours' steady walking I got a chance at a fair ram and missed. I sat down and took out my field-glasses to try to see where he went; and I soon picked up three sheep standing on a great boulder, near the foot of a mountain of the same range that we were on. They were watching us and were all ewes, but I wanted one for the museum. So I waited till they lost interest in us, got down from the rock, and disappeared from our sight. I then left Win and started toward the boulder; after some rather careful stalking I got one of them at about two hundred yards by some fairly creditable shooting. The side of the mountain range along which we were hunting was cut by numerous deep gullies from two to three hundred yards across. After I dressed the ewe I thought I would go a little way farther, on the chance of coming upon the ram I had missed; for he had disappeared in that direction. When I had crossed three or four ridges I sat down to look around. It was about half past nine, the heat was burning, and I knew the sheep would soon be going up the mountains to seek the shelter of the caves in which they spend the noonday hours. Suddenly I realized that there were some sheep on the side of the next ridge standing quietly watching me. There were four bunches, scattered among the rocks; three were of ewes and young, and there was one bunch of rams; in all there were sixteen sheep. I picked out the best ram, and, estimating the distance at 250 yards, I fired, hitting, but too low. I failed to score in the running shooting, but when he was out of sight I hurried over and picked up the trail; he was bleeding freely, and it was not difficult to follow him. He went half a mile or so and then lay down in a rock cave; but he was up and off before I could labor into sight, and made a most surprising descent down the side of a steep ravine. When I caught sight of him again he was half-way up the opposite wall of the ravine though only about a hundred yards distant; he was standing behind a large rock with only his quarters visible, but one more shot brought matters to a finish. The heat was very great, so I started right to work to get the skin off. A great swarm of bees gathered to the feast. They were villainous-looking, and at first they gave me many qualms, but we got used to each other and I soon paid no attention to them, merely brushing them off any part that I wanted to skin. I was only once stung, and that was when a bee got inside my clothing and I inadvertently squeezed it. Before I had finished the skinning I heard a shot from Win; I replied, and a little while afterward he came along. I shall not soon forget packing the skin, with the head and the leg-bones still in it, down that mountainside. In addition to being very heavy, it made an unwieldy bundle, as I had no rope with which to tie it up. I held the head balanced on one shoulder, with a horn hooked round my neck; the legs I bunched together as best I could, but they were continually coming loose and causing endless trouble. After I reached the bottom, I left Win with the sheep and struck off for our night's camping-place. It was after eleven and the very hottest part of the day. I had to be careful not to touch any of the metal part of my gun; indeed, the wooden stock was unpleasantly hot, and I was exceedingly glad that there was to be water waiting for me at camp.

I got Dominguez and the horses and brought in the sheep, which took several hours. That afternoon we were back at Tinah'alta, with a long evening's work ahead of me skinning out the heads and feet by starlight. Utting, who was always ready to do anything any time, and did everything well, turned to with a will and took the ewe off my hands.

The next day I was hard at work on the skins. One of the tanks, about four hundred yards from the camp, was great favorite with the sheep, and more than once during our stay the men in camp saw sheep come down to drink at it. This had generally happened when I was off hunting; but on the morning when I was busy with the skins two rams came down to drink. It was an hour before noon; for at this place the sheep finished feeding before they drank. The wind was blowing directly up the gulch to them, but although they stopped several times to stare at the camp, they eventually came to the water-hole and drank. Of course we didn't disturb these sheep, for not only were they in the United States, but they were drinking at a water-hole in a desert country; and a man who has travelled the deserts, and is any sort of a sportsman, would not shoot game at a water-hole unless he were in straits for food.

I had been hunting on the extreme end of the Gila Range and near a range called El Viejo Hombre (The Old Man). After I shot my ram, in the confusion that followed, two of the young rams broke back, came down the mountain, passing quite close to Win, and crossed the plain to the Viejo Hombre Range, some mile and a half away. The bands of sheep out of which I shot my specimens had been feeding chiefly on the twigs of a small symmetrical bush, called by the Mexicans El Yervo del Baso, the same, I believe, that Professor Hornaday in his *Camp-Fires on Desert and Lava* calls the white Brittle bush. They had also been eating such galleta-grass as they could find; it was on this grass that we depended for food for our horses and mules. Apparently the sheep of these bands had not been going to the water-hole; there were numerous places where they had been breaking down cactus and eating the pulp. In this country Win said that the rams and the ewes began to run together in October, and that in February the young were born. When the rams left the ewes, they took with them the yearling rams, and they didn't join the ewes again until the next October.

On the following day I left Utting and Proebstel and took the trail to the Tule tank. The two Mexicans were with me and we had two horses and three mules. We were travelling very light, for we were bound for a country where water-holes were not only few and far between but most uncertain. My personal baggage consisted of my washing kit, an extra pair of shoes, a change of socks, and a couple of books. Besides our bedding we had some coffee, tea, sugar, rice, flour (with a little bacon to take the place of lard in making bread), and a good supply of frijoles, or Mexican beans. It was on these last that we really lived. As soon as we got to a camp we always put some frijoles in a kettle and started a little fire to boil them. If we were to be there for a couple of days we put in enough beans to last us the whole time, and then all that was necessary in getting a meal ready was to warm up the beans.

It was between four and five in the afternoon when we left Tinah'alta, and though the moon did not rise until late, the stars were bright and the trail was clear. The desert we were riding through was covered with mesquite and creosote and innumerable choya cactus; there were also two kinds of prickly-pear cactus, and ocatillas were plentiful. The last are curious plants; they are formed somewhat on the principle of an umbrella, with a very short central stem from which sometimes as many as twenty spokes radiate umbrella-wise. These spokes are generally about six feet long and are covered with thorns which are partially concealed by tiny leaves. The flower of the ocatilla is scarlet, and although most of them had stopped flowering by August, there were a few still in bloom. After about six hours' silent riding we reached Tule. The word means a marsh, but, needless to say, all that we found was a rock-basin with a fair supply of water and a very generous supply of tadpoles and water-lice.

Next morning when we came to get breakfast ready we found we had lost, through a hole in a pack-sack, all of our eating utensils except a knife and two spoons; but we were thankful at having got off so easily. By three in the afternoon we were ready for what was to be our hardest march. We wished to get into the Pinacate country; and our next water was to be the

Papago tank, which Casares said was about forty-five miles south of us. He said that in this tank we were always sure to find water.

For the first fifteen miles our route lay over the Camino del Diablo, a trail running through the Tule desert—and it has proved indeed a "road of the devil" for many an unfortunate. Then we left the trail, the sun sank, twilight passed, and in spite of the brilliancy of the stars, the going became difficult. In many places where the ground was free from boulders the kangaroo-rats had made a network of tunnels, and into these our animals fell, often sinking shoulder deep. Casares was leading, riding a hardy little white mule. While he rode he rolled cigarette after cigarette, and as he bent forward in his saddle to light them, for a moment his face would be brought into relief by the burning match and a trail of sparks would light up the succeeding darkness. Once his mule shied violently, and we heard the angry rattling of a side-winder, a sound which once heard is never forgotten.

At about eight o'clock, what with rocks and kangaroo-rat burrows, the going became so bad that we decided to offsaddle and wait till the moon should rise. We stretched out with our heads on our saddles and dozed until about midnight, when it was time to start off again. Soon the desert changed and we were free of the hills among which we had been travelling, and were riding over endless rolling dunes of white sand. As dawn broke, the twin peaks of Pinacate appeared ahead of us, and the sand gave place to a waste of red and black lava, broken by steep arroyos. We had been hearing coyotes during the night, and now a couple jumped up from some rocks, a hundred yards away, and made off amongst the lava.

By eight o'clock the sun was fiercely hot, but we were in among the foot-hills of Pinacate. I asked Casares where the tanks were, and he seemed rather vague, but said they were beyond the next hills. They were not; but several times more he felt sure they were "just around the next hill." I realized that we were lost and resolved to give him one more try, and then if I found that he was totally at sea as to the whereabouts of the tank, I intended to find some shelter for the heat of the day, and when it got cooler, to throw the packs off our animals and strike back to Tule. It is difficult to realize how quickly that fierce sun dries up man and beast. I doubt if in that country a really good walker could have covered ten miles in the noonday heat without water and without stopping. We could have made Tule all right, but the return trip would have been a very unpleasant one, and we would probably have lost some of our animals.

However, just before we reached Casares's last location of the Papago tanks, we came upon an unknown water-hole, in the bed of an arroyo. The rains there are very local, and although the rest of the country was as dry as tinder, some fairly recent downpour had filled up this little rocky basin. There were two trees near it, a mesquite and a palo verde, and though neither would fit exactly into the category of shade-trees, we were most grateful to them for being there at all. The palo verde is very deceptive. When seen from a distance, its greenness gives it a false air of being a lovely, restful screen from the sun, but when one tries to avail oneself of its shade, the fallacy is soon evident. It is only when there is some parasitical mistletoe growing on it that the palo verde offers any real shade. The horses were very thirsty, and it was a revelation to see how they lowered the water in the pool.

Dominguez was only about thirty years old, but he seemed jaded and tired, whereas Casares, who was white-haired and must have been at least sixty, was as fresh as ever. Two days later, when I was off hunting on the mountains, Casares succeeded in finding the Papago tanks; they were about fifteen miles to our northwest, and were as dry as a bone! I later learned that a Mexican had come through this country some three weeks before we were in there. He had a number of pack-animals. When he found the Papago dry, he struck on for the next water, and succeeded in making it only after abandoning his packs and losing most of his horses.

We sat under our two trees during the heat of the day; but shortly after four I took my rifle and my canteen and went off to look for sheep, leaving the two Mexicans in camp. Although I saw no rams, I found plenty of sign and got a good idea of the lay of the land.

The next four or five days I spent hunting from this camp. I was very anxious to get some antelope, and I spent three or four days in a fruitless search for them. It was, I believe, unusually dry, even for the country, and the antelope had migrated to better feeding-grounds. Aside from a herd of nine, which I saw from a long ways off but failed to come up with, not only did I not see any antelope, but I did not even find any fresh tracks. There were many very old tracks, and I have no doubt that, at certain times of the year, there are great numbers of antelope in the country over which I was hunting.

The long rides, however, were full of interest. I took the Mexicans on alternate days, and we always left camp before daylight. As the hours wore on, the sun would grow hotter and hotter. In the middle of the day there was generally a breeze blowing across the lava-beds, and that breeze was like the blast from a furnace. There are few whom the desert, at sunset and sunrise, fails to fascinate; but only those who have the love of the wastes born in them feel the magic of their appeal under the scorching noonday sun. Reptile life was abundant; lizards scuttled away in every direction; there were some rather large ones that held their tails up at an oblique angle above the ground as they ran, which gave them a ludicrous appearance. A species of toad whose back was speckled with red was rather common. Jackrabbits and cottontails were fairly numerous, and among the birds Gambel's quail and the whitewings, or Sonora pigeons, were most in evidence. I came upon one of these later in her nest in a palo-verde-tree; the eggs were about the size of a robin's and were white, and the nest was made chiefly of galleta-grass. The whitewings are very fond of the fruit of the saguaro; this fruit is of a reddish-orange color when ripe, and the birds peck a hole in it and eat the scarlet pulp within. It is delicious, and the Indians collect it and dry it; the season was over when I was in the country, but there was some late fruit on a few of the trees. When I was back in camp at sunset it was pleasant to hear the pigeons trilling as they flew down to the pool to drink.

One day we returned to the camp at about two. I was rather hot and tired, so I made a cup of tea and sat under the trees and smoked my pipe until almost four. Then I picked up my rifle and went out by myself to look for sheep. I climbed to the top of a great crater hill and sat down to look around with my field-glasses. Hearing a stone move behind, I turned very slowly around. About 150 yards off, on the rim of the crater, stood six sheep, two of them fine rams. Very slowly I put down the field-glasses and raised my rifle, and I killed the finer of the rams. It was getting dark, so, without bestowing more than a passing look upon him, I struck off for camp at a round pace. Now the Mexicans, although good enough in the saddle, were no walkers, and so Dominguez saddled a horse, put a pack-saddle on a mule, and followed me back to where the sheep lay. We left the animals at the foot of the hill, and although it was not a particularly hard climb up to the sheep, the Mexican was blown and weary by the time we reached it. The ram was a good one. His horns measured sixteen and three-fourths inches around the base and were thirty-five inches long, so they were larger in circumference though shorter than my first specimen. He was very thin, however, and his hair was falling out, so that one could pull it out in handfuls. All the sheep that I saw in this country seemed thin and in poor shape, while those near Tinah'alta were in very good condition. The extreme dryness and scarcity of grass doubtless in part accounted for this, although the country in which I got my first two sheep was in no sense green. Making our way back to camp through the lava-fields and across the numerous gullies was a difficult task. The horses got along much better than I should have supposed; indeed, they didn't seem to find as much difficulty as I did. Dominguez muttered that if the road past Tule was the Camino del Diablo, this certainly was the Camino del Inferno! When we reached camp my clothes were as wet as if I had been in swimming. I set right to work on the headskin, but it was eleven o'clock before I had finished it; that meant but four hours' sleep for me, and I felt somewhat melancholy about it. Indeed, on this trip, the thing that I chiefly felt was the need of sleep, for it was always necessary to make a very early start, and it was generally after sunset before I got back to camp.

The Mexicans spoke about as much English as I spoke Spanish, which was very little, and as they showed no signs of learning, I set to work to learn some Spanish. At first our conversation was very limited, but I soon got so that I could understand them pretty well. We occasionally tried to tell each other stories but became so confused that we would have to call it off. Dominguez had one English expression which he would pronounce with great pride and emphasis on all appropriate or inappropriate occasions; it was "You betcher!" Once he and I had some discussion as to what day it was and I appealed to Casares. "Ah, quien sabe, quien sabe?" (who knows, who knows?) was his reply; he said that he never knew what day it was and got on very comfortably without knowing—a point of view which gave one quite a restful feeling. They christened our water-hole Tinaja del Bevora, which means the tank of the rattlesnake. They so named it because of the advent in camp one night of a rattler. It escaped and got in a small lava-cave, from out of which the men tried long and unsuccessfully to smoke it.

At the place where we were camped our arroyo had tunnelled its way along the side of a hill; so that, from its bed, one bank was about ten feet high and the other nearer fifty. In the rocky wall of this latter side there were many caves. One, in particular, would have furnished good sleeping quarters for wet weather. It was about twenty-five feet long and fifteen feet deep, and it varied in height from four to six feet. The signs showed that for generations it had been a favorite abode of sheep; coyotes had also lived in it, and in the back there was a big pack-rat's nest. Pieces of the bisnaga cactus, with long, cruel spikes, formed a prominent part of the nest.

After I had hunted for antelope in every direction from camp, and within as large a radius as I could manage, I was forced to admit the hopelessness of the task. The water-supply was getting low, but I determined to put in another good long day with the sheep before turning back. Accordingly, early one morning, I left the two Mexicans in camp to rest and set off for the mountains on foot. I headed for the main peak of Pinacate. It was not long before I got in among the foot-hills. I kept down along the ravines, for it was very early, and as a rule the sheep didn't begin to go up the hills from their night's feeding until nine or ten o'clock; at this place, also, they almost always spent the noon hours in caves. There were many little chipmunks running along with their tails arched forward over their backs, which gave them rather a comical look. At length I saw a sheep; he was well up the side of a large hill, an old crater, as were many of these mountains. I made off after him and found there were steep ravines to be reckoned with before I even reached the base of the hill. The sides of the crater were covered with choyas, and the footing on the loose lava was so uncertain that I said to myself, "I wonder how long it will be before you fall into one of these choyas," and only a few minutes later I was gingerly picking choya burrs off my arms, which had come off worst in the fall. The points of the spikes are barbed and are by no means easy to pull out. I stopped many times to wait for my courage to rise sufficiently to start to work again, and by the time I had got myself free I was so angry that I felt like devoting the rest of my day to waging a war of retaliation upon the cactus. The pain from the places from which I had pulled out the spikes lasted for about half an hour after I was free of them, and later, at Yuma, I had to have some of the spines that I had broken off in my flesh cut out.

An hour or so later I came across a very fine bisnaga, or "niggerhead," cactus. I was feeling very thirsty, and wishing to save my canteen as long as possible, I decided to cut the bisnaga open and eat some of its pulp, for this cactus always contains a good supply of sweetish water. As I was busy trying to remove the long spikes, I heard a rock fall, and looking round saw a sheep walking along the opposite side of the gully, and not more than four hundred yards away. He was travelling slowly and had not seen me, so I hastily made for a little ridge toward which he was heading. I reached some rocks near the top of the ridge in safety and crouched behind them. I soon saw that he was only a two-year-old, and when he was two hundred yards off I stood up to have a good look at him. When he saw me, instead of immediately making off, he stood and gazed at me. I slowly sat down and his curiosity quite overcame him. He proceeded to stalk me in a most scientific manner, taking due advantage of choyas and rocks; and cautiously poking his head out from behind them to stare at me. He finally got to within fifty feet of me, but suddenly, and for no apparent reason, he took fright and made off. He did not go far, and, from a distance of perhaps five hundred yards, watched me as I resumed operations on the cactus.

Not long after this, as I was standing on the top of a hill, I made out two sheep, half hidden in a draw. There was a great difference in the size of their horns, and, in the hasty glance I got of them, one seemed to me to be big enough to warrant shooting. I did not discover my mistakes until I had brought down my game. He was but a two-year-old, and, although I should have been glad of a good specimen for the museum, his hide was in such poor condition that it was quite useless. However, I took his head and some meat and headed back for camp. My camera, water-bottle, and field-glasses were already slung over my shoulder, and the three hours' tramp back to camp, in the very hottest part of the day, was tiring; and I didn't feel safe in finishing my canteen until I could see camp.

The next day we collected as much galleta-grass as we could for the horses, and having watered them well, an operation which practically finished our pool, we set out for Tule at a little after three. As soon as the Mexicans got a little saddle-stiff they would stand up in one stirrup, crooking the other knee over the saddle, and keeping the free heel busy at the horse's ribs. The result was twofold: the first and most obvious being a sore back for the horses, and the second being that the horses became so accustomed to a continual tattoo to encourage them to improve their pace, that, with a rider unaccustomed to that method, they lagged most annoyingly. The ride back to Tule was as uneventful as it was lovely.

On the next day's march, from Tule toward Win's tank, I saw the only Gila monster—the sluggish, poisonous lizard of the southwestern deserts—that I came across throughout the trip. He was crossing the trail in leisurely fashion and darted his tongue out angrily as I stopped to admire him. Utting told me of an interesting encounter he once saw between a Gila monster and a rattlesnake. He put the two in a large box; they were in opposite corners, but presently the Gila monster started slowly and sedately toward the rattler's side of the box. He paid absolutely no attention to the snake, who coiled himself up and rattled angrily. When the lizard got near enough, the rattler struck out two or three times, each time burying his fangs in the Gila monster's body; the latter showed not the slightest concern and, though Utting waited expectantly for him to die, he apparently suffered no ill effects whatever from the encounter. He showed neither anger nor pain; he simply did not worry himself about the rattler at all.

We reached Wellton at about nine in the evening of the second day from Pinacate. We had eaten all our food, and our pack-animals were practically without loads; so we had made ninety miles in about fifty-five hours. Dominguez had suffered from the heat on the way back, and at Win's tank, which was inaccessible to the horses, I had been obliged myself to pack all the water out to the animals. At Welton I parted company with the Mexicans, with the regret one always feels at leaving the comrades of a hunting trip that has proved both interesting and successful.

An Expedition to the Sierra del Rosario: *Sonora, 1916*

Charles Sheldon may be the closest the Mexican deserts have come to having a hunter and writer of Hemingway's skill in their midst. His terse, unaffected prose may be the most distinctive in this collection. Sheldon's journals carry with them more gorgeous images and engaging drama than most contemporary fiction.

After graduating from Yale, Sheldon supervised construction for the Chihuahua and Pacific Railroad in northern Mexico from 1898 to 1902. Before he was thirty-five years old he had acquired an interest in a silver and lead mine in Chihuahua, and its profits provided him with enough wealth to begin his wilderness explorations. Between 1904 and 1908 he devoted virtually all his time to wildlife studies in the upper Yukon and the islands of the Pacific Northwest and Alaska. These exploits sharpened his skills both as a hunter and as a naturalist and resulted in the two books he published during his lifetime.

In 1913 he began returning to Mexico for various expeditions, giving increasing attention to the wilderness of the Sonoran Desert. He ventured into the Sonoran borderlands three times during the Mexican Revolution, when *insurrectos* were making raids across the boundary for food, horses,

This account appears in *The Wilderness of the Southwest: Charles Sheldon's Quest for Desert Bighorn Sheep and Adventures with the Havasupai and Seri Indians,* edited by Neil B. Carmony and David E. Brown (Salt Lake City: University of Utah Press, 1993) and is reproduced here by permission of the publisher.

and cattle. Sheldon managed to handle himself well among these guerrillas, and his insights into their behavior are just as fascinating as his wildlife observations.

I remain awestruck by the range of skills and interests Sheldon developed despite his lack of formal training as a zoologist or ethnographer. While best known for his ability to stalk big game, Sheldon was also a diligent observer of lizards, nesting birds, and desert plants. He labored to identify as much of the flora and fauna as possible while in the field, but he also sent bighorn sheep stomach contents and other specimens back to the Smithsonian in order to obtain definitive identifications from specialists. He habitually recorded what animals were eating and where birds were nesting, often with a precision unparalleled by other naturalists of his time. Compare such details in Sheldon's journals with the scant ecological notes in the Hornaday and Roosevelt essays of the same era. And he was not limited to scientific and sportsmanly skills; Sheldon was also comfortable wielding an ax, a stonemason's chisel, or a flute.

Until recently, Sheldon has remained poorly known to modern American conservationists and nature-writing enthusiasts, at least relative to the reputations of his Boone and Crockett Club colleagues such as C. Hart Merriam, Elliot Coues, William Hornaday, George Bird Grinnell, and Kermit Roosevelt. Then, in 1978, his son, Dr. William Sheldon, donated Sheldon's Southwestern journals to the University of Arizona archives. After editing by Neil Carmony and David Brown, and publishing assistance from Paul Webb, one thousand copies of the journals were published as *The Wilderness of Desert Bighorns and Seri Indians* (Arizona Desert Bighorn Sheep Society, 1979). Although that edition is now out of print, Carmony and Brown have recently gone back to Sheldon's original handwritten journal copies and have produced a revised edition entitled *The Wilderness of the Southwest* (University of Utah Press, 1993). The version included here is from Carmony's fresh transcription of Sheldon's notes from the Sierra del Rosario, which maintains Sheldon's camp-fire journal style. The wider distribution of Sheldon's Southwestern journals and the renewed recognition of his role in preserving Mount McKinley and promoting the Denali wilderness make it doubtful that his contributions will ever again slip from public view. He was one of this century's best champions of "the mystery and fascination of forbidden terrain."

The Sierra del Rosario is a series of jagged granitic peaks about ten miles southwest of the southern end of the Tinajas Altas Mountains and forty miles east of the Colorado River. Surrounded by a belt of sand dunes, the Sierra del Rosario rises nearly perpendicular to the desert floor, with the highest summit reaching an elevation of 1,820 feet. Isolated and without permanent water, the Sierra del Rosario is the most arid mountain range in North America.

In the spring of 1910, ethnologist Carl Lumholtz, accompanied by two Papago Indians named Pancho and Pedro, made a visit to the Sierra del Rosario—reportedly the first non-native to do so. While conducting his survey of the sierra Lumholtz noted fresh tracks of mountain sheep and reported his observation in a book on his travels, *New Trails in Mexico* (1912). Sheldon, who had seen the Sierra del Rosario while hunting in the Tinajas Altas and Hornaday mountains, was intrigued. Might not the sheep in such an isolated and waterless range be a form new to science? Encouraged by his friends in the U.S. Biological Survey, Sheldon set out for the Sierra del Rosario in March 1916 to collect specimens. Win Proebstel and Staley Hovatter were hired to provide transportation between the railroad station at Wellton, Arizona, and the sierra.

Sheldon managed to kill one ram after a difficult hunt. C. Hart Merriam used the measurements of Sheldon's dwarfish four-year-old ram and the skull of a ewe Sheldon picked up on the same trip to describe the small sheep population in the Sierra del Rosario (fewer than ten animals by Sheldon's estimate) as belonging to a new species, *Ovis sheldoni*. Subsequent taxonomists, who had noted environmentally induced dwarfism in other individual sheep specimens, and also that the ewe's skull is within the range of measurements taken from other desert bighorn sheep, reclassified *Ovis sheldoni* as *Ovis canadensis mexicana,* the same race of desert sheep found in the neighboring mountain ranges of Sonora and southwestern Arizona. Biologists also know now that male desert bighorns travel many miles across broad valleys, thus precluding genetic isolation in even remote mountain ranges. Nonetheless, it is interesting that a sheep population existed in these arid and barren mountains eighteen miles from the nearest permanent water. Even cacti are rare in the Sierra del Rosario, and where these sheep obtained their moisture is difficult to say.

This transcription, newly prepared from Sheldon's field notes penciled during the trip, is the most faithful version of this journey yet published. We have added notes in brackets to elucidate obscure points or names of plants that may not be familiar to contemporary readers.

Neil B. Carmony
Tucson, Arizona

David E. Brown
Phoenix, Arizona

March 3

The sky was dull and leaden, no air was in motion, and the desert was parched as the sun poured its heat through the hazy air and beat upon us as we traveled over the road to Tinajas Altas. There has been scarcely any rain this winter, and all the smaller tanks are said to be dry. It has been unusually hot. We left Wellton at noon—Win, Staley, three mules, and "Old Bill" (same as last year). I rode "Dink." Abundant lizards skittered about, horned toads were common, but birds were not very much in evidence. Late in the afternoon we passed between some hills and saw a red-tailed hawk's nest fifteen feet up in a sahuaro. By driving up the wagon and building up the boxes, Win reached it and took two eggs. The hawk was sitting on the nest, and we approached to seventy-five feet before she went off and flew high, soaring at a distance. She did not approach as we took the eggs. She was a dark slate-colored phase.

Soon Old Bill became sick, unable to pass water. I saw one small yellow butterfly. The various points of the Gilas [Tinajas Altas Mountains] were familiar, and I recalled my difficult climbing for sheep two years ago. We passed one flock of seven Gambel's partridges, but no hummingbirds were observed. Win tells me that he was at the Sierra Pinta and tracks were numerous but sheep scarce. At eleven P.M. we camped a mile north of the Tinajas.

March 4

There was a man camping at Tinajas Altas last night who left early this morning. The morning was spent getting water—filling a fifty-gallon can, two old oil cans, and three water bags—and caching most of the stuff. In the afternoon Win and I started. I rode ahead to Surveyor Tank, which was entirely dry. Then we turned a little north and then west and came to the extreme northwest point of Republic Mountain—a high, irregular mountain mass extending west of the Gilas from Surveyor Tank. The whole desert is parched—nothing green except for the usual desert shrubs, which are always in their various shades of green. Many migrating flocks of small birds were seen, singing all the time. Hummingbirds were plentiful. Some *Encelia* [brittle bush] is in bloom, a few flowers here and there. A crimson-flowered shrub [chuparosa], very abundant along the washes, is in full bloom and very lovely. There are practically no other flowers. The galleta grass is all dead, but now and then a little patch is found with a few green blades. I saw a number of jack rabbits. As I approached the end of the point of Republic Mountain, Sierra del Rosario loomed up out on the desert, a rugged, jagged crestline of rough mountains, appearing from a distance like a section of the Gilas. It was very hot. The night was so warm that we did not sit by the fire. My hands and neck are badly sunburned.

March 5

Rather cloudy and cool in the morning, hot in the afternoon. We started at 9:00 and pulled up at the base of Rosario Mountain at 12:45, about ten miles from the nearest point of Republic Mountain. We went very fast for two hours. We carried food, two five-gallon cans of water, and two five-gallon water bags. Soon we reached sand with scattered desert vegetation. A yellow flower was everywhere. In one or two spots *Pachylophus* [evening primrose] was blooming, but not brilliantly. The greasewood [creosote bush] was in bloom, many of them. The sand became softer, the vegetation more scattered, and we were impeded by rat and gopher holes. Then two or three miles of clear, soft sand dunes, then sand with vegetation until we reached the wide wash near the mountain. Then a half mile more and we made camp in a wash right against the point of the mountain. I saw a nighthawk or whippoorwill. In a hollow between the dunes I found small fragments of fossil bones scattered over sixty or seventy feet of area, and collected some of them. A fox track was seen on the dunes.

After taking a cup of tea, Win left and I went north and around a big basin in the mountains and climbed up in several places. I saw very old sheep dung and old tracks here and there, but nothing else. Cactus was nearly absent—I saw only one Bigelow cholla [teddybear cholla] and one other small *Opuntia* [cholla]. So far, this mountain is exactly like the Gilas. There is much yucca [*Nolina bigelovii*] on the slopes, also *Elaphrium* [elephant tree, now called *Bursera*]. Ironwood trees are abundant near the washes, but only a few palo verde trees, except low along the washes. I only saw one fox track, and there are very few birds about. At least I know now that sheep have been here, but it is going to be very difficult to get them.

I reached camp at dark, a wonderful sunset covering the whole sky east and west. Tomorrow I start the hard hunting. The wind roars tonight.

March 6

Today I went around the south end of the main mountain, through the pass between this and the extreme south range, and around the midway, then climbed over to the other side and returned to camp in the dark. All day since daylight, with the exception of half an hour for lunch, I have tramped and hunted in a scorching sun. Twice I climbed to the crest, my barometer reading 1,550 feet above camp. I passed along the crestline for short distances, but it is impossible to go far. These mountains are more ragged on the crestline than the Gilas. A few very old, small sheep tracks here and there along the base, and dung (two months old) and old beds high up are all I have seen. A few small sheep have been about. No cactus of any kind except two very small opuntias. Galleta grass and *Encelia* grow high up. There is some *Ephedra* [Mormon tea], and *Elaphrium* is very abundant. A few fairly large palo verde trees are along the big wash at the south end. Ironwood is everywhere—no signs of sheep feeding on it or anywhere below.

I was in a perilous position climbing about and had to cut a yucca staff and sling my rifle. I have no right to attempt such work with a family which I love so dearly and always keep thinking about. I saw a flicker, two nighthawks, a raven, two or three kinds of flycatchers, hummingbirds, three vultures, two kinds of hawks, and a few other small birds. Bird life is scarce. Lizards, even small ones, are seldom seen. A few cottontail rabbits are in the washes. One coyote track, now and then an antelope squirrel, mouse sign in the washes, a scarce pack-rat nest in the rocks—that is about all I have seen. I could not see the Gulf from above. It is very hot and another gale of wind tonight. It is doubtful that I can find these few sheep.

March 7

This morning, as I was eating breakfast just at daylight, a coyote came trotting across the wash just above camp. He stopped opposite me, fifty feet away, and watched broadside as I took out the rifle, aimed, fired, and, to my astonishment, missed. He ran a short distance and stood until a third shot, when he ran. I fired again. All four shots missed, to my disgust. I looked at the sight and found it up at three hundred yards! I will have this Rigby sight changed as it is too uncertain.

I left and went directly to the far south end of the mountain, about two or three miles, past where the south section is separated from the main range by a half mile of flat. At the extreme south end, at the foot of a slope, I found the skull of a ewe, fairly well preserved. Passing around to the other side, my eye caught a familiar sight on the skyline of a peak—a sheep just passing over. My glasses revealed a two-year-old ewe. She jumped down from a rock, came running down what appeared to be a perpendicular slope, and quickly passed out of sight, although once she paused to browse. I was surprised to see her indifference to the perilous slope.

I was soon climbing again, around the crest of a connecting spur, risking my life, and I have no right to do it. Yet, I am more cautious than I once was. At last I was at the right point but could see nothing—all the surface is honeycombed. I climbed the peak and continued all day about the crest of the south end but did not see the ewe again, nor any other sheep. The signs seemed to show that not more than one or two sheep have occupied this south range. Yet it was a wonderful day, with views of the beautiful high peaks of Rosario, the sand dunes, the distant vague stretch of desert on the west, the haze over the Gulf, and the mountains across it just visible. Pinacate—dark blue—was clearly visible in whole outline to the east, as were the Viejos and Gilas (their whole length) and other ranges in the north. A rather strong wind blew. Vultures hovered about. Two red-tailed hawks and two other hawks, swallows, and a fly-catcher were seen. The rock and canyon wrens, though here, are not as common as elsewhere. I saw a raven catch a lizard in the rocks along the crest.

I was glad to be safe at the foot of the mountain at sunset—a glorious sky, the purple and pink glow covering the whole heavens. I tramped back to camp in the dark. Now I am sure that sheep are here. At the foot of the main range, well around toward this end, I saw the fresh tracks of a ewe and lamb crossing to the north mountain. It is quite possible that the ewe I saw picked up her lamb and came down one of the numerous canyons of the mountain and crossed over. The sheep are very scarce.

March 8

Extremely hot in the sun. Early I went to the south mountain and soon saw sheep tracks, small tracks of a ram or two. The sand butts up against the south end. After circling clear around, I saw a ram on the crest of the main range, watching me. He seemed small. I chose a spur and began the ascent. After a while the crest of the spur became more dangerous, but I kept on; near the main crest, the cliffs fell downward and I could not proceed. Nor could I descend the slope. I had to retrace my steps and lost three hours, but I was satisfied to get down alive.

I could see no other ascent, so I continued around the mountain. I came back by the west side, climbing all the canyons and watching, but did not see another sheep and only a few signs. The two or three rams here seem to be where I have been today, but how to get them when I cannot go above, I don't know. There is practically no cactus on Rosario. I have only seen a few, five or six stunted opuntias. Two jack rabbits were seen today, and the usual hawks and birds. It has been scorching hot. I reached camp after dark—tired.

March 9

This morning I was up at four, cooked breakfast, tramped two miles to the section of the mountain where I saw the ram, and waited half an hour for the daylight. I watched for a while and then found a route and, at the risk of life, climbed to the crest. As I looked over I saw three vultures lying on their stomachs on the side of a cliff with their wings spread out. They seemed to be asleep. Though a hundred yards below me, I tried a photograph. I could only proceed a hundred yards along the crest when cliffs stopped further progress. Behind, where I had started, were cliffs. I saw nothing and descended over a perilous route down the other side, cliff-work nearly all the way. I have never seen or been in mountains so broken and rough as these.

Reaching camp at noon, I found Win there with more water. After a cup of tea, he left and I went north and spent the afternoon among the mountains, but saw nothing. The sun is terribly hot. Flies buzz by the millions. I saw two cottontails and a large black bumble bee. I am to stay four more days. My chance of getting that ram is small—it will only be by luck, like finding a needle in a haystack, but I shall keep working.

March 10

No wind, intolerably hot at midday. At five-thirty I started across the desert for the north end of the main mountain to look for the ram. I could scarcely see the ground. The desert air was delightfully cool. The buzz of hummingbirds sounded among the red-flowered shrubs along the washes. Now and then the prolonged whistling chirp of insects made music, and the peeping of birds indicated the awakening of life. Several nighthawks flashed from under ironwood trees, and the cry of the small hawk, so common among the mountains, rang out against the silence. The long Gila and Viejo ranges soon became clearly outlined in the distance, and Pinacate, black in relief over the sand dunes, was more clearly visible than in the dancing waves of heat later in the day. Soon a great crimson semicircle over the lower end of the Viejos indicated the rising sun. Later it was tinged with gold; then the peaks of Rosario first caught the light and glowed in purplish hue. Then a great crimson ball began to appear, surrounded by a circle of pink and gold, and soon the whole globe of the sun rose above the rugged Viejo crest. Purplish hues overspread the desert, the sand dunes were golden, and a vague, indefinable tint of color filled the atmosphere. For fifteen minutes or more, while this silhouette of the rising sun was visible, the exquisite glow of color, the cool air, the calm, the pervading mystery of the wild desert, all were a tribute to this sun, and it did not seem possible that a little later, like a fierce tyrant, it would send down its scorching rays and lash me with intolerable heat, and that my whole willpower would be put to the test to endure it.

By the time the shining light rays had appeared and illuminated the mountains, the air began to hum with the myriad flies that now are so incredibly abundant as to cause continuous annoyance. I climbed the mountain at a point half a mile south of where I had seen the ram. I found a means of ascent up through the furrowed slope, but the steep watercourse, like all others here, made the ascent real cragwork. As I neared the top, the last two hundred feet became perilous, but with the rifle slung on my back I kept on upward, wondering how I would find a way to proceed. These mountains are so broken that, when one is hunting, every ten feet brings new areas into view and one must pause and watch. I have accustomed myself to climb as noiselessly as possible, always selecting each rock or surface to place each footstep. Therefore, progress was very slow, yet when I reached the crest I was weltering in perspiration. No breeze greeted me with its delicious cooling effect.

In the saddle the surface was smooth and there were tracks of a ram, and dung—very fresh—indicating that he had passed through this morning, shortly before my arrival. Both tracks and dung were small, of the same size that I had seen elsewhere on the mountain, and I was certain that they were made by the same ram I had seen. The displaced rocks and freshly thrown dirt up along the narrow crest to the south indicated his course. I could look down on both sides, almost perpendicular, and could view only very limited areas of the chaotic, rocky, furrowed slopes. My eagerness and strained watching were intense as I followed, but the crestline soon became pure cragwork, and I had to slowly work along cliff walls, step by step. Here and there I could straddle the crest and look down sheer cliffs for several hundred feet on both sides. A vulture was soaring along the crest, two red-tailed hawks were also soaring about, and the small crying hawk was flying about the side of the mountain. Two ravens now and then swished by overhead, and my presence did not seem to excite any of their usual curiosity; nor did it that of the vulture or hawks. These birds probably have never before seen a man up among these mountaintops. In such moments as these, one watches these birds with the deepest envy, realizing how easily they float about and see the ram that I, in continual danger, am looking for at less than a snail's pace.

The crest became even more difficult, and I had almost decided to stop and not attempt to go farther, but a displaced stone indicated the ram had gone ahead and I followed. At last I was on a little pinnacle, not a foot wide, above an abrupt cliff twenty feet high which terminated in a little saddle with a smooth surface—an old, unused sheep bed. There I could see the tracks of the ram where he had jumped from the side of the cliff, and just beyond, the displaced rocks and fresh dirt where he had started up the wall of the peak ahead, the highest peak of this section of the mountain. Before I saw the tracks, I had decided the ascent of this peak was impossible. The narrow crest rose up 150 feet, almost vertical, with sheer slopes falling away on each side. But when I saw the tracks of the ram going up, I studied it and, provided the rock was not too loose, felt there was a possibility of ascending it.

I went back and found a way (hazardous) around and down to the saddle, and once there, the ascent to the peak looked impossible. Yet, I pondered long. Perhaps if I should start, a possible way might be found. I could at least go up ten feet. The success of my whole trip probably depended on my getting to that peak. Slinging my rifle, I went up the ten feet. The rock was fairly firm. I found that I could go another ten feet. I did so, and went still farther. Each advance caused me to try to go up still farther. Then I could not turn around and had to keep on, almost straight up along a knife edge. I was clinging to a wall of rock with steep, perpendicular slopes falling away on either side. The whole aspect of the mountain was so savage that it required all my courage not to become nervous and make a false step or take hold of a loose rock. While I was clinging to the rock with both hands, not even daring to look down, a vulture soared easily and gracefully overhead, right up along the crest. I had the feeling that if I ever reached the top safely, it would be my last perilous attempt in these mountains, realizing strongly the claims of my dear wife and family. I worked upward, twice feeling that all had ended, yet I reached the top and then lay flat on my back in the broiling sun and closed my eyes to get relief from the strain I had undergone.

At last, cooled down and courage regained, I sat up and looked around. The top of the peak was fairly broad and I could easily walk about. All sense of danger soon passed. Three spurs fell away from the peak to the east. On only one could an attempt be made to go along its crestline. I saw a possible means of descent down a furrowed watercourse. There was no sign of the ram's tracks—where had he gone? His descent on this side of the peak was almost impossible—the slopes on all sides were precipices. My only chance, and this was undertaken with great disappointment, was to sit, endure the sun, and watch. Even then I felt, should the ram be seen, he would probably be in a place where I could not stalk him, or if he was killed, he would fall where I could not find him or get to him. But I sat there and moved about so as to bring all possible areas in view for two and a half hours, and not a sign of him did I see. It was twelve noon. I was feeling the sun, so I started toward the canyon in order to descend a little way, find a rock where I could get in the shadow, and wait for two or three hours while the ram would probably be lying down. Then I would ascend and resume the watch.

As I started toward the point of descent, my eye caught something in motion about four hundred yards out on a spur, just below the crest, and I saw the ram pass over a rock and disappear. In less than three seconds he appeared on the only spur with a ragged crestline along which I could proceed. The ram was on the north slope. As I started to "crest" the spur, I knew that the whole success of my trip depended on my resolution to do my utmost in careful and noiseless walking and alert watching. I had carefully marked the spot. No opportunity to watch the points near it was missed. Many difficulties and some dangers were experienced as I advanced. Even with my eagerness and excitement, I was punished by the sun.

I came to within 150 yards without having caught sight of the ram. Then I selected a good point and waited, watching for a few moments. He did not appear. About 50 yards ahead was a little pinnacle on the crest that offered a good chance to inspect ahead. I made for it with extreme caution and practically no noise, the rock being firm. This was the first time among these mountains when I did not have to pause every few steps and inspect all new areas. I watched only ahead, the possible point where the ram might appear. As I reached the pinnacle, conical and sharp pointed, I paused to get breath and then had to sling my rifle to ascend it. Reaching the top, I could see nothing in the way of a ram at the expected spot. The slope fell away very sheer in precipices among broken surfaces, boulders, and ravines. On both sides of me were the jumbled masses of rocks lifting up into the form of mountains. The wavy sand dunes stretched in a circle around the mountain, and beyond them the flat, parched desert and the long line of the Viejos, while Hornaday Mountain and blue Pinacate appeared blurred in the distance through the heat waves. A small hawk flew overhead and soared across to the next spur, all the time uttering its cries.

Then, after a few moments, the ram suddenly jumped up in sight on a rock ten feet beyond where I had seen him before and stood rigidly, looking downward. He seemed very small, but his horns had a fine curl. He blended somewhat with the gray rocks beyond him. I shot and heard the bullet strike him. He reared and then brought his forefeet down hard on the rock. My cartridges all fell out as I tried to pump in a new one, each sticking, owing to badly made clips. I pushed one in by hand. He still stood on the rock and at the next shot he humped up in such a way that I knew I had hit his belly. Quickly pushing in another cartridge by hand, I fired and he fell, having received a bullet squarely in his heart. He rolled downward and disappeared.

I hurried forward, fearing that he might have rolled into some inaccessible place. Arriving, I saw that, although in a very steep furrow of broken rock, he had been caught and held by a yucca a hundred yards below, where he lay dead. I simply sat down, lighted a cigarette, and enjoyed the supreme exultation always following the successful stalk of a ram, with the additional satisfaction of feeling that now my trip was a success. Then I worked downward to him. The first shot had struck him three inches below the spine but above the heart. Already the air was ahum with the flies around him. The slope was very steep, the rock very loose. After photographing him as best I could as he lay, I went down and selected the best spot I could find and dragged him down, fifty yards below, nearly losing him as the rocks began to slide. Then I ate a piece of bread and drank almost a canteen-full of water. The sun blazed hotter and hotter. The air became stifling. I measured him as best I could on such difficult ground. He seemed to be very small—a ram four years old with compact, curling horns proportionately massive. I suspect that owing to isolation and inbreeding the sheep here are below normal size.

The slope was so steep and the rock so loose that I had great difficulty in taking off his skin and keeping the carcass from falling. While doing so, the flies increased to incredible numbers. I have never experienced anything like it. They covered me and the ram. At last the skin was off. I found his stomach full of food, much *Ephedra* in it and other leaves and stalks. His bladder contained almost no liquid and was shrunk to two inches. The sheep of this mountain have thus adapted themselves to living without water except for such as can be obtained from their food. They don't even have recourse to the juices of cactus.

I cut off the whole hindquarters, took a good quantity of stomach contents for study by the botanists in Washington, put the skin and horns in my rucksack, drank up the rest of my water, shouldered all, and struggled down to the foot of the mountain. In doing so, owing to the load, the soles of my shoes were completely torn off. I cannot forget the misery of my struggle under the load, more than three miles around the mountain and across the sandy desert to camp. It was at the period of the day's greatest heat, and my suffering was intense. On reaching camp I was pretty near a state of exhaustion. Throwing off the load, I poured out the cool water from the desert water bag. My thirst was not satisfied until I had drunk two quarts. Then I made a cup of tea, which seemed to invigorate me. A rest restored my strength as the shadow of the mountain extended to include my camp.

I salted and put away the hide. Then I cooked supper. It was dark when I finished eating it. The moon was half full, the heavens brilliant, a cooling breeze was blowing. I went a short distance from camp and stretched myself flat on my back with the firmament spread out above me. With delicious contentment I lay there for two hours, giving myself up to thoughts of my dear Louisa and the little ones. Then I wrote these notes of the events of this day—one that has brought a reward for all the work and risks undertaken. Never before have I earned more fairly the trophy now in camp—a trophy only until I reach Wellton, from where it will be shipped to the Biological Survey for the interest of science.

March 11

Insufferably hot, no breeze. Until yesterday, a strong wind blew continually from the north, night and day. It was a hot wind, yet when climbing a mountain and perspiring it cooled me. The wind now seems to have stopped. In the morning I took a much needed rest about camp and cared for the skin and skull. In the afternoon I walked south, halfway around the base of the main mountain, going close to the slopes and carefully examining for signs of sheep but saw only very small old tracks, none fresh. I found a verdin's nest in an ironwood tree close to camp. It contained five eggs.

Houseflies swarm about camp. My buckskin shirt, now somewhat tainted with mutton from bringing in the meat, attracted a swarm to me all day, and they were almost intolerable. Biting flies were equally abundant, and I have never suffered more from insects. Where these flies breed in this dry country I know not. The flies made a perpetual hum about camp all day. At dark all the flies retired, and the relief is a satisfaction. I shall never again attempt desert hunting so late as March. But the nights are balmy and deliciously cool. I sleep with but a canvas over me.

March 12

The same heat. At daylight I was off for the extreme north mountain. On the way I found a Costa hummingbird's nest in a small palo verde with two young about half grown. All about these mountains on the flats are numerous badger holes. I have not before seen them so abundant. All the greasewood is in full bloom and very lovely, giving a cheer to this desolation. Most of the *Encelia* has passed bloom and has nothing but dry stalks, yet, here and there, some of it blooms. It is rare that another flower of any kind is seen, except the red flowers in full bloom on the abundant shrubs along the washes.

I found that the crest of the north mountain is not so rough, but still dangerous. I climbed through the sand at the southwestern corner and reached the crest and followed it north to the low saddle connecting it to another mountain, and then climbed over the crest of that one. The slopes on these mountains are as rough as elsewhere, and the crest nearly so. I saw no fresh signs of sheep, only old dung—very old—and all indications showed that few sheep exist in all this range. I found that the ewe and lamb whose tracks were seen at the north end of the main mountain did not cross the gap to this one as I had supposed. I found a fine cave just under the crest and lay in it, protected from the sun, for two hours. Sheep dung was in the cave.

Late in the evening I came off the mountain and returned to camp by moonlight. There are no sheep on this north section now. All around these mountains is an old faint trail just above the base. It was undoubtedly made by antelope, which must have existed here at one time. Just before dark I saw many nighthawks flying about. They are very abundant here, as are the owls which keep hooting all about at dusk and after. In some places on the south end of the north section the sand has covered the slope for fifty or a hundred feet. Far above this solid sand I found sand scattered about the crevices and irregularities of the slope. It must take hundreds or thousands of years for so much to accumulate.

At about ten P.M. Win and Staley came with the horses. Tomorrow I leave for Tinajas Altas and then back to Wellton as quickly as possible. It has been a hard trip, but successful after all. The heat has been trying, yet I have tramped just as hard as ever.

March 13

In the morning we made an early start and crossed the sand belt, which is about six miles wide, and on reaching the wagon, lunched. We then traveled through the Gila range to Tinajas Altas, covering twenty miles in about seven hours. This is the nearest water to Rosario. When out on the sand I could see the whole Rosario range. It is approximately twelve miles long, but contains only about five miles of actually high, rugged crestlines. Coming across the Lechuguilla Desert, I collected the large bulb of the scarce *Peniocereus greggii* cactus [night-blooming cereus]. After again passing through the Gilas, I must say that, as to roughness, El Rosario is very similar to the Gila range.

Upon reaching the Gilas, birds and vegetation at once became more plentiful. Staley had found three fine, large bleached skulls of big rams right here near the Tinajas Altas. They were undoubtedly shot by those miserable fellows who come here in summer and watch the water hole. Thus I have the chance to compare the skull of my Rosario ram and find it very much smaller and presenting many different characters. The sheep of Rosario are small and dwarfed, and this fact should be recognized, whatever the cause, by giving them a specific or subspecific name.

My trip is now over and my only task is to get back. It has been very hard, but more than worthwhile, for I have added an interesting fact to science—the change wrought in sheep by isolation, lack of water, and long inbreeding.

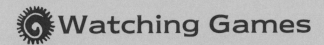 # Watching Games

*Being Observations of Bighorn and Other Beasts by
Naturalists Sitting at Water Holes or Roaming on Foot*

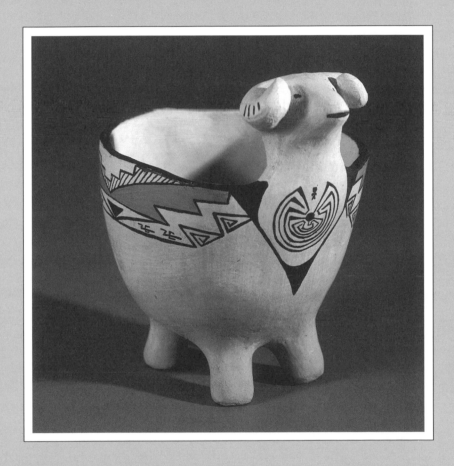

A clay effigy pot of a desert bighorn with traditional O'odham decoration motifs, sculpted and painted by Gladys Angea of Hikiwan, Arizona. (Purchased from the artist by Gary Paul Nabhan; photograph courtesy of the Arizona State Museum, University of Arizona, Helga Teiwes, photographer)

The Cabeza Prieta Wildlife Refuge Water Hole Counts

Gale Monson's original field notes from water hole counts in 1955, 1956, and 1958 are the only journal notes other than Charles Sheldon's to grace this anthology. Monson participated in the earliest water hole sheep counts in southern Arizona, and his meticulous style of presenting his observations set a standard for other biologists who have followed him in this endeavor. The next few essays are also based on water hole counts, and it is easy to see how later writers have gradually departed from Monson's precedent to explore new ground. Little movement escaped Monson's eye, and there were few organisms present that he could not identify. More than simply showcasing his talents as a desert naturalist, these notes represent the wide-eyed curiosity, ecological literacy, and graceful style that the best field scientists bring to their craft. They also tell us a little about the temperament of a man who has made tremendous contributions to desert ecology over his fifty years of involvement with Arizona's wildlife.

Gale Monson was already hooked on birds when he left the Red River Valley of the North and moved to Arizona in 1934. He continued his studies of birds on the present-day Tohono O'odham Reservation and elsewhere in the state before joining the U.S. Fish and Wildlife Service in 1940. During his twenty-nine years with that agency he was involved in some of the most significant studies of desert wildlife ecology to have been accomplished this century. Along with the controversial Allan Phillips and the highly creative Joe Marshall, Monson coauthored the classic *Birds of*

Arizona (University of Arizona Press, 1964), and two decades later served as senior author of its companion volume, *Annotated Checklist of Birds of Arizona* (University of Arizona Press, 1981). He was also involved in the earliest meetings of the Desert Bighorn Council and has published numerous analyses, reports, and reflections in its *Transactions* over the years. This led him to serve as coeditor (with Lowell Sumner) of the council's anthology, *The Desert Bighorn* (University of Arizona Press, 1980). Monson has also been a valued consultant to the Arizona–Sonora Desert Museum, demonstrating that his interest in environmental education is as strong as his commitment to research.

Through the Southwest Center's sponsorship, additional original field notes by Monson and other authors are being archived at the University of Arizona. Such notes not only give insight into what preoccupies scientists in the act of discovery, they provide benchmarks by which to measure environmental and biotic changes at particular locations through time. In the cases for which we have obtained both the raw field notes and a polished, edited essay by the same author, scholars in the future can compare these texts to understand how a nature writer elaborates his or her craft.

Agua Dulce Spring
July 12, 1955

Agua Dulce Spring area, entire 24 hrs. Two elf owls were heard at my Agua Dulce Spring camp at 0300 and later. I was up at 0430, and after a preliminary breakfast of half a grapefruit and a cup of coffee, and gathering up my stuff, I set off on the mile-long trail, much of it uphill, to the spring. It took me an hour to negotiate it—I arrived at 0600. The spring basin was overflowing, the water very green and algal.

I settled myself on a rock seat under a small palo verde just east of, and about 70 ft. above, the spring. It was a good place—I could look over the organ-pipe cacti and various other plants onto the plains and mountains of Sonora, only a few miles away. It turned out to be an interesting day. I began seeing bighorn sheep right away, and before noon I had seen 11 of them, 5 rams and 6 ewes. They hung around the vicinity, probably wanting to drink, but not daring to do so—with the exception of one ram, who came in hurriedly from the east at 0730 and drank without observing me. One of the rams chased an old stubby-horned ewe unmercifully, once right onto a rock only about 25 ft. away from me—I was ready with my camera. At one time, I had 8 bighorn on the point directly opposite me and above the tank—3 males, 5 females. I took some pictures.

These bighorns all seemed small and dark compared with the Kofa bighorns—or perhaps it was my imagination! One of the ewes was certainly a tiny thing. After I had moved about considerably just before 1200, they all went off to the north and had disappeared by 1230. I saw them no more today. One of the rams was 8–9 years old, the others from 4 to 6. An adult and an immature golden eagle lent their distinguished presence to the scene much of the day, and when first seen one of them had just swooped low over a ewe. The immature was vociferous—spent a good deal of time sailing around and uttering a series of short, shrill, piercing screams.

I was pleased to see 5 rock squirrels. This must be the extreme western limit of their range. The first one didn't come into view until 0930. The rest of the day one or more was always in sight. They climbed all over the rocks, and spent a good deal of time in the mesquites by the spring. They fed especially on mesquite beans.

After the terrific count I got on white-winged doves June 7, I was disappointed to find so few today—I counted only 743 altogether. The count is not too accurate, as the birds seem to drink, fly off some distance to return and drink again. The first one didn't drink until 0920, and then had to be shown how by a mourning dove—although this may have been due to my nearby presence. As I noted last week at Burnt Wagon Tank (on the Kofa), they seemed to water in groups, and what a melee of wings as they poured down over the rocks to drink!

The weather was of especial interest today. As I came over the trail this morning, there appeared to be fog all about the lower part of the Pinacate region. There was considerable cloudiness as the day wore on. About 1750, the solidness of the clouds in the east increased, and a "dust front" materialized between me and Sonoyta. By 1815, the dust front had hit Agua Dulce Spring, with hard blasts of southeast wind. Doves scattered, wild bees left the water, and rock squirrels took cover. I decided discretion was the better part of valor and left the spring as early as 1825 for camp. En route, the wind blew harder than ever, a few raindrops fell, and I could see a heavy storm was raging over Ajo way. In the gathering darkness and wind, just before reaching camp, I saw a male western tanager on a swaying ocotillo wand. Lightning began to flash nearby, and I scarcely had time to warm a can of stew before it began raining hard—the first break in our annual summer drought! The rain, although heavy, lasted only a brief time, followed by a second shower at 2015. I estimated .20 in. fell—no runoff. It drizzled until after 2200, so I spent part of the night sleeping in the cab of my jeep. It was wonderful to have it rain again!

[A table of birds seen during the day closes the account—*Ed.*]

July 13

Agua Dulce Spring area, entire 24 hrs. Another shower at 0200 sent me back to the jeep for an hour. I didn't get up until 0500, and due to the wet condition of my camp, it wasn't until 0540 that I hit the trail for Agua Dulce Spring to spend my second day of observations there. It was quite cloudy overhead. I saw the first millipede of the season on the trail. Reaching the spring at 0640, I saw that no bighorn had watered during the night or this morning.

Due to the rain, I suppose, doves were relatively scarce today. I saw not more than 154 all day, and not more than 4 or 5 of these actually drank from the spring. I also saw only one bighorn—this the oldest of the rams seen yesterday. He passed to the west of the spring at 1330 but did not drink. He looked for a long time at the place where he saw me sitting yesterday, so he has a memory of some sort.

The rock squirrels were busy again today. The first one popped his head out of the rocks at 0900. This afternoon I saw one eating dove droppings, and also observed them eating the fruits of the hedgehog and bush cholla cacti—it was amusing to see how they avoided the spines. They ranged a considerable distance, as I saw two of them at 1850 high on a point at least 600 ft. northeast of the spring. Their alarm call is certainly loud and jarring.

Two adult and one immature golden eagles were frequently seen. In the late afternoon, one (or both?) of the adults was twice seen to alight on a mountainside, pick up a stick in its beak, take wing, and deftly transfer the stick from bill to feet. On one occasion, the immature sailed after an adult as it (the adult) was carrying a stick, screaming all the while—for food? At 1500, 3 common ravens were seen chasing one of the adult eagles.

I am a little surprised to find canyon wrens present—not only at the spring but also near camp. I heard a roadrunner near the spring about 0830. There was a late Costa's hummingbird at the spring about 0900. Perhaps the most interesting bird of the day was one I didn't identify. I feel quite certain it was a varied bunting! It flew into one of the mesquites at 1115, and uttered its note several times—a buzzy note, but not as buzzy as the lazuli bunting's. As it flew off, I noted its size as being quite small, and its back appeared grayish. Another mystery that may never be solved.

I stayed at the spring until 1930, then returned to camp. It was a fine day—not at all hot, a light breeze, and a good many fine cumulus clouds. I passed much of the time reading W. H. Hudson's *Far Away and Long Ago*. I was fascinated by it—such an interesting account!

[A tabulation of fifteen species of birds seen that day follows—*Ed.*]

Heart Tank
June 4, 1956

Heart Tank area, entire 24 hrs. The early hour of 0400 found me up. The moon had just risen over the crest of the Sierra Pinta, and I got a quick breakfast by her light. An elf owl called from nearby. At 0450 I was hiking up the trail to Heart Tank, to begin the first day of my 5-day vigil there. At 0515, an adult golden eagle sailed over the mountains—pretty early for one of its kind to be astir! I selected a cave above and to the southeast of the tank for my hideout, not more than 100 ft. from the water. I moved into it at 0550 and set up the Exakta 35-mm camera with a 300-mm tele-photo lens I have borrowed.

The morning—and forenoon—were cloudy, a sort of high medium overcast, and warm and calm. Things were rather quiet for a time, except for the steady hum of the honey bees at the tank and the continual cooing of white-winged doves. I heard a canyon wren and a Scott oriole. The first white-wings were in to drink at 0750. They kept arriving through the day, most of them coming over the top of the mountains with a wonderful downward rushing swoop. The largest numbers, about 75, came between

0700 and 0800, and by 1200 most of them had arrived. They hung around until about 1430, when most had left. Thus, there was only one main flight during the day. A few—no more than 7—mourning doves were also seen. I saw house finches all day, but I think they were a flock of 13 or 14 that just hung around. The maximum number of white-wings present at any one time I estimated at 120, but I believe the total number that watered was about 310. Gambel's quail, too, were present—a lone cock drank at 0930, a pair came in at 1430, and a second pair (male very gray on back and tail) at 1800.

At just about 1030, a small bird in a low Mexican jumping-bean bush attracted my attention. I could scarcely believe my eyes when I saw it was a yellow-throated vireo! It didn't stick around but a couple of minutes, giving me the impression that it was ill-at-ease. This is certainly a heck of a place to see a yellow-throated vireo!—and a most unusual bird to be added to the refuge bird list.

Later in the day I was somewhat surprised to see 2 common ravens attacking a golden eagle. They flew about for a few minutes, cawing and croaking, before going off down-canyon. I also saw a female Scott oriole.

As for bighorns, I saw only ewes. A small, old, and long-horned ewe came in from the northwest at 1055, went unhesitatingly to water, took a long drink, and finally went off to the south at 1210. At 1815, another ewe appeared, followed by two more. They all appeared to be middle-aged, one of them older than the other two. They "snuffed" at me for a long time and finally went down to the tank at about 1930, but I'm not sure whether they drank or not—I doubt it. It was getting dark, so I left at 1950, scaring the trio off to the south as I did so. Score for the day—4 ewes.

I heard a spotted toad croaking down by the tank, just a trill or two at a time, from 1210 on, as follows: 1210, 1235, 1325, 1542, 1558, 1605, 1608, 1620, 1630, 1657, 1714, 1722, 1725, 1739, 1748, 1750, 1802, 1804, 1817, 1829, 1835, 1838, 1841, 1843, 1900, 1905, 1915, and 1919, and then frequently. It was really getting warmed up as I left the tank. They are peculiar creatures.

Back in camp at 2015, I captured a blind snake (an immature, very small) that came wriggling out of the fireplace after the fire had been going some time. I put it in some formaldehyde solution I had with me. Ate a big dinner featuring Vienna sausage and kidney beans, and was in bed at 2130. A good day!

Elephant tree is now utterly leafless, jumping bean nearly so.

Bighorns eat the oddest stuff. The old ewe I saw about midday browsed on brittle bush and *Franseria [Ambrosia] ilicifolia*. One of the ewes seen at evening time ate *dry F. ilicifolia* leaves.

The air force boys were over several times today with their jets. They did very little firing, however.

There is part of a case of dynamite just below my cave. It was left over from the improvement work done at Heart Tank in 1948. The tank, incidentally, is now 48 in. below the full mark, and still seems to have about 36 in. of water left.

[A tabulation of fifteen species of birds seen closes the day's account— *Ed.*]

July 25, 1958

Halfway Tank area, entire 24 hrs. Not long after going to bed last night, I was startled to hear, close at hand, a loud noise—very similar to the inhaling-grunt noise made by a common pig. I surmised it was a javelina. After several repetitions of the noise, I could hear the author up on the hillside, making a detour around my camp. . . . A little later, a poorwill began calling, and kept it up for quite some time. This is the first time I've heard a poorwill call on the Cabeza Prieta in summer!

This morning I was up at 0415, to a bright galaxy of stars—the Pleiades and Aldebaran in plain sight, Orion just rising. Venus in all her glory came over the eastern mountains as I left camp. At 0510, still in good dusk, I was settled at my post, beneath a palo verde on the hillside a little more than 100 ft. from Halfway Tank. From there I had a good view of all that went on below me.

I didn't expect to see many bighorn today—and I didn't. At 0545, I saw a large-horned ram on the ridge-top to the south. I expect he was the ram I saw yesterday. He stayed in sight only a short while. At 0940, he (possibly another individual?) came in from the southeast to within 150 ft. of the tank. He disappeared, but later in the afternoon I spotted him up in a cave, about one-half mile to the southeast. He stayed in the cave until 1615, then disappeared for good. He was an old ram, 12–14 years old, with the tips of both horns broken off square.

Another old ram—an ancient one, 14 years or older—came in from the northwest at 1750. He had very wrinkled and beat-up horns, with a large crease in the left horn about one-third its length from the base. There was nothing sprightly about him. He didn't come near the tank. He stayed in sight for just about an hour, then returned the way he came. So much for bighorn.

White-winged doves, of course, were by far the most conspicuous birds, coming in during the day from all directions. As is usual with the species, they watered in groups. These I kept track of, as well as I could. There was *no* watering except in groups. I counted 944 during the day, and 31 mourning doves. To judge by the sticky-looking bills, saguaro fruits are still the main diet of the white-wings.

As for other birds, I had a rather interesting day. House finches and lesser goldfinches were present at all times in varying, but small, numbers. My counts of them are surely subject to a high percentage of error. The largest number present at any one time was 10 and 6, respectively. There were plenty of orioles—a flock of 5 Bullocks, a male hooded plus another heard, and a female/immature Scott. Then there were a male black-headed grosbeak and 2 male western tanagers. Common ravens—2—were overhead at 1055, 1750, and 1830. What wanderers they are! Turkey vultures drifted past now and then in the afternoon. Late in the afternoon a male sparrow hawk was present.

Two amusing antelope ground squirrels were in sight much of the time, except for the forepart of the afternoon. I heard a spotted toad several times. . . . I left my post at 1920, and back in the camp I heard the clear whistle of a curve-billed thrasher three times. This is surely my westernmost record for that species on the Cabeza Prieta. . . . I went to bed at 2030—I was tired! . . . Weather was clear, hot, and mostly still—not too uncomfortable.

Counting Sheep — The Hard Way

As journalist Ed Severson once quipped, "Bill Broyles's passion for the empty spaces and his epic desert exploits have earned him a reputation among desert rats as a kind of sun-seared rat prince." The difficulty is, you hardly ever hear of those exploits straight from the desert rat's own mouth because of Broyles's nonchalance and self-effacing humor. As a case in point, I once noticed that a map of the Sierra Pinacate on his wall was riddled with pencil lines across it.

"Hey, Bill, what are those lines marking?"

"Oh, they're just trails . . ."

"Prehistoric trails?"

"Some of them . . . well, they're routes."

"Whose routes?" I probed.

"Well, they're routes I've walked or run across the Pinacate over the years . . . Hey, look at this book I just received in the mail."

Some of those routes include 45-mile stretches devoid of water and 130-mile treks that Broyles routinely runs "for fun." He has not only initiated others to the Camino del Diablo run but annually holds a "survivors" party for those who lived to tell about a summer weekend shared with him.

Remarkably, his scholarship on the history of the Cabeza Prieta is as rigorous as his physical accomplishments. While Broyles has worked as

This essay was previously published in the *Tucson Citizen*, September 15, 1984.

an English and physical education instructor at Rincon High School in Tucson he has been gathering oral histories, weather data, maps, and journal accounts which flesh out the cultural and biological history of western Pima County and southeastern Yuma County. Because it is relatively uninhabited today, this area has been overlooked by most conventional historians. Nevertheless, Broyles, Ronald Ives, Bill Hoy, and Bernard Fontana are among the few who have found more than enough there to occupy them for several lifetimes. Broyles has begun to share some of his writings on the natural wonders and cultural curiosities of that region in the *Journal of the Southwest* and *Arizona Highways,* but he still has more unpublished manuscripts than most scholars accumulate over their entire lives.

Broyles's generosity toward other scholars and writers also makes him exceptional. He introduced three of us who appear in this anthology— Zwinger, Bowden, and Nabhan—to the summer ritual of water hole sheep counts and assisted Ed Abbey and Byrd Baylor with their sojourns in the Cabeza Prieta as well. This account of one year's water hole episodes, written for the *Tucson Citizen* (September 15, 1984), remains among the best.

If I didn't want this job, it would cost the U.S. Fish and Wildlife Service a cool million. Plus expenses.

Sit for fifteen hours a day in a five-by-seven-foot wooden box? In the desert? Between Ajo and Yuma? In summer? To watch some wild sheep *maybe* drop by for a drink?

Are you crazy?

But I volunteered.

Crazy.

Each summer the Cabeza Prieta National Wildlife Refuge, some 900,000 acres of prime desert habitat, counts sheep. It monitors the size, distribution, and condition of its bighorn sheep population by posting observers at eight selected water tanks. These tanks, usually enhanced natural catchments (*tinajas*), hold rainwater for most, if not all, of the year.

The premise for this desert miniseries holds that on the hottest and driest week of the year, sheep in the area will stop in for a drink. It's rather like the census-taker staking out the supermarket to survey who buys ice cream on the hottest, driest day of the summer.

The refuge is an animal haven specializing in bighorns and pronghorns. Pronghorns apparently neither eat ice cream nor drink water, so their surveys are done by air.

Sheep also are surveyed by air, but the process is far more costly and dangerous than water hole watching. (Several sheep counters in other areas have perished on such flights.) Besides, the sheep here next to Luke Air Force Base Bombing Range are well accustomed to aircraft and seldom stir from their beds until the second or third pass of the plane.

Tank-sitting allows extended, close-up visits with the sheep, cheaply and (I hope) safely.

This tank fits neatly into a side canyon of the Cabeza Prieta Mountains. A small wash, dammed slightly, shares its rare flow with a six-by-ten-foot concrete box. The bottom slopes, so animals won't be trapped, to a depth of six feet. Corrugated metal provides a roof and helps slow evaporation.

Bees, needing water to cool their hive, are the tank's most numerous customers. Next are the white-winged doves. At one time I counted fifty-three members of The Flapping and Cooing Society in quorum. Even then others perched nearby awaiting their turns.

This multitude of birds is, as you might expect, outrageously busy and noisy. Except once.

At sunset I was near to finishing a book (fringe benefit: sheep watchers may read on duty) when my bird-battered senses suddenly heard only quiet, as if a noisy party abruptly lapsed mute.

With bewilderment, I studied the scene. Why? I didn't have to puzzle long.

Up onto the tank wall jumped a cat. It looked for all practical purposes like a spotted house cat. It sat. It looked around. It yawned. It curled its tail around itself. Sweet and innocent . . . looking.

The birds knew better. They stayed hushed and frozen. The cat didn't drink.

Instead it stretched—that rangy feline stretch. Its lanky legs must have bridged six feet of ground. There and then the semblance between a tame cat and a wild bobcat ended. A trout is to a barracuda as a house cat is to . . .

It then lay under a palo verde until I could see no more of it in the twilight.

In the predawn I found three freshly gnawed bird wings along the arroyo. The cat had eaten well last night. Death comes swiftly in the desert.

The blind's skeleton is pipe, roofed with discarded plywood and sided by saguaro ribs laced to the pipe. Five feet wide, seven long, and uncomfortably less than six tall. Real first-class accommodations for a week's vacation. It perches on the steep hillside veiled by a palo verde tree. The observer watches through breaks in the barlike ribs, much like peering at a movie through half-closed Venetian blinds.

Last year at this same time I sat for five days to count *one* ram. Ironically, a few weeks later while driving to the tank to check the water level, I met a casual ram prancing blithely down the road. Sheep watchers get no respect out here. From anything.

Still, I returned for this year's count.

A sample day begins with a ten-minute walk from camp to the blind . . . before 5:00 A.M. This predawn is the day's most serene and beautiful time. Its subtle smells, sounds, and sights, plus the air's cool touch, "make" the day.

At five and every hour thereafter, the temperature, wind, and cloud cover are recorded. Partly this provides "dryness" data, and mostly, I suspect, it keeps the observer sane and alert.

Sitting in a lawn chair with notebook, binoculars, and camera close to hand, I wait for the onslaught of doves. A four-inch scorpion prowls the blind's perimeter in search of crickets. Later, small black wasps will patrol for caterpillars. Great company for a city boy who's donating his time.

At 6:12 the doves swoop in as if called by a bell. At 6:23 the crowd hushes to a whisper. A gray fox sniffs the wash, turns into the tank for five short, nervous drinks, and then strolls on downstream. The clamor resumes.

At 8:14 the U.S. Air Force startles me to attention with the first bombardment of twenty to thirty daily sonic booms. The birds pay no heed.

By 8:30, after an apple and drink, I read, glancing every half page at the tank.

At 8:53 I hear hoof-falls on the far *bajada*. Sure enough, here come two rams. They warily stop every thirty yards to look. For several minutes they look. In all directions. They nibble browned brittle bush and nudge dried tuft grass.

Both are large. Their three-fourths curls indicate that for six to eight years they have looked very carefully. One has pointed horn tips and a sand-colored coat. The other, even heavier, bears a mahogany coat; his horn tips are blunted. Both horn sets are wide and, as are most in this area, reddish.

For the survey each sheep is numbered and charted. Sex, age, condition, and identifying characteristics are noted. A spot here, an unshed patch there, a scarred horn all serve to distinguish. No, if you've seen one sheep you haven't seen 'em all.

These are rams 1 and 2. Number 1, the mahogany, is calmer and probably older. They mill around beneath a large palo verde before stepping into the shaded wash at the tank very cautiously. They paw the sand, circle the spot, and kneel down to rest.

Occasionally, one's massive head droops to the ground for a few minutes. Otherwise they lie calmly but watchfully. The sonic booms don't startle them.

At 10:16 the sandy one approaches the tank and, after half a dozen skitterish starts, kneels to drink. And drink. And drink. By actual time he drinks for three minutes and twenty-six seconds, by no means a record. Just a moderately thirsty desert bighorn, with a canteen-sized stomach.

He returns to bed on the shady side of the wash.

Abruptly at 10:48 both rams bolt upright and with powerful fullback strides spring up the bajada amid a clattering of stones. Why?

Had they heard the camera click? Had they winded me? Even after three days in the desert I didn't think I smelled that raunchy.

The blond answer saunters down the wash: a coyote. The rams stand two hundred yards away intently watching the opportunistic coyote amble furtively past the still warm sheep beds and out into the valley. He was no real threat to them. The rams turn away and browse their way up the granite ridge, presumably to rest in the penthouse.

Midday passes uneventfully. And, actually, quite pleasantly. With adequate drinking water, ninety-nine degrees in a shaded, breeze-fanned blind is quite comfortable. We city folks seem to have forgotten the comfort of ramadas. We build solid walls and then wonder why we need cooling systems.

At 5:19, during chapter 16 of an intriguing book, I became vaguely aware of a presence, sensing that intangible, uneasy feeling of being watched. I stare at the tank. I scan the wash and trees. Nothing. Three days in a blind is too soon to go batty, so I try to read again.

Still I feel eyes on me.

Then a faint snort sounds above. Above?

Slowly I turn upward to see a ram standing not twenty feet above the blind, peering from the rock cliff through a three-inch ceiling crack. He twists his head to one side, cocks it to the opposite tilt, and sniffs the air, puzzled.

I muffle a laugh and peer back. The great wildlife observer has been snuck up on. Spied on. By a sheep. Humiliation won't be in my next contract.

For a full twenty minutes he tries to figure the mystery guest in the blind. Maybe he was reading over my shoulder. I don't know. But then he glides down to the tank as only sheep can do so wonderfully and gracefully on steep rock.

He drinks for a minute and fifty seconds and then traverses up the westward ridge.

At sundown the doves intensify their drinking before roosting for the evening. I return to camp.

By 9:20 I finish dinner and spread out the sleeping bag. A few bats flutter. An owl hoots. The stars blink. And I sleep very well. After all, I've already counted my sheep. Tough life here in the wilds.

A week of such travail—no telephone, uncomplicated duty, leisure reading, cheap entertainment, serene skies—allowed me to chart eight sheep. My most serious concern of the week: Would my oft-repaired chair survive or would it dump me unceremoniously on the ground? Oh, it was awful.

Seven other observers spent the same sort of frightful and overwrought week. (See, I'm not the only crazy on the loose.) Linda Hagen, refuge supervisor, Jusefina Mize, Lyle Williams, Dennis Segura, Dexter Oliver, and Roger DiRosa, also refuge employees, as well as Russel Haughey, all volunteered. Altogether, we counted forty-six sheep.

Roger DiRosa, assistant refuge manager, rates this year's summer water-hole survey "the best ever. The previous high was forty-two sheep in 1980. Both these years were very dry prior to the count.

"The forty-six sheep counted this year—twenty-five rams, eighteen ewes, two lambs, and one unclassified—appeared exceptionally healthy. Sixteen class III and IV rams (three-quarters curl or better) were recorded. Three state-issued hunting permits apply to our refuge.

"Overall, we estimate the Cabeza Prieta population to be stable in the range of two hundred plus members," adds DiRosa at the refuge headquarters in Ajo. "Although a thorough and complete census for the entire refuge needs to be done, it will be expensive and has not yet been funded."

Will I ever do this again? Desert? Summer? Heat? Fifteen-hour days?

Where's my cool million? I want a bonus, too! And fringe benefits this time.

If ever I go again, it'll be kicking and screaming . . . just like Br'er Rabbit to the briar patch.

The Heat Treatment: *What Kind of Fool Would Sit in the Desert Counting Sheep in June? A Hot One*

Charles Bowden's first book, *Killing the Hidden Waters* (University of Texas Press, 1977), is about the degradation of desert and cultural loss among its people. Darkly prophetic, it triggered the creation of a whole new field of environmental concern that examines how mining fossil groundwater has bankrupted natural and agricultural ecosystems and has driven cultures beyond the limits of sustainability. More recently he has dealt with a wide range of bankruptcies, including the savings and loan scandal, but there remains a common thread running through Bowden's writing: those who are disenfranchised from their own selves and cultural histories because they believe modern myths tend to destroy the natural and cultural communities around them.

Bowden's finest book, *Blue Desert* (University of Arizona Press, 1986), juxtaposes urban pathologies with the destruction of desert animals and habitats to show their common origin in rootlessness. In a style his desert rat admirers have dubbed "arroyo of consciousness" writing he exposes us directly to the horror of dead rivers, dry boreholes, endangered species, disrupted families, and emotionally crippled individuals. At its best, Bowden's spare, haunting prose embodies the challenge that John Hay has set before American writers: "The more our disengagement from nature gets out in the open, the better off we'll be."

This essay was previously published in *City Magazine* (Tucson, Ariz.), February 1987, pp. 29–31.

Bowden has done time as a social historian, water policy analyst, gonzo journalist, ecological field assistant, and free-lance writer, contributing everything from op-eds for *USA Today* to travel pieces for *Arizona Highways*. His most innovative work, however, is often the mid-length essay that takes enough twists and turns from its original objective that it finds new ground without also finding old ruts. One of his most well-worn ruts is wondering whether he or any other human actually belongs in the desert, so that his pleasure in being out in the elements is often mixed with guilt. In his "Six Part Invention" for Jack Dykinga's *The Sonoran Desert* (Harry Abrams, 1992) he says that "the game is almost over and this is the last deal in one of the last places left. That is why it still persists—our ancestors couldn't figure out how to rape it."

If many of his soliloquies sound like a codependent confessing our society's cumulative sins to the family priest, then the following essay (from *City Magazine,* February 1987) is Bowden released to do penance in the desert. It finds Bowden in his outdoor rehab clinic, alone with a million hot and thorny therapies, enjoying what he believes in most. Fortunately for all of us, Bowden spends enough time in the desert to revive his energies in order to fearlessly illuminate what few people in our society care to see or hear.

Night slides down the mountainside, and the temperature in the Tule Desert sinks to 108 in the shade. A bighorn sheep fifty yards away gawks at me while I nervously work down a steep stone slope. I can see amusement in her big, dumb eyes. Suddenly, my backpack nicks a boulder. I hear a horrible grind as the hefty stone slips, slices open my calf, and finally comes to rest on my heel. I am wearing running shorts, running shoes, and a T-shirt, and I am not pleased.

I wince from the pain and inspect the big rock now snoring on my heel. The sheep does not blink—I have made her day. I gingerly move my foot; the slab rumbles down toward the boulder-choked wash below. It can't get any better than this.

The light is a gray gauze as I reach the bottom of the rock face, and then I stagger across the half mile of wash toward my camp. Warm blood dribbles a Jackson Pollock pattern on my leg. The air is a blazing Jell-O, a solid blob of molecules that has napalmed my body since dawn. Sheep droppings decorate the arroyo, ironwood and palo verde sketch out neat red slashes on my whimpering hide. I slip and slide through a maze of boulders, visit with thorns and cactus eager for a piece of me. A vulture pops up from underneath a boxcar-sized boulder, then another grinning buzzard and another and another. I walk over to see what the fuss is about. A coyote lies stretched out on the sand, flies buzzing around the gray-and-tan body, the flesh swollen just a bit with heat and death. My nose stops me fifteen feet from the carcass.

I think: he has solved the heat problem.

Twenty minutes after exiting the rock face, I stumble into my camp. Home is a simple place: fifteen gallons of water, five freeze-dried dinners, a generous larder of Spam, sixteen granola bars, three pounds of sunflower seeds, twelve books of almost unbearable dullness, a jar of industrial-strength instant coffee, and, most importantly, no ice. A thin blue pad defines my bunk on the smouldering ground (soil temperatures here sizzle around 150 to 160 degrees), and nearby is a folding chair, the aluminum Chippendale of my genteel life.

I make a small fire of ironwood twigs, boil water for a crime against my digestive tract called Burgundy Beef with Noodles, and then relax in the blast furnace while slopping down my gruel from an aluminum pouch. Bats flutter around my face.

I call it a day, stretch out on the blue pad, note the stars puncturing the sky as night comes on, and wait for the music. At precisely 11:30 each night a coyote explodes into a mixture of heavy metal and punk about one meter from my eardrum. The concert lasts two to four minutes, and then there is nothing left to do but bake until dawn.

I have been here for five days. I am alone, forty miles east of Yuma, maybe sixty miles west of Ajo, thirty miles south of Interstate 8, and deep in the heart of one of America's favorite bombing and gunnery ranges. I am on the west flank of a rockpile called the Sierra Pintas. Nearby is a tank—a hole where the rains collect; that is, when and if they happen by every year or two. The water is green scum encrusted with a fine carpet of dead honey bees. Dung flavors this beverage.

I am here on serious business. I am counting sheep. Yes, I am.

The Cabeza Prieta National Wildlife Refuge covers 865,000 acres, and nobody lives there. The gunnery range covers even more ground, and nobody lives there either. We are talking about a couple of thousand square miles with live rounds, bighorn sheep, no paved roads, no people, and me, an official sheep counter for the United States government. Every June for the past thirty years, the feds have dispatched a handful of pilgrims to various water holes to inventory the sheep. Such workers sit motionless in the heat for five days, busily count off the herd on their fingers and toes, and then go home again. This is called science.

I would like to claim that I am here as a peculiar punishment for some act against God or man. But this is not the case. I volunteered for the job, as did a dozen other fried souls scattered about the Tule Desert, the Lechuguilla Desert, the Growler Valley, and other landmarks in hell.

I wanted to be alone. I wanted to see what heat was really like when there was no escape. I wanted to think big thoughts: I have a completely empty notebook sitting on my lap as evidence of this last goal.

I will tell you everything.

It is noon and a white flame of light sweeps across the desert floor. I am walking, a brief coffee break from my sheep-counting duties back at the tank. Heat boils up from the ground through the soles of my running shoes. I wear no socks. I wear no shirt. I wear no shorts. I wear no hat. I eat Solution No. 817. This solution is not working.

I look down at my feet and see a pottery fragment. A closer examination reveals similar debris everywhere. To the north a half mile are two small caves where early men and women and children, damnable litterbugs that they were, left busted pots, old sheep bones, and random garbage. Folks used to call this place home. In 1699, Father Kino may have ambled through here on one of his interminable marches across the desert seeking lost souls and new geography. Then, in 1939, Franklin Delano Roosevelt, at the prodding of the Ajo Boy Scouts and others, scratched his pen on a document and made the whole joint a refuge for desert bighorns. Then the war came and more ground was set aside as a shooting gallery. Now I am here. That's history for you.

I hear a big boom; my head whips toward the noise; a jet arcs across the sky and plays war games while giving the sound barrier a thorough drubbing. Then silence, absolute silence. The birds refuse to speak in the heat of midday, the insects shut up, too, and the wind has not yet started. Silence flattens the land.

I listen to the blood coursing through my veins.

It is 112 in the shade as I lie in the blind near the waterhole. The structure is a frail *ramada* (shelter) of saguaro ribs. All the wild animals know I am in here; I can see this knowledge in their eyes. But the blind is a necessary courtesy. I am that unspeakable thing to them, a human being, and it is best that I keep out of their sight as they bake through another Tule Desert day.

A golden eagle stands on the edge of the water hole. The beak is open, the tongue hangs down, the bird pants. The talons look like murder. The eagle peers up at me and then down at the water. It is 2:00 P.M., and eagle time is apparently as rigorous as factory time, since the big bird appears punctually each day. At noon, the red-tailed hawks always come in, four of them, and drink and splash in the water. The doves prefer dawn, 1:00 P.M., and dusk. Four ravens always show up around 4:30 P.M. The sheep are not so simple. They can go up to nine days without water.

The eagle pants and pants. I pant and pant. I hunker in the blind fourteen hours a day now, sitting on a boulder and exposed to the blast of the sun as it knifes through the hit-and-miss roof of sticks.

My mind stopped working days ago. I literally do not think. I sense, I know, I feel, but I do not think. I have no anxiety, I cannot think enough to be concerned about anything. Here is a sample of my mind at 112 degrees: six vultures land at the tank, they space themselves two feet apart, they drink one by one, they leave. Bees roar. Sun thuds off the stone. The eagle pants and no one pays any attention. The vultures course down the canyon and land near the dead coyote.

I can go on like this for hours. And I do.

At night I see satellites zip across the heavens. To the east, flashes of lightning suggest the monsoon has arrived in Tucson. One evening at dusk, I sit in my chair and stare at a rock face sixty yards away while I eat Sweet and Sour Shrimp with Rice. A coyote slips down the slope, the tail flowing. The animal does not hesitate and refuses to look at me.

I sprawl out on the blue pad, moths land on me, and then the bats flit by a foot off the ground and eat the moths. I am a dining room table.

I had assumed that ideas about Nature would flood my mind during this five-day stay. I am happy to report this does not happen. I see a coyote. I see a sheep. I listen to silence. I swelter in the heat. Each day I stop by the dead coyote and check on how the vultures' work is progressing. A hummingbird hovers six inches from my face, an antelope ground squirrel nibbles seeds a foot from my leg. I pick up a jug and the fluid splashes in my mouth like it was straight from a hot water heater.

But thinking about Nature here would be an insult. Thinking itself is an insult. There is nothing to contribute. I can tell by looking into the eyes of a bighorn; I have no doubt when watching the careless disdain of the coyote for my presence. This is a place to be. I am not sure how to define being, but I am getting quite good at being. I sleep very soundly and awaken an hour before dawn. The air is cooler then, in the mid-eighties, and the smells are stronger and richer and the desert requires nothing because everything that is necessary already is.

One day a huge ram, perhaps six to eight years old, walks up to the tank. His big horns have more than a three-quarter curl, his body is well fleshed, and he moves with dignity. He stands for half an hour before the tank of water, trying to decide whether to drink. He decides, moves forward, and lowers his head for six minutes and twenty-five seconds. I time him: science demands this deed.

I read a book on bighorn sheep. The author states that rams will only associate with other rams that have horns the same size as they do.

He ain't heavy, he's my brother.

Early Spanish explorers found pyramids of sheep horns in this desert. Later scholars stumbled onto a similar pyramid near the tank where I now bake. No one is quite sure what the pyramids of horns were supposed to do, but they were clearly some kind of gesture by early Tule Desert people. The Sand Papagos who frequented this area until early in this century said the piles of horns stopped the wind. The wind here is a potent force, a blazing surge that comes up around noon and streams across the flats, withering everything in its path. I drink water all the time but I cannot keep up with the power of this wind.

Scholars also found sheep bones, usually vertebrae, that had deep burns on them. They had been fired at high heats for long periods of time, far longer than was necessary to cook the flesh. The sheep had been cremated. This desert in southwestern Arizona and the Pinacate country just to the south in Sonora are the only known places in the Western Hemisphere where human beings cremated nonhuman beings.

No one is quite sure why this happened either. There are whispers of explanation. The Papago at the turn of the last century said it was to placate the sheep, to calm them and win them over so that their spirits would not be angry and go visit the living sheep and say bad things about men, things that would scare away the herds. This makes sense to me. If I ever kill a sheep out here, I am certain I will cremate the beast.

There are other variant forms of cremation taking place here. Below my tank spreads the Tule Desert, a pan of fire that officially hosts four inches of rain a year. In the first ten days of June, the Border Patrol took four dead Mexicans out of this area. They were illegals heading north toward work. There are all kinds of dead people out there, and most are never found. No one cremates their bones. No one knows how to still their spirits.

In a week it will be the Fourth of July. I peer into the volcano of the Tule Desert at noon. They are out there. But we have no striking rituals to handle this dying. When a body is found, we toss the flesh and bones into a rubber bag and tote it off to a pauper's grave. This does not seem like quite enough. We have lost the knack of desert cremation, and I suspect the spirits are not at peace, but wander this ground. And I do not want to think what they say about us.

I have not moved for four hours. Sweat streams from my body. I drink; more sweat pours out. The tank is still, just a bunch of white-winged doves sitting on the rock in the sun and broiling nicely. I hear a kind of scream; a brown form plummets, misses, wheels, and dives again. I stare into the face of a prairie falcon thirty yards away. A dead dove is gripped in its talons. The flock explodes and flees. The falcon looks up at me, and for a second or two there is nothing but the beautiful raptor, the dead dove, the heat, and death.

Then the bird vanishes. I know it leaves, I witness this exit, but in fact it simply vanishes. One second it is there with the dead dove gripped by its black talons, the next it is gone. I have no conscious memory of the falcon flying away.

The tank falls very still. A few gray feathers flutter down the rock where the kill took place. For thirty-one minutes, no doves come to the tank. Yes, I time it. Science once again. Then a flock lands, putters around the rock, sits in plain view under the sun, and returns to whatever life means to a white-winged dove.

I think there should be precautions, drills, air alerts. But there is nothing. The death is not even memory. This is the Tule Desert and it is 112 degrees and no one is up to anything but life itself.

In five days of watching, I see three ewes and two rams, or maybe five ewes and two rams. After awhile, all those ewes start to look pretty much the same.

My notebook remains absolutely empty. I sit in the morning light and wait for a truck to come by and pick me up and take me away. A stone tumbles nearby, I glance over and see a two-year-old ram romp off the rock face and then calmly walk down the wash, nibbling at ironwood shoots at he goes. He is fifty or sixty yards away and I do not interest him. Gnatcatchers and verdins and other birds flit from tree to tree.

I hike up the wash and check on the dead coyote. The vultures are gone; I can see them overhead riding a thermal. There is not much left of the coyote: the outline of the head, the empty rib cage, a pile of fluff marking the discards of his fur. He is in the Tule Desert now, powering the muscles of the vultures as they scan the bare ground for things that have run out of time.

I sit in the sun and drink a cup of black coffee. I do not think of Nature at all. I have not spoken in five days. My leg and heel are mending nicely.

An American poet once wrote, "Do not listen to the birds / They are ignorant."

Like hell they are.

Of White-Winged Doves and Desert Bighorns

Ann Haymond Zwinger, who trained to be an art historian, came to desert natural history gradually, after writing about alpine ecology, Western rivers, and the Colorado Plateau. I well remember the publication of her first book, *Beyond the Aspen Grove* (Random House, 1970), for when my college friend Susan Zwinger showed me a copy freshly sent by her mother, it dawned on me that some people had the wits to make a career of work as lovely as that; I vowed then to try my hand at nature writing myself! To this day, I remain awed by how true Ann Zwinger has remained to what Jacob Bronowski called "that quaint Victorian profession" of natural history. Her drawings and essays continue to be as artful and enjoyable as the ever-changing sounds of a perennial mountain stream.

Despite her objections to my appreciation of her skills as a field scientist, I will say in another way what I said during our dialogue in Ed Lueders's *Writing Natural History* (University of Utah Press, 1989). Ann Zwinger has over the years developed remarkable talents in interpreting botany, entomology, sedimentary geology, and biogeography, and she is faster at field identifications than most biology graduate students that I know. It may be that her eye for form, color, and texture—sharpened by years of making her own drawings, paintings, and collages, and studying those of others—preadapted Zwinger to a precise and discerning view of nature's patterns. In any case, she brings to any landscape the talents of a disciplined observer; to me, this is most evident in her Burroughs Medal–winning book, *Run, River, Run* (Harper and Row, 1975), and in *A Desert Country by the Sea* (Harper and Row, 1983).

Ann Zwinger's gifts go far beyond artistic discipline and well-paced stamina, as the following essay, truly one of her best ever, demonstrates. Originally prepared as a chapter for Ann's colorful survey of U.S. deserts, *The Mysterious Lands* (E. P. Dutton, 1989), it has also been excerpted in Stephen Trimble's *Words from the Land* (Peregrine Smith, 1988) and Robert Finch and John Elder's anthology, *The Norton Book of Nature Writing* (W. W. Norton, 1990). In this uncut version you sense that her first hours in the sheep blind were filled with apprehension—being saddled with the task of making scientifically credible field notes, surviving the heat alone, and so on. Then, miraculously, those anxieties slipped away, and we glimpse the ecstasy of a person both comfortable and enchanted with the world immediately before her. While Chuck Bowden rattled through the cholla a few miles away and Bill Broyles manned another water hole the very same week, Zwinger wove an altogether unique sheep count saga. It was the intriguing juxtaposition between the tones of Zwinger's and Bowden's essays that sparked my interest in editing this book. I urge you to read their contributions to this anthology during the same sitting, back-to-back. Truly, the heat of that week in the desert distilled Ann Zwinger down to her sweetest essences.

Cabeza Prieta means "dark head" in Spanish, and the peak that inspired that name blocks the horizon in front of us, a pyramid of pearly tan schist draped with a hangman's hood of black lava. It identifies the Cabeza Prieta Mountains, a forbidding black fault mountain range rising from an endless, boundless desert beset with a dryness and heat that devour colors and horizons and fade outlines until all that is left is shimmer.

This third week in June I enter the Cabeza Prieta National Wildlife Refuge with Chuck Bowden and Bill Broyles, both of whom have a desert fixation. When someone asks them why they go to the desert, they figure it's like J. P. Morgan's being asked how much his yacht cost. Bill, who in his sensible life is an English teacher, drives this road with an insane joy in the required high-clearance, four-wheel-drive vehicle. We enter the Cabeza Prieta from the north, and it seems to me we have come thousands of miles from refuge headquarters—where we have been briefed on bighorn sheep counting—driving first on highways, then narrow roads, then dirt roads, and now this ridiculous track.

"Road" is a euphemism. When wet, it imbibes rear axles. When dry, it buries you in sand for hours at a time. It has tracks with ruts that snap a wheel and is high-centered enough to batter a crankcase into oblivion. "Washboard" is too complimentary. We're talking lurching, jolting, tilting, loose-rock or deep-sand, kidney-busting roads that just don't care whether you travel them or not. Ocotillos, rude toll takers, thrust their thorny hands into the open window with intent to rob. On this questionable road, one not only eats dust and smells an overloaded and overheated engine, one also has to endure the squeals of vegetation dragging its fingernails along the sides of the truck, thorny plants as ill-tempered as the road itself.

We have volunteered to take part in a formal yearly desert bighorn sheep count that has been done here since 1961. In 1939 ninety bighorns were estimated to be on the refuge; today the number is approximately three hundred.

Desert bighorns roam the mountain range of the Cabeza in male and female bands (young rams are included in both) throughout most of the year, getting enough water and vegetation. They combine and come in to water holes only during the driest months of the year, May and June. The commingling announces the onset of the herd's breeding season, which is correlated to producing lambs at the most propitious time, a time that varies in each desert bighorn herd according to the particular mountain-range climate in which it lives.

We bounce into the small east-west valley that holds the tank where I will be stationed. The valley is narrow, rising to a notch between two high granite ridges to the west. Without gentling *bajadas* (slopes), the mountains bolt out of the floor, rubbled and pitted, short and steep, boldly tilted, roughed out with a chisel but never worked down or refined.

Bill offloads three jerry cans of water—enough for my six days here—a folding chair, and a cot. He and Chuck will go on to their own stations twenty miles away. I heave my duffel down, eager for them to be gone, anxious to set up desert housekeeping, ready to begin these days of immaculate isolation. The truck disappears into a cloud of dust, and for a moment I just stand quietly, blissfully alone. Then I unfold my chair, set up the tripod, and mount and focus the spotting telescope on the far slope, where I hope the sheep will be, wire the thermometer at eye level, and survey my kingdom.

The blind is half hidden beneath an ancient mesquite tree. Open in the rear and with a window facing the *tinaja,* the natural water pocket of the tank, it is made of four steel posts faced with saguaro ribs. The plywood roof has wallboard nailed underneath, and, in the space between, a heaping of mesquite twigs and pods hints at a wood-rat nest, a suspicion soon confirmed when the occupant itself sashays off to forage.

The tinaja itself is invisible from the blind. It is tucked to the right against a vertical wall, two hundred yards up the draw. Huge boulders flank it on the left; one, fifteen feet high, provides a provident perch for the several dozen birds that frequent it. Tomorrow I shall walk up to record its water level.

Promptly at 7:00 P.M. bats begin cruising the campsite, looping lower than I'm used to seeing bats fly, whishing right past my ear, winnowing the air for insects with great efficiency. After they leave, I get bitten. The light fades so gently that my eyes are adjusted to starlight by 9:30 P.M. when I go to bed. The air is a comfortable eighty-six degrees. The quiet is soporific. An infinitesimal breeze feathers my ankles and face all night long, the gentlest whisper of air in a great friendliness of night. Gazing up through the lacy canopy of mesquite leaves, I try only to doze, unwilling to miss anything. I do not succeed.

In the midst of a sound sleep, a sudden gust of wind looses an avalanche of mesquite twigs and pods and I shoot awake. The moon fingerpaints the sky with clouds. The Milky Way forms a great handle to the basket of the earth in which I lie. It is deliciously cool, enough so to pull up my sleeping bag. When I awake again, a big old saguaro hoists the near-full moon on its shoulder. By 4:30 A.M., when sheep watchers are expected to be sentient and at their task, pearly gray light seeps into the valley.

Mesquite pods litter my sleeping bag and shoes. My cup holds three like swizzle sticks. These mesquites have longer, slimmer fruits, smaller leaves and leaflets, and a larger number of leaflets than those in damper climes. Unlike other pea family pods, these do not split open but retain the seeds embedded in a hard covering, and an animal that eats one must eat pods and all. So important were they to the prehistoric Seri Indians who inhabited Sonora, Mexico, that they had names for eight different stages of fruit development. The Seris even sifted through wood-rat nests several months after harvest to recover the mesquite seeds. Their high protein and carbohydrate content made the seeds a significant addition to the Seris' diet. Other desert Indians, the Amargosa and Pinacateño, developed a special gyratory crusher for grinding them. All I can say from experience is that the fruits are as hard as rocks, as dry as bones, fall like lead weights, and truly do taste sweet.

I settle into my watcher's chair, in which I will spend so much time that I will come to feel as if it is annealed to my behind. Immediately in front of the blind wends a dry, sandy streambed about eight feet wide, in the middle of which grows a twenty-five-foot saguaro with one massive arm raised in greeting. Some fruit remains on the cactus, looking like red blossoms—indeed, an early botanist mistook them for blossoms—but most have fallen to the sand and seethe with ants. George Thurber, botanist for the Mexican Boundary Survey in the 1850s, who first collected saguaro seeds, followed the Indian practice of rolling the coarse fruit pulp into balls for storage; the seeds he thus preserved later germinated in distant botanical gardens. A mature cactus can produce more than two hundred fruits, each with some thousand seeds. Of these, perhaps half a dozen will be left after birds and rodents and ants have devoured them. Not only are they nutritious, they fulfill the water requirements of most animals.

Behind the blind a low divide centers the valley between two narrow, wiggly sandy draws. The soil of the small divide, without benefit of shading mesquite or protective creosote bush, is cement hard, paved with rough granite chips from the flanking and flaking mountains. Anthills stud it, a cholla or two, a few bristly borages, and many spiny herbs, but mostly it is bare.

On the crest of the divide is a small hill of harvester ants, whose twelve-inch-wide stream of foragers was busy long before I found them this morning. With the temperature well above their threshold of fifty degrees Fahrenheit, they likely were out at first light. They swarm on a small gilia with cottony heads, harvest white forget-me-not seeds, explore peter-grass, and cart back not only seeds but leaf scraps and bracts, anything detachable. Thus laden, they totter back to the nest's dime-size opening, rimmed with a foot-wide circle of salt-and-pepper debris. There they disappear underground to feed the larvae that serve as the colony's collective stomach. Although the adults gather the food, chew it, and prepare it, it is the larvae that digest it and regurgitate part of it to the adults, and the colony cannot survive without their services.

By nine o'clock, when it is ninety degrees, not an ant is to be seen.

The white-winged dove contingent begins calling as the day warms, a repetitive call; not the familiar measured "who cooks for who" but an erratic, petulant "don't tell me, don't *tell* me!" Their calls intermingle with those of the mourning doves in antiphonal sound.

The air between the blind and the water tank begins to waver and shimmer. More doves arrive on the big rock overlooking the water. Throughout the day they gather, sometimes twenty or so in plenary sessions, sometimes playing musical chairs as they drop down to drink and return. But always in full sun.

Judging from their numbers, white-winged doves are exceedingly successful desert dwellers. The whitewing's clutch size is always two, and population increase depends upon how many clutches are laid and reared. They are capable of producing young throughout the year, apparently oblivious of the usual environmental spurs, such as day length and rain, that govern many birds. Very resistant to dehydration, they can lose up to 20 percent of their body weight and go four to five days without water. With access to water, they can tank up within five minutes. The doves' mobility makes it possible for them to water long distances away from where they nest.

Whitewings throw together a haphazard nest that provides little in the way of insulation or protection from sun when there are eggs in the nest. A brood patch, a small area of bare skin on the bird's breast, serves as a heat sink for the eggs that prevents them from overheating. Most desert birds maintain elevated body temperatures; white-winged doves have a lower body temperature and are able to maintain it during incubation. Males have an even lower body temperature during the day than females and do most of the egg tending during the hottest periods. In the Sonoran Desert in Arizona, even in direct sun, brooding birds never leave the nest unattended.

When they take off as a flock, their white wing patches shine while their dun-colored bodies fade into the background, and from a distance they look like a flock of small white birds. But I did not come to watch birds. I came to watch desert bighorns. And not one has shown itself.

In the noon stillness, the heat presses down, lies as heavy as a mohair wool blanket on my head, on my shoulders. It's only 108 degrees; knowing it can get up to 130 in these close canyons, I am thankful for small favors. The air around the rocks near the rock tank wavers with banners of heat. I feel stooped and bent with heat as I leave the shade of the blind to walk up to the tinaja. I need to record the tank's water level so I can see how much water evaporates during the week (it goes down three and a quarter inches). Bur-sage leaves disintegrate as I brush by them. Where there is shallow groundwater, mesquite and big clumps of saltbush outline the wash, many of them festooned with vining milkweed, twined and twisted in great heaps like a giant-size helping of vermicelli. Seedpods load catclaw, how ripe the seeds are depending on where the bush is set. By the blind the seeds are still green and held tightly in the pod; lower, they are drying to a salmon color, and in the hollow at the foot of the draw they are dark brown and shiny, rattling in the twisted pods.

Up the slope, a four-foot-high elephant tree has found a purchase in the rocky slope along the trail, leaves just perceptible, ready to unfold the moment it rains. The papery-barked trunks, fat for water storage, give off a familiar turpentine odor. Hollyleaf bur sage, endemic to the lower Sonoran, marches up the slope to the ridge crest. This bur sage retains its scalloped leaves for years, the oldest faded nearly pure white. Now, nettle-like seed heads remain; blooming is over for the year.

The granite surrounding the water tank is pale gray, crystalline, flecked with sparkling black mica and roughened with large quartz crystals. Like most tinajas here, it lies in the crease of a small stream channel. A silt-holding wall has been built above the pool, and some cementing at the lower end provides an apron where animals can safely approach the water. Higher water levels limn the rocky sides with gray lines, and an inch of vivid green algae circles the present pool. It swarms with bees, ravenous for water to replace the large amount they lose in flight. I hesitate a long minute, then make my measurement as quickly as possible because in recent years I've become allergic to bee stings.

Anaphylactic shock due to bee or insect stings is not common, but on a percentage basis it kills more people than venomous snakebite does. While it would take over a hundred stings to affect a nonsensitized person, just one sting can cause anaphylactic shock within minutes in one who is sensitized. Mellitin, a basic protein composed of thirteen different amino acids, is the chief toxin. It affects the permeability of skin capillaries, instigates a drop in blood pressure followed by a swift rise, and can cause severe asthma and damage nerves and muscle tissue. In fatalities, the allergic reaction to the sting causes a drop in blood pressure so massive that no oxygen gets to the heart or brain. With immediate medical help a necessity, and none within a hundred miles, I am exceedingly conservative.

On the way back to the blind, still thinking about venomous bites, I round a boulder and gasp: five feet in front of me, on a large flat rock, is a Gila monster, a fearsome-looking lizard because it's so big. The size of my forearm, its tail is massive and thick, a repository for fat and water. Vivid warning colors of black and light yellowish orange pattern its beaded skin. With only two venomous lizard species in the whole wide world, I nearly fall over one of them.

After a Gila monster locks onto its victim with its jaws, it chews. While doing so, it injects venom from glands set just under the skin of the lower jaw. Each tooth has sharp flanges flanking the grooves through which the venom flows, making its virulent bite very painful. In small animals death comes from respiratory paralysis. Although the bite brings severe pain and swelling, quickly followed by nausea and weakness, it is not usually fatal to human beings.

Gila monsters generally hunt at night during hot weather and are out during the day only in cooler seasons. Their metabolism is so low that they need to eat infrequently, and then prefer the eggs of reptiles and birds and the young of small rodents. I cannot imagine why it is out at this time of day. I back off with more speed than grace and leave it to its meditation.

An innocent little four-inch zebra-tailed lizard, perhaps more tan and white than zebra striped, scampers across the sand, its ringed tail curled up over its back like a pug dog. One of the fastest lizards around, it has a chevron pattern on its back and legs that blends in with the flickering shadows and becomes invisible when it skitters under an acacia. I watch it dully. By comparison, my legs feel made of lead.

I spend well over an hour out of the blind, most of it by necessity in the sun. The temperature is a hundred degrees when I get back at noon, despite a high overcast. Not only does air heat envelop me, but heat billows up from the ground and radiates from everything around me: the ceiling of the blind, the sand in the wash, the desert pavement.

I gulp down a half bottle of fruit juice, made highly conscious of the necessity to drink lots of liquids by a packet of articles thoughtfully presented to me by Bill Broyles, harrowing accounts of death by thirst in gory detail, including "tumid tongue and livid lips," "unclean blow-flies" that will gather on the eyes and ears of my "already festering carcass," pierced again and again by the cruel spines of cholla.

My pulse rate is up to ninety. My face is flushed. Small blood vessels at the skin's surface dilate in order to radiate heat back to the environment because skin temperature stays cooler (around ninety-two degrees) than the surrounding hot air. The dilation of skin vessels also ensures an ample supply of blood to activate the two million sweat glands on the body because, when air temperature reaches between eighty-six and ninety-two degrees, the only way the body can lose heat is by sweating. No amount of training, no amount of acclimation, alters the amount of water that is needed to replace water lost in perspiration. Because the body can neither store water nor reduce its need, water supply is critical.

Sweating makes it possible for humans to exist in the desert and is controlled by centers in the hypothalamus that have set points keyed to temperature. Overheating can be prevented by the loss of one cup of sweat per hour, but it's easy to lose more without sensing it because in the desert sweat evaporates the minute it reaches the skin surface. But there is a limit to how much cooling can be provided by sweating because sweat removes not only water but salts in the blood, upsetting the electrolyte balance. The loss of these components of the blood—sodium and potassium chlorides and lactic acid—can bring on the muscle cramping, head-ache, and fatigue that come with severe electrolyte imbalance.

Acclimatization helps by increasing the perspiration rate and volume, lowering body temperature and heart rate, beginning sweating at a slightly lower temperature, and up to tripling the capacity to transfer metabolic heat from the interior of the body to the skin. Circulating blood increases in volume, urinary sodium and chloride are better retained, and salt concentrations in perspiration decrease. But no matter how much one is acclimated, water remains critical to well-being.

Paradoxically, even with ample water available it is difficult to drink and recover the amount lost immediately because thirst becomes satiated before one's intake equals water loss. A person, voluntarily, drinks only a third to half of what is needed for replacement. This feeling of satiation may serve as a natural governor that prevents serious upsetting of the concentration of salts in the blood. Complete restoration usually comes when water is taken with food, and food replaces the lost salts. While it is almost impossible for someone to replace in one draft the full amount of water lost, animals do so by drinking greater quantities in shorter periods of time. A mourning dove can drink ten times (per body volume) what a human can drink in the same amount of time, and bighorn sheep can gulp down enough water at one time to recover their original weight.

If water loss from sweating is not replaced, sweat glands extract water from blood plasma, and body temperature rises. The loss of plasma water increases the viscosity of the blood, placing an additional stress on the heart, requiring more work to pump thickened blood through arteries and veins, and also raising the pulse rate. Even though the heart beats faster, the amount of blood pumped per minute remains nearly the same. In turn, retarded blood flow fosters a continuing rise in temperature in the inner core of the body, where the temperature needs to be stable (the temperature of the peripheral tissue can vary without causing problems). Pulse rate and rectal temperature increase, breathing quickens. (The same reduced blood volume does not affect the heart rate in dehydrated bighorn sheep.)

At 2 percent loss of body weight due to loss of body water, thirst for some may already be fierce, accompanied by anorexia, flushed skin, and increased pulse rate. Small increments of debit have large symptoms: at

4 percent the mouth and throat go dry; by 8 percent the tongue feels swollen, salivary functions cease, and speech becomes difficult. After 10 percent water loss the ability to cooperate, or even to operate, disappears. At 12 percent loss, circulation becomes so impaired that an explosive heat rise deep in the body is imminent and deep body temperature rises dangerously fast. Death follows, although lethal limits may be as high at 18 to 20 percent loss of body weight. When liquid is available, recovery can be nearly complete an hour after drinking.

At 104 degrees, one must evaporate an equivalent of 1.5 percent of one's body weight per hour to maintain a constant body temperature. I do a quick calculation: at 110 pounds, 1.5 percent of my body weight is 1.65 pounds. Because a pint's a pound the world around, to replace what I lost means drinking at least a quart of liquid because, in addition, the body produces about eighty calories of heat per hour through metabolic activity. Dissipating this through sweat requires another five ounces of water per hour. In other words, an hour's wandering has started me toward a 2 percent deficit.

I look with new respect at the bighorn sheep that can lose 20 percent of its body weight (or a 30 percent loss of total body water), or the white-winged dove that can lose 25 percent, with no ill effects and can even drink salt water, or the quail that survives loss of 50 percent of its body weight without succumbing.

I had anticipated some anorexia. Normal enough. I had also anticipated some of the psychological by-products of dehydration, such as lethargy or depression. Lethargy just may be the better part of valor in this heat, and as for depression, I have done nothing but walk around with a grin on my face the entire time. Like one of Carl Lumholtz's creosote bushes (Lumholtz traveled the Cabeza three quarters of a century ago), I feel "radiant with health and good cheer."

Nevertheless, I take another slug of juice. It insureth my well-being.

The sheep do not come in until the second day, as if they were waiting to be sure their intruder was from a friendly planet. As I periodically scan the mountain slope with binoculars, it is some moments before I realize that the "rocks" are moving. I nearly tip over the spotting scope in my delight and eagerness to get it focused. The bighorns come downslope with a deliberate, measured tread, pausing occasionally to stand and look about or pull off an acacia twig. Either eight or nine gather at the tinaja; they change places just often enough to make them exasperatingly difficult to count.

My first impression is of smallness and grace. Less than four feet high at the shoulder, they move easily over what I know to be a ruggedly steep and treacherous slope. With their smooth coats and long legs they bear little resemblance to domestic sheep, to which they are *not* related. The genus *Ovis* originated in Eurasia more than two and a half million years ago, migrated, as man did, across the Bering land bridge, and became isolated into different groups during glacial periods. Today desert bighorns inhabit the arid mountain ranges of the Southwestern deserts.

Although I observe no pushing or shoving, clearly there exists a hierarchy at the water tank. A large, mature ewe waters first, taking two-minute and then four-minute drafts, and then stands aside. She has shed most of her winter coat, but a continuous remnant cloaks her shoulders like a shawl, making her easy to identify when she appears again. Bighorn shedding begins at the rump and moves forward. All the other sheep have less old pelage clinging, suggesting that this ewe may be an older animal. She is accompanied by two lambs with their mothers, who never do go down to drink. The ability of desert bighorns to go without water exceeds even that of the camel. Their extensive rumen complex—the first stomach of ruminant animals—holds and supplies enough water to support their needs. They produce a concentrated urine and to some extent resorb moisture from their feces. They can drink rapidly enough to get back into water balance within five minutes.

The next morning the large ewe again waters first, taking two long drinks before she leaves. Other sheep move in, young ewes and/or yearling rams—their sizes and horns are so similar that I cannot differentiate them at this distance. Mature rams are easy to identify, as the horns are much more developed and the four-year mark is usually a very prominent and readily visible groove on the horn, especially easy to see from the back. From that line one counts rings back toward the head for a fairly accurate age estimate, as each ring marks the cessation of growth for one year. The sheep remain at the tank, either drinking or standing around, for half an hour, and then slowly amble up the hill.

After they leave, a single large ram comes to drink. His horns have almost a full curl with the ends broomed off, leaving the tips worn and blunt (brooming results from rubbing the horns against rocks and dirt). The ram takes almost ten minutes to come down the hillside. After reading about bighorns' prowess in leaping rocks and sheer cliffs, covering ground with astonishing leaps and bounds, I am struck by this one's extreme deliberateness, which I take also to be a measure of his serenity. I dutifully record that he drinks for two minutes, then six, then two more minutes before mincing his way back up the hill.

Meanwhile, the earlier crew reach the crest of the ridge to the east and disappear over the rim. The ram stops twenty feet or so below the top, where a ewe and her lamb lie hidden in a shadowy niche. He nuzzles the lamb, which tags along after him over the hill. The ewe remains, entering a deep overhang I have not noticed before, disappearing into the shadow.

I am inordinately pleased. I feel as if the sheep have honored me with their presence and I find myself smiling as I write up my observations.

Three concerns haunted me before I came on this bighorn sheep count: that I would be uneasy alone, that time would hang heavy, that I could not endure the heat. Instead, I have felt at home, there have not been enough hours in the day, and the heat has become a bearable if not always welcome companion. The words of Joseph Wood Krutch, also writing about the Sonoran Desert, come to mind: "Not to have known—as most men have not—either the mountain or the desert is not to have known one's self. Not to have known one's self is to have known no one."

At noontime I am concentrating so hard on taking notes that I jump when a cicada lets off a five-second burst like a bandsaw going through metal. When there has been no activity at the tank for over an hour I opt for a can of tuna sprinkled with the juice of half a lemon.

No sooner do I open the can and get my fork out than all the birds explode from the rocks on which they've congregated. A red-tailed hawk bullets straight toward me, talons extended, tail spread. No sound, no screaming. It breaks off, rises with no rodent in its talons, wheels, spirals upward, and stoops again. Again no luck. It makes no third try. Its disappearance is followed by a great shocked silence. Half an hour passes before the doves venture, one by one, back to the sentinel rock.

I see only this one hawk stoop. The only time redtails are quiet is on the attack. Otherwise I hear their eerie *KEEEeeeeer KEEeeer* ricochet off the sky itself long before they come in to water. One afternoon a redtail sits on the steep cliff to the right; a couple of feet below it perch some house finches; a black-throated sparrow searches the bush beside it; a pair of ash-throated flycatchers rest above it; and across the tank, a batch of doves roost peacefully on their rock. All birds must be vulnerable to attack at the water hole, and many avoid too much exposure by drinking very quickly or coming in early and late, when raptors are not hunting. Yet there are also these moments when the lion and the lamb lie down together.

I put aside my field glasses and lift my fork. This time a turkey vulture alights on the big rock. The rock is nearly vertical on the side overlooking the tank, and this is where it chooses to descend to water. It gets about a quarter of the way down, contorted in an awkward position, big feet splayed out on the rock, tail pushed up behind at a painful angle, as it looks intently down at the water, a hilarious study in reluctance. Gingerly it inches down (in contrast to birds of prey such as eagles and hawks, vultures have no claw-grasping capability) until it can hold no longer and crash-lands so ridiculously onto the apron to drink that I laugh out loud. The closeness of the rocks around the pool impedes the bird's maneuvering space because of its broad wingspan, and so it edges as close as it can to ensure dropping upon the only place where it can stand and drink.

Four species of this misanthropic-looking bird existed in the Pleistocene, and this creature looks like one of the originals. On the ground, vultures are hunched and awkward bundles of feathers, but in the air, where I watch them during much of the day, they are magnificent, graceful soarers. They ascend with the updrafts coming off the hot desert floor, floating and lifting to cooler air, where visibility is superb; at five hundred feet the visible horizon is twenty-seven miles away, and at two thousand feet, fifty-five miles. Such big raptors generally get as much water as they need from the carrion they consume.

One more try on the tuna. A Harris's antelope squirrel scuttles down the wash to nibble on saguaro seeds. Tail held high over its back for shade, a single white stripe on each flank, it has quick, jerky movements typical of the ever watchful. It stands slightly hunkered up on its hind legs to eat, but its rear end never touches the hot sand. It spends little time feeding and soon tucks back into the brush near the blind, where it undoubtedly has a burrow. There it spread-eagles on the cool soil and unloads its body heat before taking on the desert again. Still, it withstands unusually high heat loads because of its lower basal metabolism.

The next day, emboldened, it hops up on the iceless ice chest in the blind and puts its head into my empty plastic cup, which tips over with a clatter, sending the squirrel flying.

I eat lunch at a fashionable three o'clock. By four o'clock, shadows cover the tank and the blind is in the sun. A cloud cover that has kept the temperature relatively low all day has disappeared, and the sun has an unobstructed shot at my back. Until the sun drops behind the ridge, it is the most miserable time of the day.

The resident robber fly alights in front of me, makes a slapdash attempt at a wandering fly, misses, and returns to watching. Flies are widely distributed in the desert, more prevalent than any other insect order, and of these, bee flies and robber flies are the most numerous. The huge eyes of robber flies give them peripheral vision; with streamlined, stilettolike bodies that allow swift flight, and needlelike beaks, they are efficient predators on the desert wafters and drifters. I've watched this one impale a smaller fly in flight, almost too quickly for the eye to follow, then alight to suck out the juices. Today it seems scarcely to care.

In the evening a caterwauling of Gambel's quail issues from the mesquite trees, where they perch in the branches. Their fussing is interspersed with a short, soapsudsy *cluck*, embellished by a silvery *tink* at the end. The first night I was here they scolded and fumed about the stranger in their midst. The second night they gossiped and fussed, and the third night I awoke to find them within a few feet of the cot.

They visit the big mesquites only in the evening, always after sunset, and they are always noisy. I would think a predator could hear them a mile off. Their drinking patterns have evolved to avoid predators: they commonly come in to water twice a day, one period beginning at dawn, the other ending at dusk. Birds of prey tend to arrive around noon, so the quail's watering time does not overlap.

Quail have been termed "annual" birds because of their variable yearly populations. In the Sonoran Desert, the number of young quail per adult in the fall correlates to rainfall during the previous December to April; in the Mojave, the same high correlation exists between young and October-March precipitation (a relationship that exists in other desert animals, among them bighorn sheep). Their reproductive activity begins before green vegetation becomes available—the amount of which would give them clues to the amount of nourishment that will be obtainable, and hence the clutch size that could survive. Although quail do not breed at all in exceptionally dry years, they are among the most prolific of birds.

They remind me of charming windup toys, painted wooden birds bustling about with staccato movements, officiously giving each other directions as they bustle among the creosote bushes. As I watch them, I remember the Kawaiisu Indian story about the tear marks on Quail's face because her young died, one after the other, when she made her cradles out of sandbar willow—a wood that the Indians therefore do not use for cradles.

The day dims and I stretch out to count the stars framed in a triangle of mesquite branches. Content, I realize I have reached, as Sigurd Olsen wrote, "the point where days are governed by daylight and dark, rather than by schedules, where one eats if hungry and sleeps when tired, and becomes completely immersed in the ancient rhythms, then one begins to live."

Yes.

Early in the morning, and again in the evening, bees create an unholy cantillation around the blind, some working the few mesquite and creosote flowers that remain, but most just circling in holding patterns of their own devising.

The number of creosote bushes in the Western deserts make it a prime source for pollen and nectar. Several bee species are closely associated pollinators of the creosote bush, although it does not depend on any single species for successful pollination. The most numerous pollinator in the summertime is *Perdita larrea*, a tiny bee just an eighth of an inch long. Because of its small size *Perdita* can harvest pollen that larger bees cannot, but its smallness may also curtail its value as a pollinator. Its size prevents it from making reliable contact with a stigma, and its foraging range is modest and limited.

While the bees are outside the blind I remain quietly inside, hoping that the shade will discourage them from visiting and, most of all, from stinging at some imagined insult. With great relief each day I watch the bees move toward the water tank as the day heats up. A thin black cloud of them is visible through the spotting scope. More than once I see a bighorn sheep make a hurried withdrawal from the tank, shaking its head vigorously from what I assume to be a bee's umbrage.

This morning bighorns remain at the tank, either drinking or standing around, for more than an hour before they leave. I follow them with the field glasses as long as I can. When I begin recording my stopwatch notations on the work sheet, I hear a strong bleating at erratic intervals. Search as I may, I can neither see around the saguaro to identify the activity nor locate the source by sound.

By default, I see a great deal of the old saguaro for the next quarter hour. The cactus is badly riddled about eight feet off the ground, so that daylight shows through the ribs, undoubtedly the work of the resident white-throated wood rat. Wood rats are the only animals that consistently eat cactus; other species may feed on it occasionally, but they cannot make it a steady diet because of its high content of malic and oxalic acids, created by the cactus's CAM (crassulacean acid metabolism) photosynthesis. The oxalic acid is in the form of insoluble calcium oxalate crystals that can cause severe renal problems in humans. For six months of the year cactus is the wood rat's major source of food, reaching a peak in late May when it may constitute more than 90 percent of its diet.

The saguaro is closely pleated, waiting to expand when the rains come. The bellowslike action, which permits expansion of the stem without tearing the inelastic skin, allows precise adjustment to water storage, an action that starts with even very light rainfall. Water loss during the dry season reduces the volume of storage tissue, shrinking the stem; as the diameter becomes smaller, the ribs draw closer together, hence the pleated look. After a rain the process reverses rapidly, with greater intensity on the south side of the stem, probably because water-conducting tissue is more prevalent there; the north side does not begin to swell until a few days later. About three feet off the ground on the north side facing me, an extra rib has been added to the basic number of twelve ribs. This onset of radial growth, or bifurcation, doesn't occur until the trunk grows to at least twelve inches in diameter.

A cactus of this immense size can absorb 95 percent of its total weight in water—sometimes up to a ton—and continues to expand for up to three weeks after the rains. Tough, ropelike roots, confined to the upper three inches of soil, may extend outward fifteen or twenty feet, placed to suck up as much water as possible before it evaporates. Lacking a stabilizing taproot, a saguaro topples if these lateral roots are severed.

The south and north sides of the cactus are measurably different. The ribs on the south side are deeper. Receiving the greater amount of direct sunlight, the deeper furrows provide a modicum of shade, reducing the time that direct sunlight heats the surface. Spine lengths on the south side are longer and may provide an insulating layer of air. Fruits ripen first on the south side. Branch ends are usually colder than the main stalk during the night, and since single flowers form at the tips only, more rapid development occurs on the warmer side. Dryness promotes the formation of flower buds; plants growing with a favorable water supply make handsome vegetative growth but tend not to bloom.

Flowering is, after all, not an aesthetic contribution but a survival mechanism.

The variety of birds in the Cabeza Prieta has been a surprise, especially at this hot, dry time of year. A pair of ash-throated flycatchers, tails a bright reddish brown, forage in the mesquite. Only gullies and washes with larger shrubs and trees support enough insects to attract the flycatchers. Three verdins squabble in a saltbush, their yellow caps bright but their bodies blending and disappearing into the fretted background. Because they feed on insects (as most migratory birds do), they can exist without free water as long as insects are available. Subject to more water loss because of a less advantageous ratio of surface area to volume than that enjoyed by larger birds, they spend the day closeted in shade and shadow. Females weave ball-like nests in the thorniest of bushes—catclaw and sometimes cholla—and line them with down and feathers for the young, while the male builds a simpler nest for protection against the chilly desert nights. A wreath of spiny twigs around each entrance protects the relatively low-placed and vulnerable nests.

Wings whir close by as a Costa's hummingbird checks out my hanging red nylon stuff sack, then perches on a mesquite twig. This three-gram female loses nearly half of her body weight on hot days, making her dependence on surface water and succulent food greater than that of large birds, which lose much less. When nectar from ocotillo, Indian paintbrush, and agaves is available, hummingbirds obtain moisture in their food, but at this dry time of the year, when no flowers bloom, they must have access to free water.

At dusk a desert cottontail rollicks down the wash, which is now in partial shade. This cottontail is lighter than the mountain cottontails with which I am familiar, illustrating the tendency of desert mammals to be paler, somewhat smaller, and have longer ears and legs than their cooler-climate counterparts. It does not hop; its front and back feet move together in a rocking motion like a hobbyhorse canter. It nibbles some fallen saguaro fruit, then beds down on the other side of the sandy strip in a thicket of saltbush. Another one appears. The first returns. They face each other three feet apart, feinting. The first one dashes for the other, who levitates straight up while the first dashes beneath, and then both bucket off. To me it looks like great good fun and I enjoy their silly antics.

My band of bighorn sheep prefer morning watering. They come with some precision to the tank. This morning there is a considerable amount of amatory exercise going on between the young rams and the ewes. Breeding season is not far off, and mating behavior patterns briefly interrupt the more unstructured ambles to the tank.

A ram follows a young ewe downslope, nose so close to her tail that he trips for not watching where his feet are going; the scent of a ewe's urine communicates whether or not she is in estrus. The ewe appears to ignore him, stopping to browse along the way or simply look about. I watch three different pairs, and each female, at different times, stops and urinates, a behavior that occurs only when a ram is close behind her.

A group of six sheep come in early today, with some I've not seen before. They remain for two hours, mostly standing around and mountain watching, before they move back up the hill. Busy recording, I hear the cracking of branches close by, and suddenly there are five right in front of the blind, noisily cracking mesquite pods. Although they prefer grass, there is precious little of that here, and so they have become more opportunistic in their feeding. The group includes both a young ram and the big mature ram, two lambs, and a female. They are obviously aware that I am here, and look at me with less than the curiosity I feel I deserve, but otherwise pay no more attention to me than to the saguaro. I hear them crunching mesquite pods as they move downslope.

Sweeping the slope with binoculars, I spot more sheep on the hillside. As I switch to the spotting scope to watch them more closely, I hear a jet coming in low. A sonic boom rips the air and reverberates so close that the whole blind vibrates, and even though I know it's coming, I still jump when the sound hits.

The bighorns on the hillside never turn a hair. The ten white-winged doves on the sentinel rock never move. The mourning doves never stop calling. I later find this to be generally true; the frequency of a sonic boom resembles that of a thunderstorm, and wildlife here generally is not disturbed by either. This observer is.

At midday, when tank activity has closed down and the temperature reads 106 degrees, the metal of the spotting scope burns my fingers. The water I take from the jerry can to drink is hot enough to brew tea with. I can't complain. Early travelers had it much worse. John Durivage, crossing the same desert in 1849, found that "the water was detestable and at any other time would have proved a powerful emetic, but now it was *agua dulce*. A tincture of bluelike, iodides of sulfur, Epsom salts, and a strong decoction of decomposed mule flesh were the component parts of this delectable compound." A western whiptail lizard patters out from behind a water can and prowls the edge of the blind, snuffling the dirt floor as it goes. I puzzle over its dark color—an allover deep smoky brown with a checkered back pattern and a long tail, the last three inches of which are almost black—until I realize that the soil under the mesquite tree where it forages is brown from the humus of leaves and pods and twigs built up over the years. Western whiptails are very variable in color, tending to match the ground upon which they travel. When the lizard reaches my bare right foot, to my delight, it tickles right over my toes.

I pour four inches of water into the bucket, put my shirt in, wet it thoroughly, and put it back on wet. Even though the water is hot it chills immediately and sits on my skin like salvation. It refreshes and energizes me enough to take a walk. When I return, hundreds of bees have found the water I unadvisedly left in the bucket. My blue sleeping bag is the dearest object of their desire. They cling to my blue shirt with ecstasy or joyously explore every object in the blind.

I sulk outside in the flimsy shade of a creosote bush for forty-five minutes while they enjoy my grudging hospitality.

Beside me, the next morning, are the subtle sounds in the brush that indicate small-animal movement, but peer as I may, I see nothing. Finally I pick out a dull-brown robin-size bird, which scratches the dirt, pauses, disappears, pops up on a branch and down again; it is difficult to see and to follow. I finally get a good glimpse of a fierce yellow eye and an almost raptorlike gaze: a curve-billed thrasher. With something in its beak it flies to a nearby cholla and solves a mystery: at last I know who built the large, messy nest in the cholla in which I found three fully feathered, grayish brown young, eyes tightly closed, beaks like hand-drawn brackets too big for their heads, so nondescript as to be unidentifiable. A high percentage of desert birds nest in inaccessible cavities in spiny trees and shrubs and cacti, symptomatic of the strong predatory pressures on nesting birds here, but only cactus wrens and curve-billed thrashers regularly brave the cholla.

By noon the temperature is 102 degrees and climbing. I was going to walk, for there are things I want to check out. I was going to draw, but even with a paper towel beneath my arm I still perspire enough to buckle the paper, and the drawings are out of proportion and awkward. I was going to do a lot of things, but the heat, combined with my usual after-lunch low metabolism, saps my ambition. A white-winged dove calls, repetitive, insistent, annoying. A thankless breeze comes through the blind. The little ground squirrel arrives, unnecessarily spry and lively and perky. I feel listless to the point of stupor.

Actually I may have reached the point where I can live with this heat, this everywhere, without-respite hot. My skin feels cool, so evaporative cooling is working. It would be heaven to pour a pail of cold water over my overheated heat, but all the water is hot. Not warm. Hot. I yearn for every ice cube I ever heedlessly rinsed down a drain.

The silence of noon is palpable, more an onerous, enveloping physical presence than a lack of sound. A female Gila woodpecker lands on a mesquite branch, mouth agape. When a mourning dove coos, it has a lunatic overtone. A fly's drone sounds like a freight train.

The white-winged doves sit on the sentinel boulder above the tank, in full sun. The heat radiating off the rocks must make the cul-de-sac in which the tank sits unbearable, yet the doves appear unperturbed. The thrasher, beak agape, sits on her nest, lit by full sun. In this high-heat time of day she must be there to shield the young, enjoying none of the comforts of a shaded nest but also not vulnerable to attack, a brutal trade-off.

Rather than evaporating water to lower body temperature, most desert birds allow a passive rise in body temperature. Birds ordinarily have a higher body temperature than mammals, well above 100 degrees Fahrenheit, and this higher temperature allows them to dissipate heat by radiation. Birds, with the exception of burrowing owls, cannot utilize burrows for cooling, nor can they sweat. They can sit in the shade and extend their wings to expose bare patches of skin; they can compress their plumage to reduce its insulating value; or they can gape, which is a means of evaporative cooling.

When ambient temperature rises above body temperature, there is one more option: gular flutter—fluttering the thin floor of the mouth and the soft skin under the throat. Gular flutter increases evaporation and is highly developed in several desert bird species, among them doves, quail, nighthawks, and roadrunners.

But sometimes even that doesn't suffice. On the last afternoon I check the thermometer at three o'clock, already 108 degrees on its way up to 112. Heat rolls down off the surrounding ridges like a *nuée ardente*, consuming everything in its path.

Hopping up on a bough of the mesquite against which the blind is built is a tiny black-tailed gnatcatcher, not much bigger than a hummingbird. Illustrations in bird identification books show such plump, neatly feathered creatures. This little soul is waiflike and thin, feathers disheveled and tufting out, the Edith Piaf of the bird world.

She walks up the branch in front of me, less than an arm's length away. She stands with her body high off the branch, tail quivering. As I watch her, her head nods forward in that familiar "I can't hold my head up another minute" droop. As soon as her head drops she jerks it up and opens her eyes in a gesture so reminiscent of a child fighting sleep that I have to smile. She moves to stand beside my duffel bag, which is wedged up against the tree trunk, and, as I watch, slowly lists until she leans completely against it as if exhausted by the heat. Her head droops forward and she starts awake several times more. Finally her head remains down. She sleeps.

In time my head falls forward and I too jerk awake; finally, very quietly, I scoot down in the chair so that my neck can rest on the back, and then I doze as well. I awake with a stiff neck just as the little gnatcatcher stirs.

She pulls herself upright, shakes her feathers flat, looks about perkily for a moment, and in leisurely fashion hops into the brush.

My last evening here, I walk up to the divide that separates my valley from the desert flats to the west, winding to the top, flushing a lizard, climbing over granite boulders, avoiding the barbed and the spurred. When I reach the top I climb up on a boulder that is set out of the wind that hollows through the defile. Below, saguaros stalk down a dry wash and then disappear as the land levels out into a wild, open emptiness.

Looking out over the pure sweep of seamless desert, I am surprised to realize that the easy landscapes stifle me—closed walls of forests, ceilings of boughs, neat-trimmed lawns, and ruffled curtains of trees hide the soft horizons. I prefer the absences and the big empties, where the wind ricochets from sand grain to mountain. I prefer the crystalline dryness and an unadulterated sky strewn from horizon to horizon with stars. I prefer the raw edges and the unfinished hems of the desert landscape.

Desert is where I want to be when there are no more questions to ask.

Confessions from a Sheep Blind

While it is undoubtedly inappropriate for an editor to comment directly on his or her own work, it may be admissible to place it into historical context. In this case, I admired the water hole sheep counts of Monson, Broyles, Zwinger, and Bowden so much that I wanted to experience a sheep count myself, but I felt intimidated by the proposition of writing up an essay from the experience. My first attempted count was at the Tinajas Altas in the summer of 1990; I took copious notes but saw no sheep for the first two days before my partner became dehydrated and sick, and we decided to abort our plans to stay longer.

The second time around, the Cabeza Prieta National Wildlife Refuge staff graciously provided backup support, and the entire experience was a delight.

After returning from the sheep count, I pondered over the kind of essay that might gracefully arise out of the experience; none did—at least none parallel to those I had read by my friends. My field notes, in their original form, had far too many redundancies and possessed too much surface roughness to make for a good read. Yet the style of field notes intrigued me and did provide a vehicle for building drama episode by episode. I realized that if I pruned out some of the excess brush from my notes, a steady pattern became more and more evident. By better sequencing my emotional responses to these episodes—but not the actual events themselves—the journal form allowed me to play out a simple story.

Once I had arrived at Buckhorn Tank, I became mildly amused by the notion that many of us had worked so hard to arrange our schedules so that we could be in a place "where nothing might happen." I began to remember (and miss) the hilarious stories Ed Abbey had spun about doing nothing in the desert. I decided then that I would simply try to capture the prevailing mood of the moment, in and around the blind. If the piece fails to take itself too seriously, no matter. Most nature writing has become too burdened by gravity; except for Abbey, David Quammen, and perhaps John Graves, it is as though humor is taboo in the genre. The fate of the earth is pretty serious stuff, right? And yet, if we can't laugh at ourselves and the world around us, we might as well forget about life here and head for Biosphere 2 or parts beyond . . .

This essay appeared in the summer 1992 issue of *Phoenix* magazine.

I slam my field notebook shut, frustrated, having spent the good part of four days in a small blind without having seen even one bighorn sheep. I've just heard footsteps, which probably means it is time for me to go, that my partner will be taking over the blind for the rest of the count. I gather my gear and hear someone walking nearby again, but when I look toward the trail to camp, my partner is still not in sight. Suddenly, a wave of apprehension washes over me; every hair on my skin, in my ears, perks up, alert. I take heed and cautiously scan my desert surroundings for clues that can cue me into that sound . . .

I am one of those field biologists who has contrived elaborate excuses for spending time in gorgeous places while not doing much more than watch the world turn. I run trap lines night after night that remain empty most mornings. I erect mist nets even when there are neither birds nor bats wanting to play badminton. I sit patiently for hours next to an open flower, hoping to catch an elusive pollinator, who must be on a house call to some other planet during my time in his waiting room. Whenever I get hooked into such snipe hunts, I somehow try to retrieve at least a modicum of data targeted to advance biology, so as not to appear as if I spend all my time playing the field.

Yet, if the truth be known, I can never be sure when or if the organism of my dreams will sneak right up and bite me on the seat, so to speak. To allow the seeds of scientific discovery enough open, fertile ground in which to germinate, I must observe what my art teacher once referred to as "loose time." These are periods of solitude for which there is no rigorous research plan, no persistent object of study, no cumbersome instrumentation separating me from the *materia prima* of the natural world.

Like a bloodhound, I simply sniff at random, nosing around various and sundry piles of stuff until I pick up a scent—the trajectory of another organism. As a field biologist, my most surefire stratagem is to muddle through the cluttered cosmos until I am tripped up by some critter's compelling pathway. Then I stalk that story out as if it were my own. I put on the hide of a deer, or roll along the path of seed and debris left by a tumbleweed, or zap down the trap line of floral fragrances essential to hummingbird geography.

Only by having time to get under the skin of another organism, or to fly its course, does my mind have the remotest chance of connecting with "the other."

Of course, there remains the risk of failure—the skin that doesn't fit, the flight that veers off course, the animal that doesn't show. Or a mind is too preoccupied to notice when the otherwise cryptic creature does make a momentary appearance. These are all hazards I have faced, hazards that can plague a field biologist at any time, in any place. They are the mental sand traps that lined the sheep-counting course out at Buckhorn Tank in the Cabeza Prieta Wildlife Refuge.

June 24, 1991

As Rankin and I drove down the Tacna Rut toward the abandoned outpost of Tule Well, I could not recall that I had been to Buckhorn Tank before; at least, I did not remember it by name. A lot of dry arroyos had passed under the bridge during the last decade. My mental capacity for remembering place-names as well as scientific epithets for plants and animals had been severely diminished by too many days as a bareheaded landloper out in the full desert sun.

While inspecting the shower stall at Tule Well—where the putrid juice of some dead bird flowed out of the tank's showerhead—some vague memory began to stir within me. But it was not until we drove the gravelly road into the Cabeza Prieta Mountains that I could suddenly picture the tank, a little concrete plug in a steep draw between tilted granitic ridges. I could also visualize the wildlife-watching blind a hundred yards or so below, the first sheep count station I had ever seen. I remembered saying to myself at the moment of that first close encounter: "Too bad for those wildlife zoologists, having to coop themselves up in a little saguaro-ribbed hothouse while all this gorgeous open space lies around them. They sit for hours in cramped quarters, all for a few moments' peek at some sheep's rump. While my botanical buddies and I simply stroll along, plucking the sexual organs off our subjects, those bighorn biologists must wait, forlorn, wondering if there will ever be another ewe."

Those condescending comments about my zoological comrades must have been overheard, for somehow I was "invited" to participate in such a sheep count. Somehow, I had been sentenced to four days of sweating until I had salt around my rim, drinking warm beer, listening to lonesome doves droning, watching the full moon shining and turkey vultures soaring, occupied with endless wondering: will the sheep ever show?

Alas, there had been some reform in this prison since my naturalist godmother Ann Zwinger chalked up time here in solitary confinement exactly five years ago to the week. I was now allowed to fly the coop every half day for a few hours because Rankin and I would be alternating shifts.

That is a monumental change in the history of sheep counts. For the first year ever, the refuge managers insisted that all sheep counters work in pairs. This mandate from above will undoubtedly drive into extinction the remaining misanthropic macho volunteers who, in the tradition of Ed Abbey and Chuck Bowden, prefer to spend their time in solitary confinement.

I feel relieved to have arranged a tag-team deal with David Rankin, a physical anthropologist and former understudy of one Ultimate Desert Rat, Bill Broyles. Rankin and I have worked out a logistic leapfrogging scheme. While one of us is in the shade of the blind, the other will be out in the boonies exercising or exploring.

After the handshakes and howdies, Rankin and I both confess that the disappointing lack of solitude (two of us in twenty square miles) is outweighed by another unanticipated condition. It is not really that hot. What can we possibly write home about if the temperature doesn't even peak out above a hundred degrees?

In fact, it is so cool that I have to go for a half-hour run to work up a sweat. Just before 6:00 P.M., while out bushwhacking on a new jogging course, I spot a gray fox a few dozen yards in front of me. He lopes along at about the same speed I am jogging, sporadically looking back over his shoulder with . . . what? Concern? Worry? Caution? Disgust? Fatalism? There goes the neighborhood, the humans have moved in, he thinks. There goes all the wildlife I'll get to see for a week, I think.

At 7:00 P.M. I wander from our camp toward the blind a few hundred yards away. An Audubon's cottontail scurries down the trail in front of me, probably the largest herbivore I'll see all week. I enter the blind and prepare to face the vast void.

Boredom, however, doesn't have a chance to take root here. Almost immediately, two coyotes pass by on their way up to the tank for an after-dinner drink as the last sunlight begins to leave the ridges. They lap up water at the tank lip but stay for only a portion of the happy hour before returning down along the ridge to the east of me.

They are hardly more than moving shadows in my field glasses by this hour of night. The sky above them is stained with pinks and oranges for a moment more. The coyote bitch and her scraggly youngster pause and look my way just once. Then they are gone with the fading eastern light. As inky blues seep into the darkening sky, the last tinges of russet, rose, and rust vanish from the rocks where the coyotes had stood.

The doves double in number now that the coyotes have gone. Two or three dozen at a time crowd around the tank. The beeper on my watch goes off, scaring away a few doves in the mesquite tree above me. It's 8:00 P.M., and a full moon is rising in the V-shaped patch of sky above the tank. It's time to check the thermometer.

The temperature has plummeted to eighty-three degrees! Time to put on my dove-down underwear and get ready for a chilly evening. The doves must be feeling the same chill, for they have fallen silent. By 8:15 P.M., at eighty-one degrees, I begin to nod into torpor but catch myself and head into camp.

Camp was only a concept when I left for the blind a bit more than an hour ago. It has since been transformed by Rankin from a parked car and piles of gear into a tidy, rather domestic little territory. There is a tarp-covered portico, a kitchen, a tree-shaded area for drinking and washing, and other facilities. Rankin, the backcountry architect of all this, is fast asleep on a cot with a throw rug next to it.

I shudder at the thought of civilization having advanced so far in just two hours and depart for the company of burrs, thorns, spines, and scorpions in the sandy wash nearby. Rankin stirs as I shake out my little ground cloth in the dry streambed and plop my straw hat down on the head of a young saguaro. I fade off to sleep with his last words—like a desert rat's lullaby—ringing in my ears: "Don't let the sidewinders get you . . ."

June 25, 1991

It's 5:15 A.M., and the wrens, woodpeckers, flickers, and quail are making a racket. Who said that the desert is so quiet you can hear your underwear brush against your legs? This place is so raucous I can hardly hear the Mexican trucks groaning through their gears two miles away.

Then I hear a groan closer to home.

"Ohhh, it's cooold!"

"I can't believe they've sent us out into Yuma County during a cold front."

If Rankin and I are any indication, desert aficionados are wimps when it comes to chilly weather. I recall those unbelievably bad lines from a recent Eddie Bauer ad in *Esquire* magazine: "Some call the desert hostile and want to change it. We say, save the desert. Change your clothes."

Well, I say, when is Madam Desert going to take care of her devoted boys and warm up a little?

"Heat yourself up a drink on my Coleman," Rankin urges. "I'm going over to the blind."

I am left alone, with the camp and the surrounding desert to myself for a few hours. I brew up some tea and shoot up my oat bran—health nut fix for the day. The birds in the neighborhood have not yet quieted down, perhaps because they find the cold as irritating as Rankin and I do. I drop a few pots and pans, trying to fit in with this noisy bunch. Finally, at six, I decide I should stand up, warm up, and take in some of the local attractions.

I walk out of a shadowy canyon, toward the sun just vaulting the tuff ridge forming the eastern edge of the valley. There, the birds and I are left speechless: the cosmos is suddenly luminous; every plant harbors its own halo of gentle light. Each backlit saguaro, with an aura of translucent spines along its ribs, radiates. Peppergrass skeletons left from the spring wildflower season stand like thousands of minuscule candelabras, each aflame. Spiderwebs crisscross the spaces between shrubs, shining like silver and crystal threads. The flower buds of night-blooming cereus—awaiting their one evening of show—are glowing with fuzzy white pelage that looks more like an egret's plumage.

Vireos and shrikes alight on trees nearby, but not one of us speaks. I amble aimlessly, dumbstruck by the dazzle of desert light. Had I inhaled sacred datura nectar while snoring last night, or slept atop some magic mushrooms? No, these visions have nothing to do with drugs, natural or otherwise. The desert is sometimes this enchanted, and I am fortunate enough to catch a glimpse of its incandescence now and then. The rest of the time, either it is not glistening or, more likely, I am not looking.

I hike with no destination in mind for two more hours, over chocolate brown tuff, over pale pink granite, over sand, keeping my eyes open for sign. I take on the persona of hunter—ready to stalk any creature whose path I cross—as a means of sharpening my senses. I remember Ortega y Gasset's insight that the relative scarcity of large ungulates has much to do with why we place so much focus (and hocus-pocus) upon them. Because bighorn sheep, mountain goats, and elk are usually beyond sight and beyond reach, you sing for them and paint pictographs to make them appear. You use sympathetic magic to move them from the invisible realm and into your presence. You make them offerings, as an interspecific diplomat might: I'll let your family be, I'll let your habitat rest, I'll hunt more humbly in the future should you surrender your flesh to my family today.

For the moment, the meat of the issue stays out of reach. I walk their trailing paths, step on their droppings, brush past branches bent by their trampling, check barrel cactus damaged by their browsing. I return to camp, blissfully empty-handed and empty-headed, yet engaged with this place.

Meanwhile, my amigo Rankin has been diligently holding down the fort. I hope he is not as tenacious as the nameless volunteer who, a few sheep counts back, did not leave his blind-embedded seat even when he needed to urinate. When I seek Rankin out at 11:05 A.M., I find that he has not been so orthodox in his rituals. In fact, he has risen from the crypt and is now as invisible as the sheep we are supposed to be counting. His last communication as a blinded mortal lies there on the holy clipboard: "31'C, wind E, 10% clouds."

I look around again, then back at the notebook. No one in sight. Did Rankin actually leave the blind unattended for an entire five minutes, or could this be for good?

Then I think I hear wing beats.

It is Rankin rounding a bush not far from the blind. "It's me. I had to find a boy's room . . ."

"Oh, okay. See much this morning?"

"No big sheep, if that's what you mean. A lotta doves, but the doves left when two vultures went down to the water for a while."

"No rams! Well, what self-respecting bighorn would want to enter the pool while we're gawking at them?"

"Well, I leave you the best seat in the house," and then Rankin adds, "as well as a cooler full of canteens filled at home. And help yourself to the homemade beef jerky if you wish."

This guy has come camping with sweet water, homemade treats, fresh meat and vegetables, and a nice setup for real cooking. I have come with a few bent-up cans, some dermestid-infested Rye-Crisps, and a dozen stale tortillas to scorch over a microscopic zipstove. I feel rustic in comparison with Rankin, yet appreciative of his generosity. I want to reciprocate.

"Thanks, Rankin. And you feel free to help yourself to any . . . any of the hot sauces I left in camp," I stammer. "Take your pick. There's nearly a full case of salsa there in my pack if you need to perk yourself up."

I spend the next forty minutes trying to figure out if the white-winged doves coming to the water hole are speaking English, Spanish, or both idioms. I had learned on various trips to Sonora that most doves there call "Coo-coo-coo-coor-pe," in honor of a small pueblo, Cucurpe, where people actively plant cottonwood hedgerows that make fine dove habitat. In ranch country on the Arizona side of the border, however, the consensus around the chuck wagons is that the doves are asking, "Who cooks for you-all?" Here, just a few miles from the international boundary, I hear everything from "Cuck-you-all" to "Who cooks in Cucurpe?"

Suddenly, the droning of the doves is broken by the one who cares not whether the meat is cooked or raw: a single turkey vulture on the rocks. I have recently been fascinated by the fact that no other vertebrate ever has vultures for dinner. Why? Because they eat dead meat? We do that too. Road kills? We publish astonishing new road kill recipes every year. Food that sits out in the elements too long? When I swapped shifts with Rankin, he spent a couple of minutes brushing ants off that homemade beef jerky he had been storing in my cooler. He had placed it out to dry in the sun (near an ant hill, unfortunately) after it had fallen into the ice water of the cooler.

Despite my affinity with carrion eaters, I lose track of the first turkey vulture (alias TV 1), distracted, perhaps, by a pair of cactus wrens fussing around in the mesquite tree east of me. At 1:00 P.M., TV 2 casts his circling shadow between me and the tank, then lands on the round rock above the water. The doves all shift positions. TV 2 helps himself to some water but leaves shortly after. He was apparently bored.

Up through two in the afternoon, nobody's here except us doves and house finches. TV 1 comes in a second and a third time for a drink. While I am admiring him, an antelope ground squirrel visits me in the blind.

"Go away until you've grown some horns and put some meat on you," I scold him. If I can't see sheep, I would rather watch feathered scavengers than see any more diminutive mammals.

TV 2 arrives just about the time some larger mammals finally make an appearance. They're wearing clothes and speak an idiom I recognize. Laura Thompson from the Fish and Wildlife Service has joined Rankin, and they have come by to shoot the breeze with me. Might as well. Nothing else to shoot. By 4:30 P.M., when Rankin goes on shift, I've gotten intimate enough with the vultures to be able to distinguish four individuals from one another. As Laura leaves to camp down the road a few miles, a dozen more vultures arrive to do crazy eights between Rankin in the blind and me in the camp. That means that we have arrived as well: after little more than thirty hours out in the refuge, Rankin and I have begun to smell like dead meat.

June 26, 1991

After jogging, puzzling over Indian place-names in the area, and wolfing down a dinner of hot sauce and hot sauce helper, I fall asleep before 9:00

P.M. to the sound of bats echo-locating around my head. I awaken at 3:00 A.M., cold and somehow resolved that by going to the blind in the middle of the night I will see the "missing sheep" by moonlight. But the moon is so low and clouded over that the tank is shrouded in shadow.

No matter, I conjecture. If sheep come while it's dark like this, they could walk within feet of here without noticing me. Wishful thinking raises its weary head at the oddest hours!

While I am still settling into my chair, three unanticipated guests arrive: a pack rat and two kangaroo rats. Unfortunately, I become too groggy to properly entertain them. Nevertheless, they become more curious and come right on up to my toes. When they realize that I'm not going to be the party animal in the bunch, they take up the task on their own. They skip across the saguaro rib that my back is leaning on and tap-dance on the plywood over my head. Every time I nod off, they increase the clatter and startle me back to semiconsciousness. I spot one of the kangaroo rats in my flashlight beam; it doesn't faze her in the least. These rats aren't supposed to be active on full moon nights, so why are they out basking in the flashlight glow? Unaware of what the animal behavior texts say about them, they continue their revels.

By the time 3:30 A.M. rolls around, when several coyotes begin yapping nearby, I wish I had the strength to place a work order with them for some rodent control.

Between 3:30 and 4:30 I doze off dozens of times, only to be rudely awakened by pounding on the apartment walls and ceiling. Sleep deprivation is indeed one of the worst forms of torture. Then the hallucinations begin. I see, dreamily, another party going on in a rock shelter "condo" on the slope opposite the tank. There, out on the balcony, are bats and bighorns in formal wear, sharing drinks and conversations with a band of desert botanists. Apparently I was not invited, perhaps for lack of a tux to complement the long black gowns the ewes are wearing.

At 6:05, as light edges into the canyon, I regain what senses I have left and switch from mammalian dreams to avian antics. The next hour of family entertainment is brought to me by the following feathered friends: loggerhead shrikes, cactus wrens, white-winged doves, gnatcatchers, a loud-cawing raven, a pair of flycatchers, a verdin, Gambel's quail, a canyon wren, and an unseen but often heard hummingbird. At 7:30, while the tank is still in the shade, its faithful congregation of doves and house finches begins matins.

Over the next few hours, the variety show switches from birds to herps. A collared lizard comes around. Later, I spot a whiptail on the struts of the blind and a zebratail running down the wash, tail curled and flashing its stripes.

Next, the invertebrates have their amateur hour, as the talent show extravaganza slides down the evolutionary ladder. I have succumbed to counting ants on my crushed pineapple can and timing the length of each cicada buzz within earshot. Little did I know when I arrived here that I would spend less time observing bighorns than I would logging in how long a cicada can hold a note. The data set itself has a lovely ebb and flow to it: 7.0 seconds, 6.4, 7.6, 8.2, 7.9, 7.5, 8.4, 7.3, 8.1, 7.4, and 9.4 seconds. I am reminded of Gale Monson—one of the early sheep counters—spending hours keeping track of spotted toad croaks. Human inquisitiveness can take so many forms!

It is now 10:00 A.M., the temperature in the blind has hit eighty-six degrees, and I have hit the desert doldrums. The big guys—bucks, rams, pumas, and eagles—have left me to be entertained by the humbler members of the wildlife society, the ones that don't have football teams or sports cars named after them. It's okay. If he knew that I was making peace with the ants and chanting "Amazing Grace" with the cicadas, Saint Francis of Assisi would open his heart to me.

Could this be the moment that I must shed the part of my male ego obsessed with big game in order to see the rest of the wild and vibrant world? I feel as though I am no longer waiting in the absence of sheep, for I am alive in the company of red ants. There may be little wind to pull me out of the doldrums and toward the next continent, but it sure is interesting out here in the middle of the Sargasso Sea.

Rankin comes to spell me and asks how it's going.

"Keep an eye out for some fish," I murmur.

"What?"

"Never mind."

I return to camp, which is a much hotter place than the ramada, and am at a loss what to do. Although not hungry, I crack open a can of Husband Pleasin' beans and douse them with green chile sauce. I begin to

sweat for the first time all day. Once I have the evaporative cooler working, I decide to take a nap in the shade of the tarp that stretches out from
Rankin's four-by-four. I sleep until the heat and the intestinal gas wake me.

"Who fired that shot?" I inquire as I bolt out of my sleeping bag,
drenched in sweat. I forget the shot, the dream, the circumstance. All I
know is that I ought to move around a little, get back in touch with a
larger world.

The temperature has reached 105 degrees in full sun at breast height,
and Lord knows how hot on the tuff beneath my feet. The heat I wanted
from the start has finally come. I decide to give in to my desire to do some
desert running.

At least I am wise enough to put on an impenetrable sheen of sunblock
before I head out onto the glittering desert pavement for some recreation.
This kind of runner's ritual is known in the sports fitness world as "training for skin cancer." I drench my hair and T-shirt with water before I
leave camp, but they are bone dry in a matter of moments. As I run over
decomposed granite and quartz, the ground glares back at me with the
brilliance of a million footlights. For a while, I lope along after a coyote,
but even he is pressing for shade and bows out of the race.

Yet, it's great to feel some bona fide heat after six months of unusual
coolness. Hell, by this date two years ago we were nearly halfway to the
new Arizona record of 165 days over a hundred degrees. By contrast, this
year has been so cool that flowering times for many plants have been
delayed by roughly a month.

Here at Buckhorn, ironwoods are still in bloom, five or six weeks after
their usual peak. Saguaros also remain in bloom, but I have yet to see a
single ripe fruit, whereas last year fruit picking was on the decline by this
time. The night-blooming cereus I saw here was still in bud, perhaps a
month later than usual. Oddest of all, last week I spotted a penstemon
blooming near Sonoyta nearly two months after they typically wane.

While a good part of the earth's surface may be warming up, perhaps
some weather cells are shifting in a manner that brings us cooler pulses
now and then. On the other hand, maybe I'm making too much of a
random event. Or it could be that we're suffering from wilder oscillations
that make us feel as though there are wider swings in the weather's course.
Or my memory is poor. Or I'm brain-dead. Did I not begin this soliloquy

while out jogging in 105-degree heat and end it by complaining that it has been atypically cool lately?

I return to the tank to spell Rankin, and much to my pleasure, the vultures return promptly. They scare away the horde of house finches that had been lolling around the water hole. At first, none of the vultures moves down to the water; they just hog the boulders around the hole. I wonder if they are just there for the cool breeze off the water's surface, or for a few drinks—I recall that turkey vultures have been known to go a full year obtaining their moisture from food (or blood!) without drinking once.

Not the case here: one of them hops down to a boulder edging the pool, then gingerly touches the water itself. He must be deciding: Should I go ahead and sip from a tank where house finches have drunk before me? The hygienic risks of living around a man-made tank; house finches and even an occasional starling show up, as if this were a birdbath on an urban lawn. I'm surprised he does not spread out one of those sanitary paper seat covers before perching his rear end on the lip of Buckhorn Tank.

I watch one rather dapper vulture through the Bausch and Lomb scope for a while. His smell may be repugnant to other species, but he is handsome by anthropocentric standards. He wears his conservative black plumage well; it absorbs radiation when heating is needed but has enough fluff to it to insulate him from sweltering surface temperatures on scorching days. He sports stylish white spots on his feet, for he defecated liquid crud onto his feet earlier in the day to help with evaporative cooling. And he has the luxury of choosing between a poolside seat in the shade of the canyon and a soaring height above the whole hot stinking desert.

Again I wonder why no one ever entertains vultures. They are far more punctual than bighorn sheep, who won't show up for a drink even when I've traveled 150 miles to meet them here at Buckhorn. Nevertheless, the ants are good company, as are the vultures, and I can leave the little/big game dichotomy by the wayside. I'm now enjoying whoever happens to be present.

Rankin comes over with Mari Hoffman of the Cabeza Prieta Refuge staff—she will give me a ride out at midday tomorrow while Rankin will stay on for another dozen hours in the blind. But for now, the three of us decide to spend a couple of hours together and go for a walk as the full moon rises. When it enters our camp's little canyon around 7:30 P.M., the walls shine tall in the low-angled light. Saguaro flowers open around us and bats dance above our heads. The air is sweet, the mood is relaxed, and the conversation is playful.

June 27, 1991

I leave my moonlit swag a bit after 4:00 A.M. and wander to the blind, bats swooping in front of me as I go. It's sixty-four degrees in the blind, cooler where the trail crosses small washes. I feel a comfort this time when the k-rats begin their ruckus, the way one's heart warms when friends at a party start on a familiar routine. At 5:00 or so the cantor of the dawning hour circles the canyon, repeating the same emotive, fluttery canticle from different perches, as if moving through the stations of the cross. I am not sure whether this soloist is a mocker or a thrasher, but he sings a lovely song of the twilight, *la madrugada*.

As muddy light washes into the range, a canyon wren chimes in, cascading through his scale, to remind me that there are other voices in the choir. By the time direct sunlight breaks across the cliffs above the tinaja, I can hear mourning doves, Gambel's quail, gilded flickers, white-winged doves, and thrashers. The sunlight strikes my skin at 6:00 A.M. and activates gnatcatchers nearby. A vireo or Lucy's warbler stirs in the tree to the west of me. The morning proceeds as a patter of various sounds, none predominating. I simply lean back, read a little, watch a little, and listen, savoring my last few hours in the blind.

At 7:15 I hear someone walking up and figure it is time for Mari Hoffman and me to go and leave Rankin with the rest of the day's work. I rise and slam my field notebook closed, saddened that my time is over and surprised by my residual frustration that I've not seen a sheep all week. I noisily gobble down some leftover fruit cocktail, then squash the can it was in. I put it into my knapsack.

When I turn around to greet Rankin or Hoffman coming up the trail, there is no one in sight. Then I hear the shuffling noise again. Instantly, my whole being becomes still, except for the hairs standing on end on my arms and in my ears.

Slowly scanning the scene behind the blind, I catch out of the corner of my eye a steel gray rump, brown-tinged and small, smaller than I could imagine a bighorn to be. I hear a grumbling and assign these sights and sounds to some other mammal, not sheep. But when I pull my field glasses up to my eyes and focus past the shrubs between me and the ridge, I see that it is a lamb, perhaps not half a year old. A mature ewe is two yards above it on the ridge; both are eighty yards or so from me.

Their eyes are fixed dead-center on my position, as if that was the first time they had heard the twang of a fruit cocktail can as it was smashed underfoot. I look further and see another, then another, then another bighorn on the low ridge northeast of me, eyes cautiously turned my way. Additional ones come over the ridge as the first few move on, now obscured by the rolling topography below the granitic ridge.

I then realize that I am but half hidden and will soon be in full view of the oncoming sheep. As if in modesty, I move behind the saguaro ribs, crouch, and refocus the field glasses. But the first few are hardly twenty yards from me now, and binoculars can hardly take them all in. I look up and count six immediately in front of me. They pause for a moment, then, as a group, hustle up another bedrock ridge toward the tank.

One immature ram pauses for a minute, as close to me as any of them have come. He is small-horned but sleek, and curious. He takes a good look my way, then bounds up the ridge to join the others over the west side of the tank. Three drop down from the ridge to the water.

Suddenly I hear a huffing, almost a bellowing, from the opposite direction, northeast of me. I can't place it. Soon there appears a mature ram with a three-fifths curl in his widely splayed horns. He moves swiftly along the slope opposite the others, then crosses and joins them. The younger sheep shift positions, making room for him on the rocks. The ram wastes no time and drops down to the water as the first three come up from it. The others gradually join the fold at the water hole, but none drinks for more than five minutes. They all give the elder ram some leeway whenever he repositions himself.

My day for big game is finally culminated—by the arrival of vultures, which causes the ewes to move much as they did when the ram came too near. By this time, however, most of the drinking is finished, and the ram starts them through a slot up-canyon from the water hole.

As soon as they move past the sand-filled concrete dam above the water hole, they are gone from my sight, never to return. I write madly, pouring words onto the official forms and into my notebook, vainly trying to catch their coloration, their muscularity and alert disposition. I am still in the same position—knapsack at my feet, field journal in my arms, looking up at the tank—when Rankin comes to take over the counting. He has seen part of the group and is eager for more.

June 28, 1991

Tucson: dreams all night long, *cimarrones* slowly ambling and browsing before me on an elevated ridge. I am at herb and grass level and follow a pale color—of ancient desert dust from caves—up the forelegs, the fetlocks, to the rump and out onto the tail. I feel the nervous tension in their sigmoid loins. I see only where they touch the rocky ground: four legs, eight legs, more. They simply go about their foraging, unconcerned that I am among them.

June 29, 1991

Organ Pipe Cactus National Monument, just west of Cabeza Prieta National Wildlife Refuge: I am unsure if this is a dream or simply a sensation. The night is hot, the breeze not enough to cool us off into deep slumber. Our sleeping bodies are spread out across the bed like desolate ranges scattered over an arid plain. Our ridges hardly touch but for the bighorn migrating between us, joining us into one gene pool.

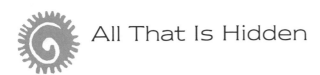

All That Is Hidden

More than any other writer over the last decade, Terry Tempest Williams has stretched the limits of the nature-writing genre to accommodate and celebrate other realms: a sensual feminism; a richness of oral histories regarding family and culture; a sense of humor and ritual that cuts against the stereotypes of "politically correct" behavior; and an ethical stance against nuclear testing, weapons proliferation, and other government actions she considers to be immoral. These explorations are not digressions from her natural histories but are embedded within them. She has given mouth-to-mouth resuscitation to a dying Victorian art form—the nature essay which nurtured her during her youth—and has revivified it into something altogether fresh and vigorous.

Having grown up as an avid birdwatcher under her grandmother's tutelage, Terry took double majors in English and biology at the University of Utah; she later completed a master of science degree in environmental education at the same institution. She continued to learn more biology outside the classroom than within—at Grand Teton National Park, the Teton Science School, and, more recently, at the Utah Museum of Natural History, where she has served as naturalist-in-residence. Through these programs and innumerable field courses she has interacted with dozens of other naturalists, biologists, archaeologists, and geologists, in the process further developing her already keen skills in nature observation and field journal writing. Many of her essays use these skills as points of departure that are then elaborated through her talents for dramatic story telling, which have been refined over the years through her association with Navajo and Mormon elders conversant with oral literature and with contemporary storytellers Laura Simms and Barry Lopez.

Although she is best known for *Refuge* (Pantheon, 1991)—her unnatural history of family and place—Williams has published two children's books, a chapbook of poems, two collections of essays, and a history of the Teton Science School. Her concerns with nuclear testing and the military's abuse of the land expressed in this essay are also evident in her other writings and in her continuing participation in nonviolent protest at the Nevada Test Site. The following essay was commissioned for this book but first appeared in the March–April 1993 issue of *Sierra* magazine.

I refuse to sign the "hold harmless" agreement issued by the Barry M. Goldwater Air Force Range. We need this piece of paper before legally entering the Cabeza Prieta National Wildlife Refuge that fall within its boundaries.

The document absolves the United States government from "any claim of liability for death or injury arising out of their usage of, or presence upon, the said Range."

Those who sign are warned of four facts:

(1) that there is "danger of injury or death due to falling objects, such as aircraft, live ammunition, or missiles"; (2) that there is "danger of injury or death due to presence of not-yet-exploded live ordnance laying on or under ground"; (3) that there is "danger of injury or death from the presence of old mine shafts and other openings or weaknesses in the earth, as well as other natural and/or man-made conditions which are too numerous to recite"; and (4) that the land "cannot be feasibly marked to warn the location and nature of each danger."

"It's a formality," my husband says. "Just sign it." He is irritated by my unwillingness to do what we have to do to get into beautiful country.

"It's not a formality for me," I answer. "I want my government to be accountable."

And so I enter the Cabeza Prieta invisibly, with a map from our friend Doug Peacock.

I am traveling with my husband, Brooke, and our desert compadre, ethnobotanist Gary Nabhan. We are here to count sheep—desert bighorn. Nothing official. Simply for ourselves.

The night before, in Organ Pipe Cactus National Monument, some fifty miles from the Cabeza, I dreamt of searching for a one-eyed ram. Brooke and Gary tease me at breakfast when I tell them of my night image.

"Sounds phallic to me," says Brooke.

Gary offers a retort in Spanish or O'odham or both and does not translate.

I ponder the symbolism and try to locate its place within my psyche. I know of the ram's association in Celtic lore—that the spiral horns are attributes of war gods. In Egyptian mythology the ram is the personification of Amon-Ra, the Sun God. "Ra . . . thou ram, mightiest of created things." It is virility, the masculine generative force, the creative heat. In Islamic culture it is the sacrificial animal.

Conversation shifts in base camp as we load our day packs for a seven-mile walk to Sheep Mountain. I take two water bottles, sun block, rain gear, a notebook and pencil, and lunch of raisins, cream cheese, and crackers. I also slip in some lemon drops.

Gary hands Brooke and me each a black comb.

"A subtle grooming hint?" I ask.

"For cholla," he grins. "To pull the spines out of your legs when you bump into them."

We begin walking. It is early morning, deeply quiet. Each of us follows our own path in solitude, meandering through mesquite, palo verde, ocotillo, and cholla. The giant saguaros with their animated postures create a lyrical landscape, the secret narratives of desert country expressed through mime. Perhaps they will steer us toward bighorn.

Ovis canadensis. Bighorn walk on the tips of their toes. Their tracks are everywhere. In the vast silences of the Cabeza Prieta, these animals engage in panoramic pleasures. Hidden on steep, rocky slopes, they miss nothing. Elusive and highly adaptive to desert extremes, desert bighorns are graced with a biological patience when it comes to water. Research shows that bighorns on the Cabeza Prieta National Wildlife Refuge have gone without water for periods extending from July to December—six months, maybe even longer. But most sheep find water holes or small depressions in the rocks that hold moisture after a rain, enough to drink daily or at least weekly.

Bones. White bones are scattered between the lava boulders. Given the terrain, tracks, and scat, it's a safe bet they're bighorns. There are ribs, vertebrae, and a pelvis that looks like a mask. Where the balls of the femurs once fit is empty space. I see eyes. I look around—nothing stirs, with the exception of side-blotched lizards. Now you see them, now you don't.

Brooke and Gary are ahead of me. They wait. Before I catch up to them, I see a saguaro that looks like the Reverend Mother, her arms generously calling me toward her. I come. At the base of her feet is an offering of gilded flicker feathers.

The men tell me the sheep tank is around the next bend. According to Peacock's map, we are less than a mile away. Bighorns could be watering there.

Gary has found a pack-rat midden made out of cholla and sheets of shrapnel. He tells us how opportunistic and enterprising these creatures are in building their dens. "Quite simply, they use what's available," he says. The glare from the silver metal blinds us. "We can trace the history of desert vegetation in the arid Southwest through these middens, sometimes as far back as forty thousand years. Food remains become cemented with pack-rat urine. Such crusty deposits represent centuries of seed gathering. There are stories here."

Brooke accidentally brushes against the den as he turns to leave. He winces. A cholla hangs from his calf, spines embedded in flesh. Out comes the comb, out come the needles. The clouds are beginning to gather and darken. Barrel cacti are blooming, blood red.

Bighorns are tracking my imagination. I recall the last one I saw, a young ram with horns just beginning to curl. He was kneeling on wet sand as he drank from the Colorado River. His large brown eyes looked up, then down to the flowing water. In the Grand Canyon, we were no threat.

Threat. Rams. Rivals. The bighorn was the mascot of my high school. The football song comes back to me ("Oh, the big rams are rambling, scrambling, rambling . . ."). As Pep Club president, I cut ram tracks out of black construction paper and then taped them to sidewalks leading to the front doors of athletes' homes. Where the tracks ended, we placed Rice Crispy treats with a "go-fight-win" letter wishing them luck. In the desolation of the Cabeza, I wonder how I have found my way from the pom-pom culture of Salt Lake City to this truly wild place.

No sheep tank in sight, although Sheep Mountain is. We decide to climb the ridge and eat lunch. The view will orient us and perhaps even inspire us to think like a ram.

Gary pulls out of his pack a small glass bottle filled with something resembling red beads. "Try a couple of these on your cream cheese and crackers," he says.

"What are they?" Brooke asks, taking a handful.

"Chiltepines. The Tarahumara believe they are the greatest protection against the evils of sorcery." We trust our friend and spread the beads on our crackers.

One bite—instant pain; red-hot and explosive! We grab water and gulp in waves, trying to douse the flames dancing in our throats. Gary, blue-eyed and blissful, enjoys the culinary fire, adding more and more to his crackers. He is native to this heat.

"I once ate thirty-two chiltepines in one mouthful during a competition," he says nonchalantly. "In fact, in all modesty, I am the Arizona state champion."

I bypass lunch altogether and suck on lemon drops, praying for a healing.

It begins to rain, lightly. As far as we can see, the desert glistens. The Growlers, jagged black peaks, carry the eye range after range into Mexico, no national boundaries exist in the land's mind. The curvature of the earth bends the horizon in an arc of light. Virga: rain evaporates in midair, creating gray-blue streamers that wave back and forth, never touching the ground. Who is witness to this full-bodied beauty? Who can withstand the recondite wisdom and sonorous silence of wilderness?

All at once, a high-pitched whining shatters us, flashes over our shoulders, threatens to blow us off the ridge. We look up. Two jets scream by. Thunderbolts. Within seconds, one, two, three bombs drop. The explosions are deafening. The desert is in flames.

The bombers veer left, straight black wings perpendicular to the land, vertical rudders on either side of their tails. The double engines behind the wings look like drums. The jets roll back to center, fly low, drop two more bombs. Flames on the desert explode; columns of smoke slowly rise like black demons.

The dark aircraft bank. I have seen them before, seabirds, parasitic jaegers who turn with the slightest dip of a wing. I am taken in by their beauty, their aerial finesse. And I imagine the pilots inside the cockpits seeing only sky from their clear plastic bubbles that float on top of the fuselage, jet jockeys with their hair on fire following a cross-line on a screen, that is all.

We are now in a cloudburst. The land, the mountains, and the aircraft disappear in a shroud of dense clouds. Rolling thunder masks the engines, the explosions. Everything is hidden.

"Basic ground warfare. Tankbusters," Technical Sergeant Robert Sexton tells me. He is the spokesman for the Fifty-eighth Fighter Wing at Luke Air Force Base, twenty miles west of Phoenix. "What you witnessed were Warthogs at work."

"Excuse me?"

"Warthogs, known by civilians as the Fairchild A-10 Thunderbolt II. They are extremely maneuverable machines that can stay close to their target." He pauses. "Did you watch the war?"

"Yeah, I watched the war."

"Then you saw them in action. These babies carry sixteen thousand pounds of mixed ordnance: bombs, rockets, missiles, laser-guided bombs, and bullets. They are specifically designed to destroy enemy tanks, and they do. Twenty-three hundred Iraqi vehicles were knocked out during Desert Storm."

"And the action we saw below Sheep Mountain?"

"Mock air-to-surface missile strikes. Some twenty to thirty aircraft use the South Tactical Range each day. This is a 'live fire' area where we train our pilots. It has been since the 1940s."

"Have any ordnances accidentally been dropped on the refuge?"

"Never."

"And how do the jets, the noise, affect the bighorn sheep?" I ask.

"They don't," he replies.

Not everyone would agree. John P. Russo, author of "The Desert Bighorn Sheep in Arizona,"[1] observed "bighorn going into headlong flight when the scream of rockets on military reservations were heard nearby." Jerry T. Light, a U.S. Forest Service official, states that "sonic booms have startled bighorn, causing them to leap into the air and lose their footing."[2] Monte Dodson of the U.S. Fish and Wildlife Service maintains that "bighorn continually exposed to sonic booms, as on the Cabeza Prieta Wildlife Refuge in Arizona, may develop severe stress problems that inhibit normal daily living patterns, as well as reproduction."[3]

What I know as a human being standing on the ridge of Sheep Mountain on the edge of the Cabeza Prieta National Wildlife Refuge is that a primal fear shot through my bones. I froze. In that moment I glimpsed war.

Instead of counting sheep, I am counting bombs. The A-10s sweeping the sky at high noon are gone. F-16s have taken over. They are silver and sleek. I will learn from Sgt. Sexton that these are one-person, single-engine aircraft designed for air-to-air attack, hence the nickname Fighting Falcon. Like the peregrine, speed is its virtue. Five hundred miles per hour is a usual clip. The F-15E, also employed above the Cabeza, is a two-person, double-engine craft capable of defending itself in air-to-air battles as well as air to ground. It is known by intimates as the Strike Eagle. Lying on my back with binoculars pointing up, I realize I am seriously engaged in military ornithology.

Four jets screech above me—close, too close. Every cell in my body contracts with fear. I am reduced to an animal vulnerability. They can do with me what they wish: one button, I am dead. I am a random target along with cholla, ocotillo, lizards, and ants. In the company of orange-and-black-beaded Gila monsters, I am expendable. No, it's worse than that: we do not exist.

Over the ridge, bombs batter the desert. The ghosts of war walk across the *bajada*. They turn. I imagine their grief-stricken faces, gaunt, cheated. Bombs counted: 23. Sheep counted: 0.

We have dropped down from the pass. Gary and Brooke continue hiking up the canyon. I choose to sit near a windmill where there is a cistern of water, still hoping for a look at a desert bighorn.

More jets. More bombs. The machinery of freedom. Eduardo Galeano writes: "*Democracy* forms part of the title of various regimes of terror."

Another blast stops my heart. Birdsong ceases, then resumes. Even the canyon wren's song is silenced. It is late afternoon. I drink some water and put on my sweater.

I scan the hillside with my binoculars. The small black boulders are covered with petroglyphs. The etched images are pink. I walk across the wash for a closer look. Miniature rock murals are everywhere. Who were these artists, these scribes? When were they here? And what did they witness? Time has so little meaning in the center of this arid country. The land holds a collective memory in the stillness of open spaces. Perhaps our only obligation is to listen and remember.

Bighorn. I walk toward him, stoop down, and run my fingers over the primitive outline of his body. Stone. Wavy lines run out from the hooves like electrical currents. This ram is very old. His horns spiral close to a circle like moons on either side of his head. And then I stand up, step back. This stone sheep has one eye.

Night in the Cabeza restores silence to the desert, that holy, intuitive silence. No more jets. No more bombs. Not even an owl or coyote is heard. Above me is an ocean of stars, and I wonder how it is that in the midst of wild serenity we as a species choose to shatter it again and again. Ivan Illich says, "Silence threatens to introduce anarchy." It is our national security. It is our civil defense. By destroying silence, the legacy of our deserts, we leave no room for peace, the deep peace that elevates and stirs our souls. It is silence that rocks and awakens us to the truth of our dreams.

Tonight in the Cabeza Prieta, I feel the eyes of the desert bighorn. It is I who am being watched. It is I who am being counted.

NOTES

1. J. P. Russo, "The Desert Bighorn Sheep in Arizona," *Arizona Game and Fish Department Wildlife Bulletin* 1 (1956): 1–153.

2. J. T. Light, personal communication, 1991.

3. M. M. Dodson, "A Review of Management Objectives on the Kofa Game Range and Cabeza Prieta Wildlife Refuge," *Transactions of the North American Wild Sheep Conference* 2 (1976): 38–41.

Changing Contexts

Being Reflections on the Ways Human Interactions with Wildlife Are in Flux, in Peril, or in Conflict

A red-on-buff ceramic censer of a desert bighorn by a prehistoric Hohokam potter of the Sacaton Phase, ca. A.D. 950–1150, from the Snaketown site. (Courtesy of the Arizona State Museum, catalog no. GP43312; photograph courtesy of the Arizona State Museum, University of Arizona, Helga Teiwes, photographer)

PETER STEINHART

Looking for Sheep

"What is being substituted for nature," Peter Steinhart has said in critiquing wildlife films, "is a mass-produced, homogeneous experience. We will all have the same nightmare."

Steinhart has been measuring the pulse of public appreciation of wildlife for more than two decades, in part through his former role as contributing editor and columnist for *Audubon* magazine. Along with David Quammen, Roger Swain, and David Ehrenfeld, he is among the finest craftsmen of the short narrative essay working today. Like Quammen, Steinhart has made the feature column in journalistic nature magazines more literary, more provocative, and more open to a range of issues that seldom find a forum in other contexts. For example, his eye opening essay on "environmental racism" propelled several organizations into dealing with this issue. Fortunately for students, Steinhart also shares his skills through teaching at Stanford University.

The following essay, set largely in the Sierra Pinacate, reminds us that the desert is pervaded by a chimeric quality revealed only to those who are tenacious enough to stick with it. It is from Steinhart's collaboration with photographer Tupper Blake: *Two Eagles/Dos Aguilas: A Natural History of the U.S.–Mexico Borderlands* (University of California Press, forthcoming), which has also inspired a Smithsonian Institution traveling

This essay is adapted from *Two Eagles/Dos Aguilas: A Natural History of the U.S.–Mexico Borderlands,* by Tupper Ansel Blake and Peter Steinhart (1994).

exhibit of their work. When not traveling himself, Steinhart lives "like a dangerous lunatic in a part of California where there are more people than sheep."

This is a land of glimpses . . . of the bobcat that darts across the road, the coyote that slinks behind the cactus, the shadow of a lizard skating over the rocks. We are in the Pinacate, one of the more spectacular desert land-scapes of North America. It is named for a shield volcano at the edge of the Sonoran Desert, forty miles southwest of the Mexican border town of Sonoyta. The broad, rust red bulk of Pinacate Peak rises high into the haze of the desert sky. It is warted with smaller cinder cones and old volcanic vents. The lava beds strewn like bedclothes around it are black and tortuous but enlivened with the green of ocotillo, creosote, cholla cactus, and other desert shrubs and forbs. Here and there are old calderas, yawning a mile or two across. The Pinacate is said to be the driest place in North America. Archaeologist Julian Hayden, who knows it more inti-mately than any other human, took photographs of the same locations, year after year, and showed thereby that they saw not a trace of rain for seven years. Far to the west, the lighter beige of sand carried down the Colorado River, dropped at its delta, and blown by wind into the dunes of the Gran Desierto traipses into the black of the lava. The dunes seem to be a mile or two away. In fact they are twenty miles. This is a country of wide vistas. If you have eyes, you can see far enough to glimpse your own divinity.

But if anyone were to ask, we would have to say we are looking for sheep. William Hornaday came here in 1907 and with his companions shot seven bighorn sheep. It was, he said, "the vanishing point of the genus in America," referring to the sheep's geographic range rather than its vulnerability to the lust of hunters and scientific collectors.[1] We are just hoping to see one.

Looking for sheep is an exercise in patience. For me it is usually rhymed with disappointment. I have looked for sheep in the Colorado Rockies, Alaska's Talkeetnas, and the desert ranges of California, and only a few times have I seen anything more than the absence of their thoughts. In the Sierra San Pedro Mártir, I tramped with a hunting guide for six hours, clambering over the tumbled boulders of mountain gullies, panting over the fractured rocks of the ridgetops, and clattering down the other sides. We walked and walked, stopping now and then to glass the ridge lines. The confidence of good intentions faded with the clear light of morning, and in the afternoon haze, will and resolve faded. We returned without sighting a sheep. In Joshua Tree National Monument, I walked miles to a remote palm oasis, hoping to find sheep drinking. All the while, over a distant ridge, the boom of tanks and rockets, the sky-ripping mutter of jet airplanes, and the rising black pillars of smoke announced that the U.S. Marines were playing out games of war. Apocalypse over my shoulder, hope down the trail, I walked and walked. And when I reached the oasis, it offered up only the uneasy confidence of a pair of cactus wrens and the distant regard of ravens. I saw no sheep.

Here in the Pinacate we bobble and bounce in a Range Rover over a rocky track. The landscape seems as empty of life as a parking lot at midnight. There is not even birdsong to punctuate the waiting.

It is as if sheep live in another dimension. The landscape is plain enough that you ought to see them easily. There is abundant sign of their presence. There are day beds and piles of dung. We have seen trails over the black lava where sheep have, for millennia, placed each footstep in exactly the same spot, leaving a beaded strand of sand-colored circles etched into the black of the desert varnish. These careful hieroglyphs contrast sharply with the hoof-dragged plow welts cattle have bulldozed across the same landscape.

But we have searched for hours and have seen no sheep. Sheep seem to live in seams of time. One can imagine that they're up there on the ridges, standing silently, watching whatever passes with a lofty indifference, invisible to mere humans. Perhaps their thoughts run to realms so remote that they lift bighorns right out of the material world.

More likely, they are invisible because they are rare. Bighorns were once abundant all across the border region. They were much reduced by hunting and then by diseases transmitted by domestic cows and sheep. Two of the three California subspecies are on the endangered species list. One of them is the peninsular bighorn, which inhabits the mountains of Baja California and the California desert. Bighorn sheep are not abundant anywhere in Mexico. They are protected by law; that is, the Mexican government limits the number that can be hunted. But they are hunted illegally just the same. There are bighorns in the mountains of Baja California and here in the Pinacate. Everywhere they are hard-pressed.

The Pinacate, like all the borderlands, offers all kinds of tests to the vision. No country so challenges the links between eyes, mind, and heart. And perhaps no creature so tests the connections as bighorn sheep. The Indians of central Baja California painted sheep under rock overhangs in the narrow canyons of the mountains. Their paintings show shamans in sheep headdresses reaching out to touch the sheep. Why sheep and not deer, coyotes, roadrunners, or any of the more common residents? What charms did sorcerers and sheep once exchange in these lands?

Such questions arise because to see in this landscape, you have to think differently. This is not the waterlogged north, where the spring snowmelt signals a rush of life, where herds rumble over the grass and immense flocks wheel over the mudflats. In most of the borderlands water is scarce and life must go on without the ceremony of crowds splashing into water. There is not the industry or the sense of appointment with the seasons; there are few of the calendared arrivals and departures. There are long periods of sunbaked stillness, when nothing seems to stir. The desert demands patience.

And then there are sudden apparitions. Once, riding in a National Park Service vehicle through the numbing hundred-degree heat of the Chisos Mountains of Texas's Big Bend, miles from any water, I was more asleep than awake. As the car roared over a culverted arroyo, I cracked open an eye to see, spattered in a leafless tree like spots of paint, a flock of egrets. They were cold white patches of snow against the fiery oranges and browns of the desert rock. I could not hold my eye on them as the car sped past, and even today I am not altogether sure I saw them.

To see here may also demand the willingness to look for those seams in time into which things dimly seen may fall. There is about the desert an air of unreality. And what is real is unfamiliar. There is more variety to life in the desert than in the northern forests. There are more kinds of plants and animals because winter brings no annual eviction and the scarcity of water discourages travels. But few of the creatures grow in masses. Desert life forms don't sweep across the landscape. They watch and scurry, gobble and hide. Many go underground to evade the aridity and heat. There is waiting where we expect decision. There is silence where we expect song. Reptiles, by not having to use energy to keep their bodies warm, get along on as little as one-thirtieth the food it takes to support a bird. They can close down, not eat for weeks or even months. So, much of the biomass of the region is clothed in scales. There are more lizard species in these borderland deserts than anywhere else in the North America. They hide like private thoughts under rocks, then streak between bushes like half-heard mutterings.

The desert is certainly not lacking in landmarks to steer by. But as you pass, your perspective changes. The mountains contort. They change shape and color. There is more exposed rock, and, fractured by the heat and cold, it tosses sunlight in extravagant ways; as the sun passes overhead, color, shadow, and tone are constantly changing. If you look away from a mountain for a few minutes and then look back, you can't be sure it's the same peak. It is easy to get lost.

And we do just that, missing a fork in the track and following the wrong wheel ruts off to the northeast. We bounce along over rock and gully. We know quickly that we are on the wrong track. But the desert's heat and insubstantiality have jellied our wills, and rather than turn back, we just keep driving.

We come to a large saguaro on the edge of a rocky jumble of hillside. A red-tailed hawk perches on top of it, unconcerned by the spines under its talons. We rattle right up to the cactus, but the hawk does not fly. It sits on top of the saguaro, looking off into space, neither threatened by nor interested in us. Perhaps we take this as a sign. Wordlessly, we turn the Range Rover around and rattle back the way we have come.

We are driving along a low ridge of crumbled lava. The heat of the day numbs our brains and drags at our eyelids. To the west, we look down on a tossing sea of rock and small pale green shrubs. A dust devil stirs from the valley below. It rises like an awakening giant, bending from the knees and hips, straightening out slowly and stiffly, and then whirls slowly across the landscape. It grows as it moves, forty, then fifty, then sixty feet tall. We stop to watch.

The dust devil whirls faster. It dances over the rock, picking up bits of cactus and grass and the fallen leaves of creosote. Feeding on all this desert debris, it fattens and grows taller. Suddenly, it divides—that is, a partner steps out of its ribs, a wraith of equal size and rhythm—and the two begin to dance around each other. Like mating snakes they whirl and writhe and spin together. They fade back into a single column, then divide and dance again, then come together and couple again.

For fifteen minutes the dance goes on. The wraiths circle and dart over the valley floor. We watch intently and wordlessly. And when at last the wind settles and the dust fades into puffs of cloud and the scatter of leaves, and then into the thin air of invisibility, it is as if a curtain has drawn open on the landscape. My eyelids are no longer heavy. My mind is no longer asleep. The blue of the sky seems bluer. The green of the creosote seems greener. It is then that I look over my shoulder and see the sheep.

They are silhouetted against the ridge behind us: four ewes and two lambs. Only two stand, their curving horns outlined against the clear blue sky. The others sit, with legs tucked under their bodies, chewing slowly and staring out into space. The sun is low now, and the sheep are bathed in a golden glow. Even though they are perhaps half a mile away, the scarlet of the ocotillo blossoms among them leaps across the air at us, strikingly red.

We get out of the vehicle and stalk. Our aim is to photograph the sheep and thus take something material away from the meeting. The sheep are clearly aware of our approach. They stare down at us. They hardly move a muscle. We move slowly, a few feet at a time, and then stand still, always keeping our arms close to our bodies.

Before we cut the distance between us in half, two of the sheep clamber to their feet. Another 50 yards and all are up. Only one seems to look at us at a time. The others seem to browse, picking up a mouthful here and chewing awhile, a mouthful there and chewing awhile. But they are clearly intent on keeping us out of their world. As we close the distance to 250 yards, they slowly, almost aimlessly, turn and walk over the ridge and disappear behind it. They vanish just as quietly and quickly as they appeared. We clamber around the side of the ridge and look up to where the sheep ought to be. But there is nothing there.

There are other worlds—worlds we remain for the most part blind to. Every once in a while we stumble in, like a skater breaking through the ice or a reveller stepping out of a brightly lit room into the dense dark of the night. We flutter our hands before us and blink our eyes, trying to shake vision into our brains. But we see nothing clearly. So we scramble back to the security of light, not at all sure where we have been.

Could it be that other creatures travel better than we? Could it be that this house of life rambles through more rooms and corridors than we yet illuminate? It is a sad fact of human existence that we see only what we know. And we know only a little bit about sheep.

NOTE

1. William Hornaday, *Camp-Fires on Desert and Lava* (New York: Charles Scribner's Sons, 1908).

Rambo: *The Desert Bighorn Sheep as a Masculine Totem*

David E. Brown epitomizes what can happen when a wildlife biologist turns to nontechnical nature writing. His attention to detail, to zoological accuracy at a level unobserved by most general readers, communicates an authenticity and care for "the particular" in many of his works. After years of serving as a biologist for the Arizona Game and Fish Department, Brown "spread his wings" to become an interpreter and popularizer of Southwestern natural history topics. Along with the dean of Sonoran Desert ecologists, Charles "Chuck" Lowe, Brown published a series of maps and descriptions of the biotic communities of the binational Southwest that revolutionized biogeographic appreciation of the region. He then began an editorial collaboration with historian Neil B. Carmony that has led to seven books (including *Mexican Game Trails* [University of Oklahoma Press, 1991]), ranging from edited journals of pioneering naturalists and hunters to a humorous look at Gila monsters in truth, myth, fiction, and film. Brown has also published overviews of grizzlies, game birds, wolves, and waterfowl in the Southwest, covering considerable historical as well as technical ground.

The essay included here—one of several he has written on bighorn sheep—is among his most penetrating pieces. It looks hard not only at the animal but at the men who have historically made it their business to stalk and study bighorn sheep. In critiquing the means through which game managers study wild sheep today, he also brings us a chilling look at their ends, their motives, and their self-images. This essay first appeared in the May–June 1992 issue of the *Game Journal*.

It's a long haul from Pas, Manitoba, to Phoenix, Arizona, especially in November. Alternating between driving, keeping the driver company, and napping in the camper, the three of us had fought ice-slicked roads for thirty-six hours. Now, peering out the window from the bunk in the camper shell, I am again treated to the familiar sight of pinyons giving way to ponderosa pines as the truck hums southward on Arizona 89A. Utah is behind us; soon I will be home.

As the driver pulls into the gas station at Jacob Lake, I can see that the deer season is on. A jerking caravan of pickups and campers festooned with cheesecloth-draped carcasses, hocks and antlers protruding, is winding its way through the hunter check station. Wildlife managers are harvesting the weekend crop of weights and ages. A compelling urge to break out of my chrysalis and help gather the accumulating data overcomes me. For too many years the Kaibab check station was an integral part of my life.

But the gas tank is full now, my companions are anxious to get going, and no one even opens the camper door to see if I am awake. As we ease back onto the highway, an Arizona Game and Fish truck pulls into the service station. I do not know the face of the driver. Nor am I able to identify any of the coverall-clad people directing traffic. The hustle and bustle of the check station retreats rearward, its personnel oblivious of my past or presence. I am reminded of the departure scene in *Lawrence of Arabia* when Peter O'Toole stands up in a staff car to acknowledge his former Arab comrades-in-arms, who no longer recognize him. A part of my life is over.

As we drop down into House Rock Valley, the late afternoon sun bathes the Vermilion and Echo cliffs in their finest magenta, a hue so incongruous with the surrounding duns and grays that the scene must be the product of an artist's imagination. For the briefest moment, the cliffs glow with the same intensity that they did on the morning I first passed this way to interview for a job with the Arizona Game and Fish Department nearly thirty years ago. Bighorn sheep, or the promise of them, was the reason I came to Arizona. No other animal played so pivotal a role in my career as a wildlife biologist.

Why this animal so fires my imagination is hard to say. I first saw desert bighorns in southern California's Santa Rosa Mountains on a field trip during my senior year in college—a sight that thrills my memory still. Perhaps it was the romance of their desert setting that so captivated me. The earth's "wastelands" have certainly cast their spell on more than one neophyte adventurer. If so, the presence of bighorn sheep gave the desert mountains meaning, and a purpose to prowling about "unmanaged country." Bighorn sheep symbolized the essence of a wilderness without farmers, foresters, and graziers. Looking for bighorns, conducting sheep surveys, evaluating potential bighorn transplant sites, and, later, restoring desert bighorn sheep to historic habitats became my pleasure and my passion. Although we began our honeymoon in Las Vegas, the ultimate oasis, my wife and I were quickly sated with the neon glitter, and I persuaded her to spend our remaining week in Nevada's Desert Game Range looking for sheep. Nor was my life complete until I one day drew a permit and killed a desert bighorn.

Memories rush back. A collage of a hundred special days comes to mind. My memory shifts southward to real sheep country. It is one of those crisp, still mornings that one awakens to only in the desert. A winter sun hurriedly erases a topaz dawn to create an eerie gathering of mirages on the horizon. Shimmering nipplelike buttresses and inverted trapezoids temporarily complement the familiar ranges of granite and lava that characterize this part of the Sonoran Desert called the Cabeza Prieta. My waking thoughts are a fantasy, wishing that these disappearing apparitions of castles and mesas were real, thus multiplying the habitat for desert bighorn tenfold.

Our campsite west of Ajo is ugly, as man's intrusions into the desert always are. Two house trailers, towed in the night before, and a dozen or so pickup trucks squat randomly among the creosote bushes, their spoor parallel gashes in a veneer of desert pavement. The focal point of the camp is a smoldering ironwood snag protruding from a residue of snowlike ashes ringed by a myriad of footprints—the altar of the night before.

The camp is coming to life. Already a few men—there are no women here—are gathering around the still-living coals, drinking coffee and talking earnestly. Soon bands of twos and threes emerge from campers and bedrolls to augment the huddle. Some wear tan Arizona Game and Fish uniforms. Others, veterinarians and Sheep Society volunteers, are in Levis and denim jackets. Most of the participants sport Stetsons or baseball caps adorned with bighorn emblems and pithy epithets in praise of sheep—the war paint of technological-age hunters. A few of us have donned fluorescent orange coveralls. We are the ones who will fly today.

Inside the trailers our medicine men grease O rings and load syringes with drugs amid an odor of bacon and eggs. Outside, others are test-firing net guns and dart guns. A partylike atmosphere prevails. This will not be a day for individual contemplation and solitude in soft light and shadowed mountains. What will take place today will be a tribal endeavor not unlike a military campaign in which victory is expected but not assured.

Our mission is to capture four ewes and four rams, put radio collars around their necks and plastic tags in their ears, and release them to go about their business. Because we do not have to transport any animals our assignment is regarded as "a piece of cake," even though the same feat would have been deemed virtually impossible only a few years ago. Using a mixture of new technology and old mathematics, we will use the ratio of ear-tagged sheep to unadorned animals observed as an index for estimating sheep numbers on subsequent surveys. The radio collars will enable us to track the sheep from one mountain range to another and allow us to learn if and when any animals leave the sanctity of the Cabeza Prieta National Wildlife Refuge.

Helicopters are spotted in the eastern sky. In a few minutes the throaty roar of their supercharged jet engines and the whop-whopping of aluminum blades shatter the morning peace. Marvels of the twentieth century, the Bell Jet Rangers appear today as ominous giant locusts, enveloping the camp in a whirlwind of stinging dust and debris. As the engines whine down I can see the clean-cut faces of the pilots—invariably military veterans of untold overseas adventures. With ships and men like these we are all Titans more powerful than any conjured up by gods or Greeks.

Not unlike members of a football team, we each have a function and specific duties. The pilot will be forward on the left, my observer on his right. I will be the gunner in the back, the quarterback, if you will. The custom-built Coda net gun, which fires a triangular rope web out of a bucketlike muzzle, will be the weapon of choice. Propelled by a .308 cartridge, any one of the four buckets of prefolded nets should capture a sheep caught out in the open, whether running or standing. For backup I have a Paxarm capture rifle and four dart syringes loaded with M-99 as an immobilizer and Azaperone as a tranquilizer. We have sixty gallons of aviation fuel—enough for four hours of flying time. All that is needed for success is that we find sheep and keep them in sight, and for the pilot to get me within twenty yards of our quarry. I will not admit the possibility of not shooting well.

The pilot goes through his litany of procedures. *Keep your head down when leaving the ship. Always get out on the downhill side. Remember the tail rotor. Don't leave your seat belt unbuckled.* The manufacturer of the net gun issues other warnings. *Never fire upward lest you hit the rotor blades* (a fatal error). *Don't hold the gun down so the tape gives way and the net falls out of the bucket. Don't close the bolt until you are ready to fire. Always point the gun outside the ship* . . . All this and more I have memorized. But I listen intently. What we are doing *is* dangerous. More wildlife managers' careers have ended in a helicopter than anywhere else. Three of my coworkers have been badly hurt on similar operations. All of us have a repertoire of horror stories.

The doors are taken off the ship and the guns are taken on board. I cinch the seat belt and test the safety strap that will allow me to lean out of the helicopter and fire downward. The white plastic helmet fits, a good omen. Cables are plugged in; the radio both receives and transmits. The pilot and observer glance back over their shoulders. I give the thumbs-up sign.

A whine and a cough start the aluminum blades churning. The noise builds to a deafening crescendo. Then the pitch changes; the angry engine becomes a monotonous symphony, the whipping rotor blades a metronome. The helicopter strains upward ever so gently, tilts forward, and slowly rises. Seconds later, I am watching the helicopter's shadow pass over the widely spaced creosote bushes and clumps of kangaroo-rat holes. The background noise is now a comfortable, pulsing whisper. Blue palo verdes and ironwoods trace the courses of arroyos. The morning light casts the trees in chartreuse and spinach, giving the landscape the appearance of a tropical veld. Within minutes we are ascending a bajada leading us upward into the Growler Mountains. I sense the comfort of knowing exactly where I am. A vague feeling of apprehension gives way to supreme confidence.

Silver-crowned saguaros and glistening teddybear chollas, backlit by the morning sun, replace bronzed creosote bushes. In seconds we ascend a ridge that would be an hour's hike. We are now over the crest of the Growlers. Without any instructions the pilot begins working the sun-kissed spine of the mountain, giving us an eagle's-eye view of the slopes on either side. He has played this game before and knows his stuff. We begin our search for the white rump or the glimpse of a crooked leg that betrays a sheep.

Suddenly I see them. The sight of sheep is always a surprise. Half a dozen animals are standing on a shady slope staring up at us. "Sheep at eight o'clock," I shout into the mike. Instinctively aware that they have been seen, the sheep bolt and scramble up and over a saddle between two ragged peaks. For a few seconds, as the helicopter wheels around the pinnacles, they will be out of sight. This is their chance to lose us.

But the pilot is on them. As we cross over the crest of the ridge the animals are directly below us—at least some of them are. Some innate defense against disaster from above has caused the band to split ranks. A ewe and a lamb are holding their ground below a steep cliff face. Two ewes and a young ram are bailing off into a broken canyon, heading downslope in pounding bounds that make me fear for their safety. Another ewe, an older animal, has cut back toward the saddle above where the sheep were initially spotted. She, I tell the pilot, is the one we want.

Time is the ewe's ally. Like a bronc rider, I am only to keep on the animal for an allotted time. To stress a sheep by running it too long is to risk capture myopathy and death. We want prisoners, not carcasses. The pilot knows this and backs off to keep the ewe from panicking. My observer starts counting off the seconds.

But our sheep is not prone to panic. After a run of only a hundred yards she hunkers down under a palo verde to await our next move. The pilot eases in to nudge her out. I lift the no-longer-heavy net gun from my lap and close the bolt. Out comes the ewe, bounding through a patch of teddybear cholla. Reluctant to risk a running shot so early in the day, I hesitate.

After running another sixty yards, she again takes refuge under a palo verde. Three times she breaks, runs, and then attempts to hide again.

The ewe seems to comprehend that she has a defense that works. Even though the helicopter is hovering but ten yards above her, she will not move. I decide to attempt to ensnare her head as she peers out at us from beneath the spindly branches. Aiming two feet over her head, I pull the trigger. I do not hear the report of the gun. I am only aware of the net unfurling over the stubby tree. Off she goes to the next palo verde. I load another canister while the pilot jockeys for position.

This approach is more open, and the tree provides poorer cover. I lean out the door and look directly down at her, waiting for her to flush while the helicopter edges ever closer. I can age her horns at six years. When she bolts, it is a dash of only a few yards. Here she hesitates, standing defiantly in the open, wondering what tactic to use next. I hold my aim three feet over her head. This time the net drops directly over the gentle arch of her horns. One lurch and she is hopelessly entangled.

Instantly the pilot heads for the nearest saddle, where my partner and I clamber out beneath the whirling umbrella. At our approach, the sheep resumes her struggle to free herself. I can see the fear in her eyes. Grasping the protruding horns, we blindfold her as she fights the net. Unable to see her tormenters, she immediately calms down and makes no objections as we rivet on the radio collar and punch in an ear tag.

When handling Arizona's game animals, I am conscious of subtle differences between the species. White-tailed deer are perfect in every way, each muscle sculpted and every hair in place. Pronghorn antelope strike me as somehow unfinished, perhaps because they appear so diminutive and fragile up close, and they shed great patches of brittle, synthetic-looking hair when handled. Mule deer possess a faint gamey odor; once recognized it is forever remembered. Desert sheep have a ragtag look about them and seem more prone to mortal ailments than other ungulates. Chipped horns, torn ears, and knots and scars showing through a too-stingy pelage are more the norm than the exception. Our ewe, too, has an unkempt look. She has ticks in her ears, mucus draining from her nose, and cactus spines in her hocks. Hershey's Kisses dribble out of her anus. But eking out a living in an arid mountain range like the Growlers does not make for a refined existence.

Removing the net from the entangled forelegs and horns is surprisingly easy. The fear is gone from her amber irises when the blindfold is removed. Uncertain of our continued magnanimity, and disbelieving in her regained freedom, the ewe gives us a quizzical look before scampering off to wherever spooked sheep go. Within minutes both nets have been retrieved and folded, and we are back in the chopper looking for more prey.

It takes us close to an hour to find our next quarry. Near Sheep Peak the observer spots two rams—good-sized fellows. Even the smaller of the two, an eight-year-old, is almost too old for our purposes. But it is now 9:10 and we are no longer choosy. The thermals will soon be up and we have no way of predicting how much wind the afternoon will bring. After a short chase, our intended target seeks refuge in a cave. None of the pilot's arsenal of ruses pries him out of his sanctuary.

No matter. I pick up the dart gun and insert a Palmer CapChur dart into the breech. As if knowing my intentions, the ram presses his rump against the cavern wall and eyes us warily. Could he have been through this before? Using the helicopter's rear-view mirror, the pilot eases backward, threading the tail rotor through two saguaros. Suspicious, the ram switches his stance from one end of the cave to the other so that he can keep us in sight. For a moment his hindquarters are exposed, giving me a chance.

The dart seems to leave the barrel in slow motion. An eternity passes. The ram will certainly dodge the incoming missile or move before it arrives. But my aim is true. The sheep bolts from the cave, the green tail-piece of the dart protruding from his left hip. Immediately the pilot ascends the helicopter two hundred yards straight up. Here, we will watch and wait for the drug to take effect. I load another syringe into the rifle in case not all the drug has been injected or the dose is insufficient for so large an animal. We are committed to him now, and, unknowingly, he to us. Once again the observer ticks off the minutes.

We have not long to wait. After running downhill for two minutes, the ram slows to a walk. Another minute and the head droops and his gait becomes stiff-legged. Then comes the awaited-for stumble. He is down. The nearest the helicopter can land is a cholla-infested bench off the main ridge, leaving us a downslope scramble of three hundred yards. We are thankful to see that the sheep has come to rest in the shade of an acacia and is in no danger of overheating.

The strength of a ram, drugged or not, is impressive. While I am holding the horns so that my partner can blindfold the stupefied animal, his neck lunges violently, knocking me backward and sending me somersaulting downslope. Scratched and bleeding from rocks and cactus, I am relieved to find nothing broken. Grappling with the still-thrashing sheep, my accomplice can only grin at my acrobatics. Only when the blindfold covers the oddly horizontal pupils does the sheep calm down. The tagging and collaring completed, we swab his skinned shins and dart wound with an antibiotic. We then inject him with M50-50 to reverse the immobilizer. Within seconds the ram is staggering off wearing the necklace that makes him ours.

Our second flight of the day goes even better. The wind hasn't come up as we had feared, the day is clear and cool, and the sheep have prolonged their feeding on the slopes. I am the observer now, relieved of the responsibilities of marksmanship. My gunner is more confident than I and snares a running two-year-old ram on his second cast. Another ewe is bagged in textbook fashion as she hustles up a ridge toward the summit. Hubris overtakes me; it is not yet two o'clock and we have completed our mission. I would look for deer and other game on the return trip to camp, but I am too busy picking cactus glochids out of my fingers.

The other chopper crew is still out capturing their quota of four sheep in the Cabeza Prieta and Pinta mountains. There is nothing to do but return the equipment to the trailer, drink coffee, and talk sheep. Our praise for the pilot and the new net gun is unreserved. We have heralded in a new age in the rapidly changing science of sheep capture. No longer must we risk ourselves and our sheep with dangerous drugs. We alone could have taken eight animals today. Like Stone Age hunters, we spend the next two hours reliving our prowess over and over again.

The sun is close to setting when the other chopper comes in. Their final animal was hard to come by; the last one always is. Never mind that we have one more ram than we wanted and one less ewe. We have fulfilled our quota in the time allotted without losing any animals. Our little campaign that is waged both for and against the sheep has been an unqualified triumph.

196

The helicopters crank up once more. The pilots are headed for the Plomosa Mountains, where another camp and another crew await. Tomorrow other bighorns will be captured for transplantation to the Buckskin Mountains—a much more difficult operation. The sheep will not only have to be captured, but also transported to camp in cargo nets before being loaded into crates for their trip to the release site.

Rooster tails of dust mark the retreating pickups, speeding from their brief rendezvous in the desert like a covey of Road Warriors. A haze fills the evening sky. It is time for me to go as well. But I am reluctant to leave. I am still elated by the day's events. I want more. I wish that I was in one of the departing Jet Rangers, their running lights now hurtling through the twilight like shooting stars.

Now, years later, I am still puzzled by what it is about bighorn sheep that so intrigues us. The bighorn's relative scarcity and proclivity for myriad ailments explain the need but not the desire to intervene on its behalf. No doubt the bighorn's tolerance for being managed explains some of the appeal. We not only capture and release them; we also provide them with water, study their diseases, and rid their habitat of burros and other competitors. But are not such animals as kit foxes and desert antelope equally appealing and just as deserving of our attention?

Obviously not. When it comes to desert sheep, forces more powerful than human empathy or a need to demonstrate management expertise are at work.

I remember when we once inadvertently killed a doe Sonoran antelope. She tripped and broke a vertebra on being netted in full flight, and no magic of modern medicine could save her. With one pitiful bleat, a ruminant scream that only distressed antelope make, the doe convulsed and expired. The accident put the entire camp into a depression that forever canceled our euphoria over what had heretofore been a flawless operation. None of us ever felt quite that way about a dead sheep.

Yet, no other animal has more organizations dedicated solely to its well-being. Each year Southwestern biologists talk sheep and present their data at meetings of the Desert Bighorn Council. For more than thirty years Nevada sheep aficionados have gathered under the auspices of the Fraternity of the Desert Bighorn. For twenty-five years the Arizona Desert Bighorn Sheep Society has promoted bighorn welfare projects, and a

California Sheep Society now champions sheep in southern California. On a broader scale, the aim of the Foundation for North American Wild Sheep is to fund sheep research and other sheep enhancement projects throughout the continent.

Membership and executive board rosters show that sport-hunting males are the driving force behind these organizations. Contractors, construction workers, veterinarians, and engineers are heavily represented occupations. Moreover, participation in programs beneficial to sheep appears to be primarily a masculine pursuit. The bighorn sheep is a male totem. From my viewpoint, women seem drawn to big cats, wolves, and other predators—a gender bias reflected in the membership of such organizations as the International Society for Endangered Cats and Preserve Arizona's Wolves. Could it be that the bighorn's masculine appeal has as its source some innate striving for dominance, while women identify more with animals that have a better-defined social structure? Or is the attraction of many men to mountain sheep as enigmatic as the infatuation some prepubescent girls have for horses?

A masculine bias carries through to how we visualize and portray sheep. Bighorn sheep and rams are almost synonymous. Nevada's state animal is the desert bighorn, but it is a ram that appears on the Silver State's license plates. Dodge trucks are "Rams" with charging-ram hood ornaments. We have the Colorado State University Rams and the Los Angeles Rams. The Embraceable Ewes are only cheerleaders for the latter. The slang term *horny,* now widely used by both men and women, was until recently almost entirely confined to the lexicon of males and has its origin in ramlike behavior.

The bighorn ram's freewheeling social life certainly evokes the image of a male fantasy role model. On approaching puberty, young rams join bands of other rams, with whom they continually joust for individual dominance, the smaller rams following the larger ones. Dominance is established and maintained on the basis of horn size. Territories are neither established nor defended. Clashes and displays throughout the year characterize the individual ram's relations with his colleagues. The more passive ewes are ignored except when they are in heat, a time when the rams vie among themselves for the right to mate. Possession is a temporary phenomenon that goes to the largest ram, who does not gather a harem but goes from one receptive ewe to another. All of this is accompanied by much lip curling, tongue flicking, and nudging—behavior not unlike that of a drugstore cowboy at a honky-tonk.

And, like many a man, a ram in middle and old age grows diffident. Chances are he will become a wanderer, either a solitary animal or traveling in the company of others of his sex and age class. More than once I have seen several trophy rams bedded on the same ledge, staring out into space like old men on a park bench.

One does not have to spend much time in sheep country to see that man's fascination with sheep is long-standing. No other animal is more prevalent in the prehistoric rock art of the Southwest than the bighorn. Why did the Patayan, Anasazi, and Hohokam laboriously peck so many bighorn sheep on basalt rocks patinated in desert varnish? Perhaps the artists were hunters—males who, like their Paleolithic brethren in Spain and France, depicted the game animals most special to them. Why else would pictographs rarely represent predators and rabbits? Nonetheless, it is doubtful that all of these bighorn drawings are merely commemorations of successful hunts—badges of prowess like the mounted heads that line the dens of present-day trophy hunters or the miniature swastikas below cockpits of World War II Mustangs. While most of the sheep depicted are rams, many of them appear to be pregnant. Clearly, some greater fertility-related mysticism is implied. Most anthropologists believe such art was ceremonial in purpose, and that these drawings were meant to favorably influence the abundance and availability of this most prized and hard-to-get game animal by invoking its image and appealing to its spirit. That such Stone Age attempts at intervention on the behalf of mountain sheep parallel the water hole projects and other sheep enhancement efforts of modern sheep-hunting organizations lends credibility to such a hypothesis.

One wonders if a yearning for a return to pre-Neolithic times plays a role in our fascination with sheep. Wild sheep would be a natural totem for men longing for the life they had before they enslaved themselves by enslaving animals. This yearning for a better time appears to be especially strong in desert peoples, many of whom have been prone to deep religious beliefs in messiahs, from Jesus of Nazareth to Wovoka of the Ghost Dance. Was not the desert the source of all three great Western religions? And are not the teachings of many of these desert traditions replete with sheep symbolism and metaphors including ritual sacrifice—Cain's and Abel's gifts to their father, a sheep substituting for the sacrifice of Abraham's son, the Good Shepherd, Lamb of God, separating the sheep from the goats, and so on?

I guess I will never get desert sheep out of my blood. I think fascination with the animal is an inherited trait imperfectly passed down from Paleolithic times. It goes back to a time when *sheep* country and *our* country were the same wild place, and we did not yet know who would come to own it. For those of us who still do not know, or do not want to know, the bighorn sheep remains the ultimate symbol of the desert's wildness and our longing for identity with it. To those of us who love the desert, the sheep are us and we are them. Perhaps this is why the singular and plural of *sheep* in so many of our languages are one and the same.

The President Spoke

Eric Mellink is one of a new generation of Latin American ecologists who write in a variety of genres, from research reports in technical journals to creative nonfiction essays in *El Imparcial*. Along with prominent Mexican ecologists such as Exequial Escurra, Arturo Gomez Pompa, Victor Toledo, and Humberto Suzan, Mellink underscores the relationship between culture and nature no matter what form his writing takes. Mellink, who was educated at the University of Chapingo and the University of Arizona, emphasized ethnozoology throughout his academic studies of wildlife biology, evolutionary ecology, and cultural anthropology. His studies and field excursions with paleoecologist Paul Martin encouraged him to take the long view of human interactions with the environment. Although his early work documented bird and mammal diversity associated with traditional agriculture in Mexico, more recently he has focused on human impacts on the endangered species of Baja California and the islands of the Sea of Cortez. His numerous monographs, journal articles, and published lecture notes are indications that his perspective on conservation biology is having a widespread influence in the Mexican universities and the research centers of the desert regions he frequents.

This essay might be called a "political ecology" of bighorn sheep in Baja California. It is not a natural history per se; rather, it demonstrates how the Mexican people have come to use bighorn sheep as a symbol in their quest for control over local resources whose fates now lie in the hands of bureaucrats in Mexico City. Although not a nature essay in the

Anglo-American tradition of Gilbert White, Ralph Waldo Emerson, or Henry David Thoreau, it *is* representative of a Latin American intellectual tradition of essays that contemplates how public policy (or lack of it) affects real people (and real animals) in places remote from where that policy is made. Marxist ecologist Victor Toledo perfected this form of political ecological essay in his discussions of the Lake Pátzcuaro region and its Tarascan Indian inhabitants, but it is not limited to Marxist intellectual writers. In Latin America, where essayists often become diplomats and engineers of new social programs, innovative thinkers from Octavio Paz to Mario Vargas Llosa have used the extended essay to move their readers to understand the ever-widening web of interactions that surrounds any single event. Dr. Mellink, a scientist in the ecology program at the CICESE research center in Ensenada, Baja California Norte, accomplishes this through weaving together numerous statements from newspapers and public meetings into a tapestry which pictures people in conflict over the control of the *cimarrón*.

In a speech on December 10, 1990, President Carlos Salinas de Gortari of Mexico said, "He dado órdenes que mientras la Universidad Autónoma de Baja California [UABC] no termine el diagnóstico que está llevando a cabo, se decreta la veda total en lo que hace al borrego cimarrón."[1] This statement—declaring a total ban on bighorn hunting in Baja California—was the culmination of a long series of events, but it might also be seen as the closure of just one more episode in the continuing saga of bighorn sheep management; or, indeed, the management of all natural resources in Mexico. For that reason, I would like to describe the controversy leading to this presidential decree. As far as possible, I have tried to present the various sides of the controversy. And, as with many stories in the history of game management, this one reveals more about human behavior than it does about the behavior of bighorn sheep.

I begin my story with some background on the bighorn sheep of the peninsula.[2] Baja California cimarrones are highly regarded because they offer superlative trophies for sportsmen and are particularly attractive to

"Grand Slam" hunters who wish to exhibit the four most prized sheep on their walls: Dall's, Stone's, Rocky Mountain, and desert bighorn. Baja California claims the largest cimarrón populations and the world record desert cimarrón trophy (205 1/8 points on the Boone and Crockett system). Hunting conditions in Baja are rustic, and the countryside is scenic, wild, and rugged. These factors have contributed to the high price of the hunt (U.S.$12,000 for a fourteen-day guided hunt in 1987,[3] and as much as $28,000 more recently).

Despite its current popularity, cimarrón hunting before the turn of the century is poorly documented by historians. Very few persons other than determined Americans ventured out to hunt cimarrón because of the hardship involved.[4] Even by the early 1900s, however, some populations had been hunted to extinction.[5] It is clear that great numbers of cimarrones were killed for their meat, which was "dried or jerked to supply mining camps and other communities."[6]

After the turn of the century, President Porfirio Díaz posted army troops in the borderlands, allegedly to protect wildlife, especially cimarrones,[7] although this action may have been made less from environmental concern than from a sense of violated sovereignty and a fear of Americans annexing more Mexican land. After all, the nineteenth century had seen the annexation of more than half of Mexico's territory, and there had been unsuccessful attempts by the United States to conquer the peninsula of Baja California as well as part of Sonora.[8]

On October 19, 1917, E. Cantú, governor of Baja California, issued a notice indicating that bighorn sheep hunting was prohibited within his jurisdiction.[9] By 1922 there was substantial concern within the federal government over the decline of this species, and President Alvaro Obregón established a ten-year prohibition on cimarrón hunting.[10] The prohibition was extended for another decade in 1933 by President Emilio Portes Gil[11] and declared permanent by President Manuel Avila Camacho in 1944.

Poaching remained commonplace despite these prohibitions, both because the public was ill informed about the laws and because there were no penalties enforcing them.[12] Corruption at various levels of the government exacerbated the problem, as officials were paid by hunters "to look the other way."[13] In any case, certain sheep populations were dramatically reduced because of poaching.[14]

In 1959, Bernardo Villa, now a renowned Mexican mammalogist, felt that the populations in Baja California could probably support hunting, and the Department of Wildlife Conservation requested studies to assess the suitability of allowing a hunt.[15] A hunting season was proposed shortly thereafter, and in 1964, 1966, and 1968 private outfitters organized experimental cimarrón hunts.[16] Participants during these three years left their camps with hunting successes of 30, 54, and 72.6 percent, respectively.[17]

Apparently the outfitters ignored the agreement made to prevent poaching. As a result, there was little that game wardens could do. Wardens J. Rivera Oliver and J. Samano Sánchez found themselves "faced with trying to catch hunters who have planes while all we have is a burro."[18] Cimarrón populations continued to dwindle.

In 1969 the government began a series of yearly cimarrón hunts for "trophy rams only,"[19] with a minimum legal size of 180 points (later reduced to 160 points). Hunters who shot undersized rams were fined. While in the field, hunters were provided with guides and meals and were accompanied and supervised by two biologists. But even this did not solve the poaching problem.

In 1974 the federal government established the Programa Nacional de Borrego Cimarrón (PNBC, National Program of Bighorn Sheep)[20] in efforts to forestall poaching by trophy hunters (mainly Americans) and to eliminate local poaching for meat. Hypothetically, the money obtained from carefully regulated hunting would be used to pay local campesinos for building and maintaining water holes for sheep and other desert animals. This program, which became internationally famous, attained its climax in the mid-1970s, when it had several employees and vehicles in Baja California.[21]

Beginning in 1974, annual estimates of the sheep population were made to assess the success of the government's program. Estimates ranged from a low of 4,000 to a high of 7,800.[22] The 1989 population figure estimated by the Consejo Nacional de la Fauna (CNF), an organization formed by wealthy big-game hunters to promote wildlife conservation, was even higher at 12,500, although its wildlife managers did not indicate how this estimate was reached. Overall, there seemed to have been an increase in the cimarrón populations in the peninsula as a result of the PNBC.[23]

Hunting success figures, however, seem to place in doubt the generally assumed beneficence of the program. Between 1969 and 1970 one hundred permits were annually issued at the national level; seventy of these were issued in the state of Baja California.[24] The reported hunter success averaged 87 percent (reaching 98 percent in the 1978 hunting season).[25] Between 1979 and 1985, the total hunt was reduced to a yearly average of sixty-four permits, but the average success rate diminished to 84.5 percent. From then on, hunting success continued to fall, and the number of permits issued dropped accordingly, to forty-five in 1990.

In 1982, the new president of Mexico, Miguel de la Madrid, created the Secretaría de Desarrollo Urbano y Ecología (SEDUE, Secretariat of Urban Development and Ecology), which took control of the Department of Wildlife from the Secretaría de Agricultura y Recursos Hidráulicos (Secretariat of Agriculture and Water Resources). This change caused resentment, communication problems, and lack of cooperation between agencies, both federal and state.[26] These problems were in addition to those identified by A. W. Sandoval:[27] SEDUE's low budget (the money gained from game utilization was not being invested back into game management) and the presumption that overhunting was the only important problem facing the sheep. Moreover, some consider that this administrative change ruined the program by putting game management into the hands of "ultraconservationist desk biologists."[28]

However, the PNBC's decline seems to have started even before this administrative change. In an interview for a Tijuana television station on May 27, 1991, Dr. Graciela de la Garza, then head of SEDUE's General Directorship of Ecological Conservation of Natural Resources, commented that while formerly the hunt had responded to the demands of tourists, now it would meet the demands of population management. In essence, she was implying that overexploitation had occurred during the first period. Similarly, the CNF claimed that the official cimarrón-hunting program had failed because it had come under the control of a coterie.[29] Indeed, former governor Xicoténcatl Leyva Murrieta (who was impeached early in Salinas's presidential term, presumably because of alleged irregularities) was said to hunt cimarrones from helicopters with his cronies.[30]

In 1986 SEDUE contracted with the UACB to study cimarrón biology. Of the 2,331 animals counted in the study, only 171 were considered to be huntable trophy males. The principal conclusions of the study were that cimarrón hunting should be stopped due to low numbers, that further studies should be carried out, and that vigilance should be increased since much evidence of poaching was found. Unfortunately, the study had a major flaw that was to have serious repercussions in the future. Although the authors recognized the existence of two peninsular subspecies of cimarrón (*O. c. cremnobates* and *O. c. weemsi*), they failed to notice that the boundary between the two subspecies actually occurs within the state. Accordingly, they erroneously considered all the cimarrones in the state to be *O. c. cremnobates*.

Cimarrón policy changed rapidly after the Consejo Nacional de la Fauna was formed in 1974. Within a decade, President Miguel de la Madrid (1982–88) decentralized certain functions of the federal government, and the CNF was officially given the status of consulting and support organism for the federal government in 1986. More important, in 1987 the CNF obtained the concession to manage cimarrón hunts. The CNF is a lay association, but its members often claim that they were officially appointed.

The activities of the CNF started with some administrative irregularities. The CNF did not stop the poaching, and it was widely rumored that even some SEDUE inspectors were guiding poachers to sheep. Its research director later resigned as a result of charges that the activities of his CNF staff had gone too far out of line with the original objectives of the program.[31]

In 1989, growing public dissatisfaction with the program became evident. The most outspoken critic was Alberto Tapia Landeros, a hunter, wildlife artist, and taxidermist who writes a popular Sunday column on fish and game for *La Voz de la Frontera,* a Mexicali newspaper.

In January 1989, Tapia Landeros said that the concession to the CNF was allowed only because of SEDUE's poor administration of the resource, and he joined the voices of hunting outfitters in requesting that the cimarrón hunts be administered locally, and not by a group from Mexico City.[32] He also argued that the drawings of permits should be held locally and in front of a public notary to prevent lucky Mexico City "*chilangos*"[33] from obtaining them, implying irregularities in the drawing process. On January 23, Luis Arnoldo Fragoso Salazar, president of the Association of Hunting and Fishing Clubs of Baja California, wrote a letter to President Salinas de Gortari indicating that the private businessmen who were now administering the hunt included former wildlife functionaries who were marketing rather than protecting the wildlife during their terms.[34]

In March, Marco Antonio Pastrana, the general director of the CNF, and Fidel Alfaro, CNF's state director, showed up at a public auction in Reno, Nevada. That was where Greg Waldom and Bob Center offered high bids of $22,000 and $28,000 for cimarrón permits during the 1989–90 hunting season.[35] Officially, however, permits for foreigners cost $12,000 and could be legally allotted only through official in-country drawings. The official drawing for the coming season was not held until seven months later in Hermosillo, Sonora.[36]

On March 22 a gathering of hunting clubs demanded that a state organization be created to manage the state's wildlife resources. During the annual meeting held to plan the next season's hunting calendar, SEDUE's representative in the state claimed that the CNF's role had been suspended, and its delegate was asked to leave. Clearly, CNF's Pastrana and Alfaro had to take a defensive stance. In a letter published in the newspapers and distributed to SEDUE authorities in Mexico City as well as to local interest groups, Pastrana and Alfaro claimed that everything Tapia Landeros had said against the CNF was either false or misleading.[37] They indicated that the Reno auction was sanctioned in their agreement with SEDUE. Pastrana and Alfaro claimed that all the money from the program, except that which was turned in to the federal treasury, was invested to benefit the cimarrones. Suspension of the CNF's program, they said in retaliation, was being pursued by the very people whose poaching activities had been disrupted by CNF personnel stationed in the field. Finally, they contended that all attacks on the CNF could be traced back to Hector Sánchez Limón, president of the state's association of game outfitters and a good friend of Tapia Landeros, whom they called "the main poacher in the state."

Tapia Landeros quickly offered a rebuttal. He referred to a letter from Graciela de la Garza in which she stated that SEDUE had never agreed that the administration of cimarrón hunting was an exclusive prerogative given to CNF by presidential decree. Furthermore, SEDUE itself had never sold or auctioned any permits and was entitled to offer permits only through drawings.[38]

Despite Pastrana's and Alfaro's claims of legality and technical competence, their last season as administrators produced a hunting success of only 73.7 percent, and nine of twenty-four trophies taken were below permissible size.[39] Another amazing coincidence was also detected. The hunters who had most often been chosen to hunt cimarrón in Baja California were none other than CNF board members! In response, residents of nineteen ejidos, including those in charge of the best areas for cimarrón in the southern part of the state, declared that they were not going to allow hunting on their ejidos. They asked the governor to stop the CNF's abuses.[40] During the previous hunting season they had been hired as guides, cooks, haulers, and hunting assistants but were paid a salary 29 percent lower than that of the year before. Furthermore, after the ejidatarios traveled all the way to Mexicali to cash their paychecks (because no branches of the authorizing bank exist in the southern part of the state), the checks bounced. Moreover, they had not received compensation for the food they had provided to hunters, for the rental of the mules, for promised bonuses, or for per diem to cover some costs of the hunts.[41]

In response to these charges Fidel Alfaro claimed that the CNF was losing money with the cimarrón program. This was difficult to believe, considering the low (and still unpaid) salaries the CNF was paying to field assistants and the low-quality services being provided. In comparison, outfitters offering mule deer hunts in Sonora and black-tailed deer hunts in Baja California charged $2,500 and $700, respectively. They offered excellent food and wine, paid good salaries, and still showed a good profit.[42] According to Alfaro, the low net returns from Baja cimarrón hunts occurred because the CNF invested the money in other parts of the country, such as a zoo near Mexico City.

The conflict over control of desert resources was suddenly heating up. Governor Oscar Baylón Chacón called an open hearing on May 24 to address the problems of wild animals and plants of the state.[43] Invitations were sent to hunting clubs, the media, game outfitters, the CNF, SEDUE, campesinos, biologists, military authorities, and heads of various governmental offices. The southern ejidos reaffirmed that they would not allow the hunts in their area to proceed. Many other speakers petitioned for local administration of cimarrones.

The first CNF representative to speak at this hearing was Alfaro, whose talk centered not on policy issues but on the technical details of a dazzling new telemetry study. Alfaro was followed by Hector Gracia Galván, another state CNF director, who informed the audience that the CNF had been created by presidential decree and that all of their activities were reported to Mexico City officials. With regard to the bounced checks, he conceded that even the governor issues checks with no funds in his accounts!

When his turn to speak came, Arturo Lara, a SEDUE biologist, removed all the glitter from the highly touted telemetry study. He further contended that the CNF was supposed to carry out a census before starting the hunting programs, but after two hunting seasons no census numbers had been made available. Outfitter Hctor Sánchez Limón then shared Dr. de la Garza's letter refuting many of the statements that CNF representatives had made. José Angel Sánchez Machuca, the campesinos' representative, waved several bounced checks in the air. Other people gave accounts of private use of CNF vehicles by CNF directors and employees. The CNF officials left the meeting with their credibility mortally wounded.

On May 28, 1989, the southern ejidos published a statement directed to the president of Mexico presenting their view of the problems and reiterating their decision not to allow the hunt to proceed. Remaining oblivious to these concerns, the federal government granted the concession to manage the next cimarrón hunting season to the CNF.[44] However, on August 20, Alejandro Moreno Medina, third director of the local chapter of the CNF, resigned from his position on the grounds of internal conflicts.[45]

About this time Ernesto Ruffo Appel, the new governor of Baja California came into office.[46] He was immediately presented with the cimarrón problem and sought to address it. Several state representatives soon assembled a dossier which stated that the hunts were "an aggression to the state's sovereignty, a transgression to the natural heritage that we have the obligation to leave enriched for our offspring, and an offense to the dignity of Baja Californians." Following this report's recommendations, the state legislature instructed the governor to terminate the cimarrón hunt, ban the CNF from performing services within the state, and request the army to deny any firearm transport permits solicited by cimarrón permit holders.

And yet, the 1990 cimarrón hunt proceeded. On March 15, 1990, at a hearing to gather public opinions regarding the next hunting season, the state's agriculture department petitioned that bighorns be excluded from the hunting permits sold for the following season. Not long afterward, the CNF began to disintegrate; massive resignations of the Baja California board were followed by the resignations of the vice presidents of the national board and the Sonoran board of CNF, and of other important members of the national board. These turnovers culminated in the replacement of the Baja California CNF director with Hector Gracia Galván.

Many reasons were given for the resignations, including "prostitution of the objectives of the organization." The resigning officials all agreed that the principal culprit was Marco Antonio Pastrana. The CNF circulated rumors to the effect that the Baja California board had gotten into trouble with the opposition party, the Partido de Acción Nacional (Party of National Action).

Despite all the opposition, the *Diario Oficial de la Federación* nationally distributed a notice on August 10 that the CNF was once more in charge of the cimarrón hunt. César Villalobos, an agriculture-oriented journalist with a very influential column, charged that the CNF under the direction of Pastrana had never fulfilled its obligation to the campesinos.[47] Soon afterward, Rubén Castro Bojorquez, SEDUE's new delegate in the state, announced that the CNF was no longer offering any game warden services in cimarrón areas.[48] Poaching was rampant, and cimarrón meat was sold openly in San Felipe markets for $20 per kilogram.[49]

In an effort to downplay the severity of the game depletion problem, Castro Bojorquez declared to a local newspaper that there were still 2,000 cimarrones, so there was no reason to halt the hunting.[50] However, the tenacious critic Tapia Landeros learned from confidential sources that the hunting parties of the last season, most of which had taken undersized trophies, had seen only 323 animals.[51]

On September 9, 1990, the Confederación Nacional Campesina (National Peasants' Confederation) called a meeting in Bahía de los Angeles, a town in the southern portion of the cimarrón range.[52] There, the campesinos reaffirmed their desire for local management of the cimarrón in order to return benefits to the ejidos. On September 11, Manuel Ramos, the head of the sports department of *Novedades de Baja California,* a major newspaper, joined their cause. On three consecutive days he published articles demanding the suspension of cimarrón hunting on the basis of managers' lack of knowledge about the status of cimarrón populations and lack of control over the number of animals taken. Immediately, Castro Bojorquez issued a counterattack. He said that banning the hunt would cause shortage of funds for vigilance, that funds from permits had also been used in special studies and in the (supposed) construction of water holes, and that there was no risk of extinction.[53]

On October 3 the Club of Columnists invited the CNF's current spokes-man, Hector Gracia Galván, to its weekly meeting. There he said that thirty-four permits would be issued that year and that the drawing would be held in La Paz—as usual, outside the state. He argued that the state government did not have any basis for requesting a halt to the hunting. Still, when he was cornered during a question-and-answer period he conceded that a temporary suspension of hunting would be prudent. He also admitted that forty American poachers had been successful in taking cimarrones during the previous season.[54]

Later, Gracia Galván conceded that undersized trophies had been taken.[55] He said that the state SEDUE had instructed the guides to allow this in order to undermine the CNF, because of that organization's differ-ences with SEDUE's delegate. He attributed the lack of vigilance which had allowed the poaching to continue to interference by SEDUE's workers' union. At the same time, Gracia Galván asserted that there were nine thousand cimarrones in the state and that the species was not in trouble.

To follow up CNF's assertions, SEDUE's Castro Bojorquez was invited to speak at a later meeting of the Club of Columnists.[56] He declared that there was no basis for any statement that the population was too small to be hunted. In fact, he said, a ban would only increase poaching.

In a press conference on November 15, Sergio Reyes Luján, accom-panied by Graciela de la Garza, declared that regardless of the state's ban, the old male sheep must be removed "to improve reproduction." This opinion came despite the SEDUE technical staff's own view challenging the validity of the old-male elimination argument.[57] It also flew in the face of Reyes Luján's earlier support of the 1987 UABC study which had first proposed the ban. Reyes Luján further argued that if the state wanted to participate, it had to pass and enforce its own environmental laws. Before a week was over, the Alianza Ecologista de Baja California and Club Madrugadores de Tecate had joined the opposition to cimarrón hunting.[58]

In a final meeting between Luis Gonzalez Ruiz and CNF's Pastrana, the latter argued that wildlife management was a federal issue, while the former replied that allowing access to hunting grounds was a right of the ejidatarios.[59] The final lines had been drawn. Local sovereignty had be-come the central issue.[60] It came as no surprise when someone at the Primer Foro de Conservación del Borrego Cimarrón threatened to set off firecrackers on the hunting grounds to scare the bighorn away from the hunters.[61]

At this stage, the UABC was the seedbed ready to receive the presidential declaration. Since approximately May 1990 the Consejo Universitario had been addressing the bighorn issue in its meetings. At its November 27 meeting the Comisión para la Defensa del Borrego Cimarrón, a special task force, was created. This task force prepared a document to present to the president at his forthcoming visit. Upon his arrival at the UABC campus in Ensenada on December 10, President Salinas de Gortari was greeted by representatives of the commission, who briefly explained their concern about cimarrón management in the state. To the surprise of many, Salinas informed the group that he had already ordered the prohibition of cimarrón hunting.

So, what seemed to have started as a fight between two groups wanting to administer the cimarrón hunt had come to an end, or at least to a recess. What exactly triggered the president's decision is, however, difficult to interpret. José Luis Aguilar, a local SEDUE biologist and the leader of the UABC's 1987 study, believed that, after three years, the federal government was finally responding to the conclusions of the study. I personally doubt that the study was ever taken into account. Was the president's declaration a spontaneous reaction to the three-minute argument presented to him by the Comisión para la Defensa del Cimarrón? Obviously not, since President Salinas had already given orders to initiate the ban before he heard the argument. Was it triggered by a need to gain popularity in a state that had recently voted in favor of an opposition party? I doubt that, too, because despite all the hoopla, too few politicians and laypeople were actively involved in the conflict to warrant the president using the issue to gain greater political support. Was it media pressure? I am not convinced of this either, since only one journalist was involved during most of the controversy. Was it the benevolent recommendation of the higher echelons of the national board of the campesino organization? Or was it, perhaps, President Salinas's own concern for bighorn sheep?

Whatever the reason for the president's decree, the initial joy at its announcement soon dissipated.[62] When the *Diario Oficial de la Nación* published the prohibition of cimarrón hunting on December 24, only the subspecies *cremnobates* was protected, and only in Baja California. The populations in the south—where ejidatarios were most concerned—were still unprotected. "Treachery!" was the claim by many, who believed that SEDUE had simply tried to distort the president's intention in order to keep management out of the hands of locals.

More likely, SEDUE policymakers just copied the technical mistake in the 1987 study without realizing that by designating only *cremnobates*, the anticipated effects would be negated. Actually, no cimarrón hunting was allowed for the 1991–92 hunting season in Baja California.[63] By the end of December, however, the CNF had neither informed the hunters who had obtained their permits that there would be no hunt in the state nor reimbursed them.[64] Future reopening of the hunt will depend on the results of the study to be completed in 1994.[65]

And so, the president spoke. A ban has begun and the lines have been drawn. Now what? What will be the fate of each of the participants: the cimarrón, the CNF, local outfitters, the campesinos, the UABC, President Salinas, and the society as a whole?

Will the cimarrón benefit from this ban? If stopping the government-controlled hunting program means less vigilance, as the CNF has claimed, the number of sheep taken might very well increase through poaching, and the net results could be counterproductive.

Nobody knows what the CNF's future is. The resignation of prominent members and the governing boards of three state chapters was a severe blow. However, it is apparently maintaining a strong relationship with agencies in Mexico City, which might help its recovery. The CNF has claimed that it voluntarily removed untrustworthy people from its ranks, to draw attention away from those who resigned in protest. One thing is quite certain, however. It will be very difficult for the CNF to operate in Baja California in the near future. Nevertheless, the CNF was granted the management of the 1991–92 cimarrón hunts in Sonora and Baja California Sur.[66]

The local game outfitters must wait until the university concludes its studies to see if hunting will be recommended. If so, they will certainly try to obtain a piece of the pie. The local outfitters will be competing not only with outsiders' groups like the CNF but also with the local campesinos, who have already demanded a greater involvement in the issue.

The ejidos and private landowners might have a good chance to administer the wildlife on their own holdings. The National Association of

Diversified Ranchers has already been successful in obtaining the concession for its members (mainly private owners) to administer the game on
their properties. The organization was born in the Texas white-tailed deer
country of Mexico, and its membership is rapidly expanding to other
parts of northern Mexico and to Baja, where the cimarrón issue has stimu-
lated interest in a more integrated use of natural resources.

The UABC now has the responsibility to carry out a definitive cimarrón
study. SEDUE approved a three-year project that will cost an estimated
$100,000.[67] The university, however, does not have any trained wildlife
professionals, and most of its faculty from biology, agronomy, and veteri-
nary science departments have only undergraduate-level training.[68]

President Salinas de Gortari has definitively reaffirmed the status of
the president in natural resource policy. At the same time, he has argued
that Mexico is a mature country capable of taking care of its own environmental problems on the basis of studies by its own scientific consultants.
This is an argument against those in the United States who oppose the
signing of a free trade agreement with Mexico, claiming that competition
will be unfair because of Mexico's less restrictive environmental regulations and paucity of trained scientists. Finally, Salinas may well have been
personally satisfied by making such an environmentally sound decision.

What about society? It is clear that only a very small part of Baja California's inhabitants were involved or even interested in the cimarrón controversy. The biological and political relevance of Salinas's declaration
was not understood by many, and the decree did not receive extensive
media coverage. Although La Voz de la Frontera did include a full description,[69] El Mexicano, the largest daily newspaper in the state, did not include the president's decree at all in its extensive accounts of Salinas's visit
to Ensenada. To counteract the sparse coverage by reporters, the UABC
published a full-page ad in El Mexicano,[70] thanking the president for his
decision. A celebratory poster from the UABC came later.

This ambivalence is not difficult to understand. Baja Californians often
care more about business enterprises and financial gain than about environmental health. Many consider the issue to be no more than a fight between two groups (CNF and local outfitters) over an economically valuable
resource, and they discount complaints from ejidatarios. Even the majority of hunters were not necessarily interested. Due to the high cost of
cimarrón hunting permits, the great majority of them do not anticipate

ever participating in a legal cimarrón hunt. Some people fear that the bighorn ban will stimulate actions by anti-hunting groups to ban the hunting of other species. Mario Herrera, who writes for *Zeta*, has already sided with the animal rights groups and has asked the government to take additional steps to ban all sport hunting.[71]

A final matter relates to biological conservation in general. It could be argued that the whole issue has been useful in awakening a concern for the environment. Nevertheless, the cimarrón has been so surrounded by glamour and so ardently defended that attention to it has eclipsed that offered to other pressing problems in wildlife conservation.[72] For example, when I first started working in wildlife biology in Baja California in 1989, the most frequently asked question was: "Are you studying cimarrones?" Many other concerns, including the survival of truly endangered species (such as several rodents), the impact of off-road vehicles, ecovandalism, habitat modification by ranching and farming, and inadequate forestry practices, have been left in obscurity. To make matters worse, cimarrón poaching is perceived differently from wildlife poaching in general, as if other species are not as vulnerable.[73] Law enforcement will be biased toward attending to bighorn sheep, as will other management actions. Considering all this, the protracted focus on the cimarrón might ultimately be an impediment rather than an open door to the overall conservation of Baja California's flora and fauna.[74]

NOTES

1. "I have ordered that until the Autonomous University of Baja California finishes the evaluation, a total ban on cimarrón [hunting] is decreed."

2. The bighorn sheep north of approximately Bahía de los Angeles are *Ovis canadensis cremnobates;* those south of it are *O. c. weemsi* (L. M. Huey, "The Mammals of Baja California, Mexico," *Transactions of the San Diego Society of Natural History* 13 [1964]: 85–168). The difference is mainly in the darker color of the latter (I. M. Cowan, "Distribution and Variation in the Native Sheep of North America," *American Midland Naturalist* 24 [1940]: 505–80). The Mexican name for bighorn sheep is *borrego cimarrón,* which means "wild" or "untamed sheep." It is shortened to cimarrón in the remainder of this essay.

The desert cimarrón includes five subspecies: *O. canadensis nelsoni,*

O. c. mexicana, O. c. texiana (questioned by E. R. Hall, *The Mammals of North America,* 2d ed. [New York: Wiley, 1981]), *O. c. cremnobates,* and *O. c. weemsi* (B. Lawson and R. Johnson, "Mountain Sheep," in *Wild Mammals of North America,* ed. J. A. Chapman and G. A. Feldhamer, 1036–55 [Baltimore: Johns Hopkins University Press, 1982]), which range from southern Nevada and southern California east over most of Arizona, southwestern New Mexico, and a small area in Texas, and south to include all of Mexico's cimarrones.

3. C. K. Winkler, "Desert Bighorn Sheep Hunting Regulations and Methodology for Determining Harvest Quotas," *Transactions of the Desert Bighorn Council* 31 (1987): 37–38.

4. C. M. López and C. López, *Caza mexicana* (Mexico: Vda. de C. Bouret, 1911); C. B. Slade, "Hunting Sheep and Antelope in Lower California," *Outing* 39 (1902): 505–12; O. H. Van Norden, "Hunting in Laguna Salada," *Outing* 74 (1919): 209–13, 260, 280–84, 316–17, 349–53, 380, 386; J. Cudahy, *Mañanaland: Adventuring with Camera and Rifle Throughout California and Mexico* (New York: Duffield, 1928).

5. W. T. Hornaday, *Camp-Fires of Desert and Lava* (New York: Scribners, 1908); Hornaday, "Saving the Big Game of Mexico," *Nature Magazine* (1924): 213–19, 236.

6. E. W. Nelson, "Lower California and Its Natural Resources," *Memoirs of the National Academy of Sciences* 25 (1921): 1–194.

7. A. Salas C., "El borrego cimarrón de México," in Subsecretaría Forestal y de la Fauna, *Fauna silvestre: expresiones y planteamientos de un recurso, 1964–1970,* 109–27 (Mexico: Secretaría de Agricultura y Recursos Hidraúlicos, 1970).

8. J. A. Rubial C., *Y Caborca se cubrió de gloria . . . !* (Mexico: Porrua, 1981).

9. Nelson, "Lower California and Its Natural Resources."

10. See Hornaday, "Saving the Big Game of Mexico," for a detailed account.

11. Salas, "El borrego cimarrón de México."

12. A. W. Sandoval, "Status of Bighorn Sheep in the Republic of Mexico," in *Wild Sheep: Distribution, Abundance, Management and Conservation of the Sheep of the World and Closely Related Mountain Ungulates,* ed. M. Hoefs, 86–94 (Yukon, Canada: Northern Wild Sheep and Goat Council, 1985); G. Medina G. and A. L. Martinez C., "Aspectos

generales de la biología, ecología y aprovechamiento cinegético del borrego cimarrón *Ovis canadensis;* Artiodactyla, Mamm.," in *Memorias del VIII Simposio sobre Fauna Silvestre,* coord. M. A. Roa R. and L. Palazuelos P., 432–70 (Mexico: Universidad Nacional Autónoma de México, 1990).

13. J. A. Dávila, "Hunting Season in Mexico," *Transactions of the Desert Bighorn Council* 5 (1961): 80–83; Medina and Martinez, "Aspectos generales de la biología."

14. L. Macías Arellano, "Bighorn Management in Mexico," *Transactions of the Desert Bighorn Council* 5 (1961): 51–52.

15. B. Villa R., "Brief Notes on the Present Status and Distribution of Bighorn Sheep in Mexico," *Transactions of the Desert Bighorn Council* 3 (1959): 77–79; J. A. Dávila, "Borregos y berrendos en México," *Transactions of the Desert Bighorn Council* 4 (1960): 101–3.

16. Dávila, "Hunting Season in Mexico"; Medina and Martinez, "Aspectos generales de la biología."

17. Salas, "El borrego cimarrón de México."

18. J. Rivera Oliver and J. Samano Sánchez, "Status of the Bighorn in Baja California," *Transactions of the Desert Bighorn Council* 14 (1970): 771–78.

19. In this management option, the old males are eliminated to allow younger, supposedly more fertile, males to take over the mating, presumably increasing the number of offspring (M. L. Cossio, "Report from Mexico," in *The Wild Sheep in Modern North America,* ed. J. B. Thetethen, 72–74, 138–142 [Alexandria, Va.: Boone and Crockett Club, 1975]). It was also argued that the old males would die anyway in the next couple of years, and it would be silly not to use them for the hunt. However, Valerius Geist has indicated that because they are socially immature, young males are more likely to hurt females during the rut (Geist, "On Delayed Social and Physical Maturation in Mountain Sheep," *Canadian Journal of Zoology* 46 [1968]: 899–904; Geist, *Mountain Sheep: A Study in Behavior and Evolution* [Chicago: University of Chicago Press, 1971])

20. M. L. Cossio, "Report from Mexico," in *The Wild Sheep in Modern North America,* ed. J. B. Thefethen, 72–74, 138–142 (Alexandria, Va.: Boone and Crockett Club, 1975).

21. E. Araujo, "Development of the Program for Protection of Bighorn

Sheep in Baja California," *Transactions of the Desert Bighorn Council* 20 (1976): 12.

22. T. Alvarez, "Status of Desert Bighorns in Baja California," *Transactions of the Desert Bighorn Council* 20 (1976): 18–21; Cossio, "Report from Mexico."

23. Medina and Martinez, "Aspectos generales de la biología."

24. Ibid.; Cossio, "Report from Mexico," indicates forty permits for the peninsula. I am unable to find the source of the discrepancy.

25. Tapia Landeros, *La Voz de la Frontera*, August 19, 1990.

26. Mendoza, in Sandoval, "Status of Bighorn Sheep in the Republic of Mexico."

27. Sandoval, "Status of Bighorn Sheep in the Republic of Mexico."

28. Tapia Landeros, *La Voz de la Frontera*, January 29, 1989.

29. *Novedades de Baja California*, April 5, 1990.

30. Raúl Marín Durán, *Zeta*, November 24, 1989.

31. Tapia Landeros, *La Voz de la Frontera*, October 21, 1990.

32. Tapia Landeros, *La Voz de la Frontera*, January 21, 1989.

33. *Chilango* is a contemptuous term used for people from Mexico City.

34. Durán, *Zeta*, November 24, 1989.

35. Tapia Landeros, *La Voz de la Frontera*, May 21, 1989.

36. Cruz Aguirre, *El Mirador*, December 1989. A note about the drawing appeared afterward in *El Imparcial*, October 13, 1989.

37. *Novedades de Baja California*, April 5–7. A summary appeared in *La Voz de la Frontera*, April 5, 1989.

38. *La Voz de la Frontera*, May 21, 1989. The letter was directed to Héctor Sánchez Limón.

39. Tapia Landeros, *La Voz de la Frontera*, September 30, 1990. The information was based on an internal confidential report; see F. Alfaro Melendrez, O. Chacón Alvarado, and G. López, "Reporte técnico; temporada cinegética enero-marzo," Programa Integral del Borrego Cimarrón, Mexicali, Mexico, 1989. Tapia Landeros indicated there were ten undersized trophies, but I counted only nine mentioned in the report.

40. *La Voz de la Frontera*, April 16 and May 18, 1989.

41. Tapia Landeros, *La Voz de la Frontera*, May 28, 1989.

42. Tapia Landeros, *La Voz de la Frontera*, May 21, 1989.

43. The account of this meeting was presented by Tapia Landeros in *La Voz de la Frontera*, May 28, 1989.

44. Published in the *Diario Oficial de la Nación* on July 11. The *Diario* is the official gazette where all important decisions of the federal government are posted.

45. Tapia Landeros, *La Voz de la Frontera*, June 3, 1990.

46. Ruffo Appel was the first governor elected from any opposition party in the history of the country.

47. *La Voz de la Frontera*, August 15, 1990.

48. Tapia Landeros, *La Voz de la Frontera*, September 2, 1990.

49. Tapia Landeros, *La Voz de la Frontera*, September 2 and 9, 1990.

50. Tapia Landeros, *La Voz de la Frontera*, September 23, 1990.

51. *La Voz de la Frontera*, September 30, 1990.

52. The National Peasants' Confederation is the most important farmers' union in the country. It is part of the Partido Revolucionario Institucional.

53. Tapia Landeros (*La Voz de la Frontera*, September 23, 1990) said that these water holes had been contructed by the National Commission for Arid Lands, and not by SEDUE or the CNF. Also see Ramos, *Novedades de Baja California*, September 14, 1990.

54. López Yañez, *La Voz de la Frontera*, October 4, 1990; and Tapia Landeros, *La Voz de la Frontera*, October 7, 1990.

55. Tapia Landeros, *La Voz de la Frontera*, October 11, 1990.

56. Anonymous, *La Voz de la Frontera*, November 1, 1990.

57. Medina and Martinez, "Aspectos generales de la biología."

58. Tapia Landeros, *La Voz de la Frontera*, November 22, 1990.

59. Villalobos, *La Voz de la Frontera*, December 7, 1990.

60. Tapia Landeros, *La Voz de la Frontera*, November 18, 1990.

61. Tapia Landeros, *La Voz de la Frontera*, November 22, 1990.

62. See Tapia Landeros's article in *La Voz de la Frontera*, December 16, 1990.

63. *Diario Oficial de la Federación*, August 1, 1991.

64. Tapia Landeros, *La Voz de la Frontera*, December 30, 1990.

65. Herrera Cienfuegos, *La Voz de la Frontera*, September 13, 1991. Incidentally, the length of the study makes it very likely that the decision on reopening the hunt will be made by the next federal administration, since Salinas's term ends in December 1994.

66. *Diario Oficial de la Federación,* August 1, 1991.

67. Herrera Cienfuegos, *La Voz de la Frontera,* September 13, 1991.

68. The staffs of most Mexican universities are made up of professors without graduate degrees. The reasons for this and other problems associated with science are discussed in Mellink, "La ciencia en Mexico: el caso de la fauna silvestre en el norte del país," in *Memorias del VIII Simposio sobre Fauna Silvestre,* coord. M. A. Roa R. and L. Palazuelos P., 359–93 (Mexico: Universidad Nacional Autónoma de México, 1990).

69. Bustos Perez, December 11, 1990.

70. December 11, 1990.

71. December 28, 1990, to January 3, 1991.

72. See E. Mellink, "Conservación de los vertebrados terrestres en el estado de Baja California," in *Memorias del II Simposio Internacional sobre Areas Naturales Protegidas en México* (Mexico: Universidad Nacional Autónoma de México, forthcoming).

73. In late 1990, the secretary of an opposition municipal board was caught with a poached cimarrón. The stir this caused was so great that he was removed from office. Shortly afterward, some other hunters were caught with poached does (mule deer), but the incident received little attention in the media.

74. This essay was essentially completed in February 1992. Relevant events occurring after this date are not included.

Only Prey

Harley Shaw can surely be called a legend in his own time without embarrassing him too much; no doubt he would claim that he merits such a distinction only because he is older, ornerier, and luckier than most contemporary nature writers. His tenacity in the field and his accumulated wisdom have earned him recognition from his peers; he has been featured in an essay by Charles Bowden entitled "Love Among the Lion Killers," in the anthology *On Nature's Terms* (Texas A&M University Press, 1992), and in an essay by Barry Lopez published in the early 1980s in now-defunct *GEO* magazine. Yet the best expression of his multifaceted relationship with cougars comes from his own words in *Soul Among Lions* (Johnson Books, 1989).

Within that balancing act between recognizing the needs of mountain lions and recognizing the chronic fears and economic needs of their rural (human) neighbors, Shaw's wisdom shines through on every page. Undaunted by the quick fixes of game management agency bureaucrats, self-ascribed "deep" ecologists, and fast-buck hunting guides, Shaw looks for the common ground that we all may need to rely on over the long run.

And yet, he never forgets how little we know about other large mammals, even the best-studied ones. In Shaw's own words, "What you really need to know about mountain lions can't be found in the data." The same can be said of bighorn sheep, of course; whether ultimately unknowable or merely difficult to know at present, much of their behavior remains poorly understood.

Because they prey on some of the same game species that humans love to hunt, mountain lions don't elicit the following that bighorns do. The Western States Mountain Lion Workshops, in which Harley has participated since 1976, have never drawn the crowds that the Desert Bighorn Sheep Council meetings generate. There's the rub, Shaw argues; when one wildlife species has an overwhelming number of advocates compared with other animals in the same ecosystem, you can guess which will be favored in game management plans. When one species is made an icon, how do others suffer as a result?

There may be those who take issue with Shaw's view that the Yuma puma was no different from its mountain neighbors and seldom frequented true desert habitats, but rather stayed along verdant floodplains or in the mountains. Both Paul Krausman and Doug Peacock consider evidence to the contrary in their essays. Nevertheless, I doubt whether any of the other authors included in this anthology would take issue with Shaw's personal observations or philosophical stance; his seasoned view of how the world works is as agreeable as his lucid prose. This essay was commissioned for this book and appears here for the first time in print.

The man in front of me was a desert bighorn hunter and guide as well as a member of the Desert Bighorn Sheep Society. His enthusiasm for wild sheep was unbounded, and he assumed everyone else felt the same. He had caught me at the wrong moment, however, and I allowed my irritation to show, inappropriately taking it out on him. His question had been, "How's it feel to be studying bighorns?" with the implication that I had reached the pinnacle that a wildlife biologist could ever hope to attain. The answer I snapped back—and I was ashamed the instant I saw the look on his face—was, "Oh, they're just another prey species." I was being spiteful, and the enthusiast in front of me was bearing the brunt of a larger frustration. At that moment, I simply could not share his excitement for sheep.

This worthy, of course, was not the first person to be hooked on bighorns. The phrase "bighorns are special" echoes throughout forewords and prefaces of bighorn sheep books from the 1980s. The fact that a group of scholars and writers has gathered to produce *Counting Sheep* is an affirmation of human reactions to bighorns. But I like to think that *any* species (or single organism, for that matter) is special after emerging from the evolutionary processes of the millennia. Living, adapting, and surviving make them so. Beyond that, any other value judgment is hubris—an assumption that humans have the wisdom to assign status in the first place. But judge we do, and bighorns are given high rank.

At the time of the above incident, however, bighorns weren't particularly special to me. There, I said it. In fact, for three years of my life, bighorns were a damned nuisance. This had nothing to do with whether I liked or disliked sheep. I was occupied with a backlog of eight years of field data on mountain lions, much of which still needed analysis. I had, I thought, insights into additional research needed to resolve some of the conflicts surrounding that problem-ridden predator, and I had the tools—namely, hounds—to help me accomplish the job.

But I now found myself assigned to study bighorns in Aravaipa Canyon, largely because an interested layman from the town of Globe, Arizona, had provided the Arizona Game and Fish Commission with evidence that the Game and Fish Department's bighorn counts in that area were inaccurate. Floyd Krank's presentation of his weekend survey data to the commission had set off a chain of events that translated downward through the ranks of the department into an order for me to switch to sheep. With all due respect to Floyd, I felt that my research was suddenly being directed by someone who knew more about mining than wildlife. I was a pawn being shifted to suit the political needs of the bureaucracy, with no opportunity for me to assess scientifically the merits of the proposed sheep study and no concern for the species that I had previously been paid to understand.

I was sure that the sheep project was a public relations front, one that would continue just long enough to allow the issue to quiet down. It held no promise of long-term involvement. I knew how much time and energy I'd spent acquiring a visceral understanding of one species, and I felt that research on any species without such a level of total involvement was a waste of time. I wasn't sure I had the energy to do it all over again. Thus my frustration—unloaded on an unsuspecting sheep devotee.

I confess that I never became a good sheep biologist. During my association with the species I began to feel that the world was inundated with sheep experts, both lay and professional, and I was not convinced of a need for my efforts. As I filtered bighorn literature through my brain, however, I began to see an intriguing veil of uncertainty shrouding the subject of lion predation on sheep. Writers comfortable in their knowledge of bighorns seemed to approach predation, touch gingerly on it, and then retreat, leaving minor contradictions and imprecise descriptions of sheep-predator interactions. Perhaps because I was comfortable in my knowledge of lions, I could use my enforced experience with bighorns to sharpen the image of the point where the biology of the two species met. The effort became a challenge.

Superficially, defining bighorn–mountain lion relationships was easy. Lions and other predators eat sheep—domestic or wild—given the chance. Bighorns, like all herbivores, convert vegetable matter to protein usable by carnivores, so the relationship of a bighorn to a lion is about the same as that of a spring vetch to a bighorn. They're just another food (prey) species.

But, as always, things get more complicated when we look beyond individuals and consider populations. Early sheep behaviorist Valerius Geist felt that predators played a minor role in sheep populations, and he distinguished between the sanitary role of most predators and the relatively nonselective behavior of the lion: "Predators are of little danger unless a sheep is very old, exhausted into physical bankruptcy after the rut, or has a broken leg, which happens surprisingly often. The major sheep predator appears to be the wolf. Coyotes, grizzlies, wolverine, and even lynx may take an occasional sick or incapacitated sheep, while the mountain lion may take a healthy one now and again, but these carnivores appear to play a very minor role in sheep mortality."[1] As we'll see, this all depends.

Geist noted that simple avoidance was the main strategy used by sheep in dealing with predators. Bighorns do not have many of the behavioral mechanisms for protecting young that are so prevalent in deer and antelope. Ewes do not ingest urine and feces of the newborns or limit the frequency of their visits to lambs. Lambs do not hide for long periods and freeze when danger approaches. Nor do the young have a specially camouflaged birth coat or reduced scent. Instead, according to Geist, the lamb is born in inaccessible terrain which generally excludes the major predators such as wolves, bears, and coyotes. The lamb is precocious and capable of following its mother the day after birth. Within a few days it can ricochet through rocky clefts like a cannonball.

Geist also noted that juvenile bighorns are especially vulnerable to predation when they are exploring new areas, so they venture forth only when following experienced sheep. This behavior, while important for predator avoidance in healthy populations, limits exploitation of new habitats and prevents reestablishment in areas where populations have been extirpated. When habitats become reduced or segmented, such an adaptation becomes a liability, isolating sheep in relict populations.

Geist was not immune to the above-mentioned veil of uncertainty regarding sheep-predator relations. At one point he wrote, "The lamb is protected from its major predators by the terrain and its speed and from minor predators, such as eagles, by its mother." Later he said, "A close association between ewe and lamb after weaning is of no significance to sheep, unlike moose, *since ewes do not defend lambs against predators* [italics mine]. Sheep are much too small to face wolves, and their only means of escaping them is to head for safer terrain."[2] Whether ewes defend their young or not, seeking safer terrain seems to be the most important predator avoidance mechanism in the repertoire of sheep of any age.

That their habitat selection strategies allow desert bighorns to avoid mountain lions seems to be a matter of evolutionary coincidence. Desert sheep are derived from ancestral stock that crossed the Siberian land bridge and expanded into areas that are now Sonoran Desert by following the gradual southward movement of the petran and tundra vegetation types during the last glaciation.[3] Today's desert bighorns are considered to be relict populations that were stranded in xeric habitats as more mesic vegetation types receded northward during the current interglacial. Their reluctance to leave traditional territories, an apparent adaptation to avoid predators such as wolves, reinforced their isolation. Perhaps their earlier existence in cold climates with long periods of freezing—a very real form of drought—helped them to survive in the desert.

Lions, on the other hand, are most likely a neotropical species that has adapted to Madrean woodland habitats. This hypothesis has not been proven beyond doubt, for felid ancestors certainly existed on the North American continent in association with nontropical environments. One respected mammalogist, Terry Vaughan, has suggested that lions passed southward through the Panama filter during the most recent glacial and then reexpanded northward, while bighorns were stopped north of the filter.[4] If this is the case, lions probably met sheep on the return trip. The fact that lions breed year-round—even at the northernmost part of their current range—suggests a tropical origin and leads one to suspect that their northward extensions have been fairly recent.

Bighorns thus probably did not evolve in the presence of a large stalking predator such as the lion. Their defenses are not attuned to dealing with such a predator, and when they range into—or are placed in—lion country, they get eaten.

As a result of these differences in origins, the historic distribution of bighorns in Arizona is almost a reverse template of the distribution of mountain lions. Mountain lion habitat, conversely, is an overlay of the range of the lion's principal prey, which in North America is usually either mule deer or white-tailed deer. Extension of lion populations into desert vegetation is generally limited to areas where water is available and where deserts abut on more mesic vegetations, such as chaparral.

Lions are not adapted to hunting in terrain used by sheep. Killing large horned animals on five-hundred-foot bluffs is risky, and approaching groups of sharp-eyed sheep on open rocky slopes is difficult even for a master stalker. Bighorns tend to get killed by lions when they roam into gentler terrain with thick brush. Or when someone puts them into that kind of habitat.

But there are contradictions to this paradigm, and these contradictions have clouded the thoughts of more than one biologist, myself included. For example, the literature on the mountain lion, unless read carefully, would lead one to believe that lions do live in the dry desert habitats that now are the principal abode of the sheep. In fact, a subspecies has been described that appears to be adapted to the lower Colorado River subdivision of the Sonoran desertscrub biome. Because bighorns are the dominant large ungulates in desert mountain ranges, there has developed an assumption that desert lions eat, and perhaps survive on, desert sheep. This seemingly simple and logical conclusion was one that I didn't bother to question even though my own experience had told me otherwise.

On the other hand, the sheep literature suggests that desert bighorns once ranged through many of the habitats now occupied by relatively high densities of lions. This body of literature also suggests that sheep have been restricted to their present xeric habitats through pressure exerted by humans and domestic livestock. From this we must conclude either that sheep were once better adapted to predation by lions than they are now, or that lion densities were once lower in these areas. These are the contradictions that I hope to resolve in this essay.

First, the desert lion. This creature carries the subspecific title *Felis concolor browni* and is fondly called the Yuma puma by desert naturalists.[5] If this subspecies of lion truly exists, or ever existed, it must be suspected of preying on desert bighorns, for its purported range, shown on maps in accepted texts, strongly overlaps both the Mexican and Nelson subspecies of sheep. But I believe these texts have misled us.

The Yuma puma was described by C. Hart Merriam in 1903 under the trinomial *Felis aztecus browni*. Merriam's description was in keeping with the "splitter" trends of the immediate post-Darwinian era.[6] At that time, their enthusiasm over evolutionary theory led many naturalists to expect an infinite array of life forms adapted to an infinite array of habitats—Darwin's finches applied on a grand scale.

Lions occurred periodically in the Colorado River delta and riparian habitats along that river and its tributaries. Prey in the form of mule deer was present in limited numbers in the backwater sloughs, riverside bosques, Indian fields, and adjacent desert edge. This was a unique habitat many miles from areas where lions were abundant. Using a few specimens from scattered locations, most associated with this riverine habitat, Merriam described a new subspecies. He thereby, and I suspect unintentionally, set the stage for the specter of a large felid adapted to the lower Colorado River valley desert.

Subsequent workers revised the scientific name of the subspecies to its present form and mapped its presumed distribution. It is here that at least some of the confusion regarding mountain lion–desert sheep relationships originated, for these later biologists expanded the range of this subspecies, apparently with little justification, to encompass a large expanse of the lower Colorado River and Mojave deserts in Arizona, California, and New Mexico. With a stroke of the pen, the Yuma puma was converted from a creature of the river to a creature of the dry desert mountains.

While the history of taxonomic revision of the subspecies would seem moot in this discussion, even the renaming of the Yuma puma added subtly to the confusion and embedded even more solidly the image of a desert-dwelling lion. Two years before Merriam identified the Yuma puma, he had classified the more widely dispersed lion of central Arizona, New Mexico, and parts of northern Mexico as *Felis aztecus*.[7] This species carried the rarely heard common name of Sierra Madre lion. The Yuma puma (more formally called the Colorado Desert lion in texts) was to Merriam a variety of the more widely distributed Sierra Madre cat. Merriam and his contemporaries recognized several other distinct species of lions, some of which also had attendant subspecies. The rank of species was easier to acquire in those days than it is now.

Subsequent taxonomic revisions ultimately placed all mountain lions into a single species, *Felis concolor*, and recognized, depending on the authority you accept, as many as thirty-one subspecies. The Sierra Madre lion and the Yuma puma assumed equal subspecific status as *Felis concolor azteca* and *F. c. browni*, respectively.

Actually, Merriam's concept of the relationship of the Yuma puma to its widespread neighbor was probably more accurate than that of his successors. The Colorado Desert cat was an extension of, rather than a taxonomic peer of, the Sierra Madre lion. In fact, I believe it was the same race. But, regardless of the cladistic array we accept, the question remains whether a desert lion existed in nature or just in the minds of systematists. Was there a subspecies of lion adapted to the lower desert?

I believe that the validity of the Yuma puma as a separate taxonomic entity is suspect on the basis of morphological information alone. Merriam and his contemporaries did not have the statistical tools that are available to modern taxonomists. In their overly enthusiastic application of the theory of natural selection, they often made decisions based on extremely small samples. Only nine specimens of the Yuma puma were ever cataloged. More recent examinations have shown that the skulls of these specimens, or at least those still available, fall within the range of measurements of the Sierra Madre lion.

The idea of a separate variety of lion inhabiting the low deserts becomes even less tenable as mountain lion social behavior and movements are better understood through radio-tracking studies. We now know that resident lions require large expanses of land. In habitats such as the Sonoran desertscrub, where densities of ungulates are low, home ranges of adult male lions may exceed five hundred square miles. In parts of this desert, particularly the Colorado River valley subdivision, suitable prey is not generally abundant enough to support a resident lion population. Where residents can exist, they must range over areas so large as to badly blur the mapped lines of demarcation between supposed subspecies. The chance of genetic isolation becomes extremely slim. Darwin, as far back as *The Origin of Species,* mentioned that feral house cats would not long maintain great diversity because of their tendency to move about and breed with many different mates.[8] His observation is equally applicable to the nature of mountain lions.

Another form of lion mobility, discovered through recent radio-tracking studies, further reduces the chances of isolation of desert cats from those in contiguous habitats. We now know that at about two to three years of age, lions often disperse long distances from their areas of birth in search of home areas of their own. In fact, emigrations by young cats of 50 miles or more are common, and movements up to 350 miles have been documented.[9] The few lions that occur sporadically along the lower Colorado River and in the surrounding desert could be transients that originated in more mesic habitats and are exploring these dry areas, where they are not likely to remain. They could easily be connected via streamways with more extensive lion populations at higher elevations.

We know that lions periodically occur in these low desert areas. But I doubt that an established population of lions has ever inhabited what Sonoran Desert biologists now call the lower Colorado River valley subdivision. Between 1984 and 1985, the Arizona Game and Fish Department fielded a team of experienced trackers to assess lion densities in key areas around the state. The Colorado River Valley Desert was an area of particular interest because of pressure to list the Yuma puma as an endangered subspecies. Although this habitat type was more saturated with survey routes than any other habitat in the state, the team was unable to find a single lion track anywhere within the Eagletail, Kofa, Dome Rock, Castle Dome, Copper, Cabeza Prieta, Sierra Pinta, or Mohawk mountains. This agrees with the observations of W. T. Hornaday and the group of naturalists who accompanied him across this desert in 1907 and 1908. His only mention of lions says, "Of puma, we saw not a trace."[10]

It also agrees with the observations of Carl and Aldo Leopold, who found abundant small game, waterfowl, coyotes, and bobcats in the Colorado River delta and surrounding desert in 1922.[11] Deer sign was sparse, and the Leopolds found no lion tracks. Biologists Dice and Blossom, assessing desert mammals in the 1930s, also failed to document lions in the lower desert habitats.[12]

Of the mountains surveyed, the Kofas appear to have the best lion habitat. They also probably hold a higher density of deer than most of the other ranges. Even here, only one lion was killed during the period of intensive predator control efforts in the first half of this century. No records of lions killed as trophies or taken as scientific specimens exist for the Kofas.

In the desert south of Gila Bend, populations of lions are found no farther west than the Crater Mountains near Ajo. Chaparral is nonexistent in this area. In deserts to the north and west, resident lions are known to use the Bighorn and Belmont mountains and the Bill Williams River drainage. These are marginal habitats. The Sand Tank, Harquahala, and Harcuvar mountains, which lie within the Arizona upland desert and interior chaparral habitats, are the nearest true bastions of lions bordering desert bighorn ranges.

I believe that without the clutter of Merriam's early classification of the Yuma puma and with our current knowledge of lion habitat use, movements, and social behavior, no modern taxonomist would be likely to conclude that two lion subspecies range through the Southwestern deserts. The pattern that emerged from Arizona's track surveys was one of increasing lion density from the lower Colorado River valley desert to the Arizona upland desert and interior chaparral habitats. This increasing density correlates directly with increasing deer density and inversely with numbers of sheep.

A lion inhabiting the lower Colorado River valley desert is probably a biological myth. But it is a myth that kept biologists imagining frequent interactions between desert sheep and lions for several decades.

The second apparent contradiction to our paradigm—historical records of sheep in lion country—kept me confused for years as well. Early literature mentions sheep sightings throughout Arizona. These go as far east as Springerville, into the breaks of the Little Colorado, Black, and San Francisco rivers, and extend into many of the south-central mountains. Sightings occurred in the Superstitions, the breaks of the Verde River, and the red rock of Sedona. Sheep were documented in most areas where suitably open and rugged escape terrain existed, and at times, apparently, away from such open terrain. Bighorns were recorded by Mearns on top of Bill Williams Mountain and by Merriam on San Francisco and Kendrick peaks.

Current literature suggests that bighorns were eventually extirpated in all but the dry desert mountains through a combination of hunting by early settlers and the arrival of diseases carried by domestic livestock, particularly sheep.[13] Whatever the case, by 1950 bighorns were restricted almost entirely to those dry and isolated desert mountains where raising domestic sheep was not practical and where too few miners and settlers ranged to provide the coup de grace to the bighorn population.

The role of predators in this range reduction remains vague. Were these early sheep a part of a large, interconnected bighorn population across the state or just struggling remnants being slowly squeezed out by interglacial changes in climate and vegetation? How could they have cohabited with lions if our thoughts on predator avoidance strategies of bighorns are at all correct? At the time of these early sightings, bighorns had to contend with wolves and grizzly bears in addition to lions. If predators were a factor, why would the bighorn range have been reduced at the very time major predators were being eliminated?

Our veil of uncertainty crops up again in efforts to answer these questions. In discussing this transitional period, biologist Warren Kelly, in *The Desert Bighorn*, noted:[14]

> From the writings of the early settlers and explorers of the Southwest, including Mearns (1907),[15] we know there were more bighorn, spread over a wider range, than at present. The advent of the settler with his livestock and guns *upset the bighorn-predator relationship* [italics mine], and that relationship may continue to be out of balance today. The distribution of the desert bighorn has decreased since the advent of the settler. Much of this decrease in distribution has been blamed on man and his livestock, but probably some can be attributed to predators. The bighorn have withdrawn to, and now survive in, mountain ranges where they are least vulnerable to men or predators.

I'm uncomfortable with the teleological notion of a species "withdrawing" within historic times to a place where they are less vulnerable to predators, even with increased human pressures. This suggests that predators were not a factor in habitat selection prior to this time. Something doesn't quite compute.

Writers such as Merriam and Mearns, great naturalists that they were, viewed only a short window from about 1880 to 1910. From their perspective, most of the damage due to hunting and livestock had already occurred, and they saw little hope for continued existence of bighorn sheep in the Southwest. They believed that the bighorn distribution they saw was greatly reduced from the past distribution. Perhaps this was not so.

During any period, historical information must be interpreted with caution. Too often the *unusual* records of wildlife draw attention and are repeated as literary gossip. This may be true even of petroglyphs, prehistoric graffiti littered with sheep morphs but obviously not actual sheep counts. Also, historic ranges of wildlife, then as now, varied over time, and the truth was a moving target. Nonetheless, the scarcity of good historical data causes most of us to cling to each observation as a priceless view of the past. While we may qualify our sources in original writings, the qualifiers often become lost in subsequent citations. Eventually, all that remain are dots on maps, which rigidify as fact. Ultimately, someone plays connect the dots and shades in the enclosed area. For a species such as bighorn sheep, this process can create, and indeed has created, serious misconceptions regarding the habitats actually used.

The only way to put this contradictory history into context, then, is through a clear understanding of the biological nature of the species derived from good field observations. Adaptations evolved over eons are not likely to change over a few decades. But even here, the veil of uncertainty persists, and the relationship of bighorns to predators is unclear. Summarizing the writings of bighorn biologists, pathologist Rex Allen[16] said, "It seems to be the consensus that predation is not usually an important factor in limiting populations of bighorn sheep." Yet sheep choose to live where predators don't. This restriction of habitat would seem to be a limiting factor greater than direct mortality.

Kelly provided instances of a variety of predator-bighorn interactions, demonstrating clearly that under suitable circumstances, coyotes, gray foxes, golden eagles, bobcats, and mountain lions all have killed and eaten desert bighorns.[17] He ranked the bobcat above the lion as a bighorn predator but gave more documented incidences of lion predation on desert bighorns than of any other predator. The apparent difference is that lions, being predators of deer, seldom occur in the areas considered to be the best bighorn habitat. All of the smaller predators naturally seek smaller prey, which is abundant in the desert. Coyotes, bobcats, and foxes are common throughout the bighorn range and hence on an opportunistic basis alone may have more interactions with sheep. Their smaller size, however, restricts their predation to a sanitary role within sheep populations. Lion predation is not so selective.

I think it is here that we approach at least one crux of the matter. We are dealing with different predation effects. On the one hand, we have smaller predators such as bobcats or coyotes, which have limited ability to kill bighorns and to which the bighorns react with simple avoidance or even defensive behavior. These smaller predators must have all the cards stacked in their favor to take a wild sheep at all. Minor behavioral changes such as aggression or short-distance flight by the bighorn will prevent any such stacking of the cards.

Lions, on the other hand, are different. They occur at relatively low densities even in good lion habitat, and they range over large expanses. They show up unexpectedly. They stalk. They are adapted to killing bighorn-sized prey. Lions require much less stacking of the cards to kill bighorns, and the bighorns must react to them in a different way. Sheep avoid lion country. Or, more likely, they never really occupied it.

As I mentioned earlier, bighorns probably did not evolve in the presence of lions, and their selection of habitat—resulting from adaptation to other predators, perhaps wolves—is their only real protection from lion predation. Other adaptations are not as effective. Charles Hansen, another early sheep researcher, noted that "desert bighorn appear to depend primarily, though not exclusively, upon their sense of sight to detect danger. On several occasions I have seen bighorn running away from me when I was still about 1.6 km from them. In most of these cases, the wind was such that it was doubtful that the animal heard or smelled me."[18] So bighorns react strongly to visual stimuli. Lions are cryptic beasts.

Welles and Welles, in their monograph on Death Valley bighorns, stated: "The fact that they have good vision is too well known to warrant discussion. We have seen ample proof of this in distant vision and in close vision associated with the incredible surefootedness of the species. There is some question, however, involving their intermediate vision suggested by a seeming inability to recognize well known objects within certain limits." Could it be that sheep cannot see clearly at the distance at which a lion might begin a stalk?

Welles and Welles further noted that "desert bighorn apparently do not have as good vision at night as they do by day. At Corn Creek Field Station of Desert National Wildlife Refuge, Nevada, the hand-raised lamb 'Tag-along' followed people outside at night, where she occasionally walked into wire fences and other objects that also were difficult for humans to see. Her actions left the impression that she had no better night vision than a human."

Lions are mainly crepuscular. A bighorn roaming through dense cover at dusk could be easy pickings.[19]

Hansen also noted that bighorns depend on their sense of smell to detect other animals but will pause to see interlopers before making an extraordinary effort to flee. Such hesitancy could be disastrous if the interloper happened to be a stalking lion.

Bighorns in colder climates may be forced by snow depth or food requirements to cohabit with lions. In these cases, group behavior may help them survive. During his pioneering lion study in Idaho, Maurice Hornocker observed that "sheep frequent the bluff areas regularly hunted by lions, but because of their close-knit group behavior, they appear to be well able to compete [that uncertainty again—even lion biologists seem to have difficulty finding the right words] with lion predation. Seldom can a stalking lion approach the group closely without being detected."[20]

A more recent study, however, found bighorn rams to be extremely vulnerable when forced to live in lion habitat. In British Columbia, rams were actually the major item in the lions' diet (as I noted near the beginning of this chapter—it all depends). The biologist in charge of the study concluded that rams, whose large horns impede vision to the side and rear (allowing lions to stalk them without being seen), were more vulnerable to predation than bighorn ewes or deer. Also, ewes seemed to be able to select safer habitat than did rams.

Bighorns in general appear to be poorly prepared—either by senses, behavior, or anatomy—to deal on a regular basis with lions, and their best strategy is to stay out of lion country. That they do this is supported strongly by results of transplant efforts. In reviewing Arizona's bighorn transplant program, biologists Stan Cunningham, Norris Dodd, and Ron Olding concluded that "although suitable habitat exists from Goat Mountain on Apache Lake to Mormon Flat Dam and a little beyond (a distance of over 12 airline miles), the gentler nature of the upper slope and the presence of interior chaparral makes this a somewhat narrow band. The dense upper Sonoran Desert Scrub and interior chaparral combine to restrict bighorn sheep use of the area."[21]

Arizona's lion survey team found some of the state's highest lion densities in ecotones of Arizona upland desertscrub and interior chaparral. Not a good place for bighorns.

Transplantation of bighorns into the Black Mountains on the upper Bill Williams River apparently failed because of lion predation. Escape terrain was limited in this area, and many of the caves underlying bluffs were easily accessible to lions. Three of eight transplanted sheep were quickly killed by lions. Most of the remaining sheep left the area, some traveling long distances.

In another transplant, on Lion Mountain near Bartlett Lake, five of eight radio-collared bighorns died shortly after being moved. At least three of these were lost to predation, and two are known to have been killed by lions. Some of the surviving sheep in this transplant also moved long distances.

In earlier transplant efforts, where sheep were held in enclosures before being released, losses to lions were common. For the Muleshoe–Redfield Canyon transplant, four of seven known mortalities were attributed to lions. Lions entered the Virgin Mountain enclosure and killed at least two sheep before being discovered. Lion predation within an enclosure virtually wiped out early efforts at bighorn transplants in the Black Gap area of Texas. All of these enclosures, with the possible exception of Aravaipa Canyon, were built on relatively gentle terrain in known lion country.

When bighorns were placed in new habitat with adequate escape terrain, they became established. When they were planted in areas without adequate escape terrain, predation—usually by lions—disrupted the groups, disturbed the sheep, and sent survivors looking for a less violent neighborhood. Contrary to biblical hopes, lambs will never sleep peacefully near lions.

Why, then, were sheep able to survive in so many scattered locations in the Southwest before 1900? What habitats did they use then? James Ohio Pattie made a pertinent observation during his travels on the San Francisco River of eastern Arizona during the mid-1820s: "The banks of the river are for the most part incapable of cultivation being in many places formed of high and rugged mountains. Upon these, we saw multitudes of mountain sheep. These animals are not found on level ground, being there slow of foot, but on these cliffs and rocks they are so nimble and expert in jumping from point to point that no dog or wolf can overtake them."[22]

I rediscovered this passage after assembling the above historical and behavioral quotes and interpreting them from what I hoped to be a profound neo-Darwinian point of view. Pattie made his observation sixty years before Merriam and Mearns even came to the country, and his notes were published in 1831—the year Darwin left England on the *Beagle*. Sometimes it is hard to beat good observation by uncluttered minds.

Based on modern studies of sheep adaptive behavior as well as observations such as Pattie's, I believe that Southwestern bighorn sheep, then as now, occurred in scattered populations restricted to suitable terrain. This alone allowed them to survive in areas surrounded by lions. The cause of their ultimate demise in these scattered areas is beyond my present purpose. The point is that sheep and lions don't mix.

This can perhaps be usefully contrasted with the behavior of whitetailed or mule deer, species that naturally cohabit with lions. North American deer are adapted to short-range detection, quick response, and evasive tactics within habitats that harbor predators. In addition to this, they have all of the fawn-saving strategies that Geist found missing in bighorn lambs. Even with such adaptations, deer also move in response to predator pressures. Results of radio-tracking studies of lions and mule deer on the north Kaibab, for example, suggest that deer winter at elevations below the normal range of lions; and while lions dip into these wintering areas, taking deer on the upper margins, they seldom reside within prime deer winter range. Use of this lower habitat by deer occurred even in mild winters when food or snow was not limiting, suggesting that deer have evolved their migratory habits in response to something other than climatic or nutritional effects alone. Adaptations to lion predation could certainly be involved.

Biologists M. E. Nelson and L. David Mech, in studies of wolf-whitetail relationships in Minnesota, noted that whitetail winter yards often occur in areas where wolf territories overlap. The overlap areas are avoided by resident wolf packs. Nelson and Mech speculated that traditional winter yards have become used by deer through long-term avoidance of wolf predation.[23]

Although the differences in adaptation of deer and bighorns to predation are a matter of degree, deer live closer to lions and finesse their way through subtle habitat differences to survive, while sheep, simply put, do their best to stay out of lion country.

So what does all of this mean to a lion biologist viewing sheep? More than one concern comes to mind. In the world of modern wildlife management, single-species advocate groups have become increasingly dominant. Sheep advocates are among the most successful. These societies contribute funds and labor to sheep transplants and water improvement projects. Their results are undoubtedly beneficial to sheep. However, the failure of expensive transplants, such as those at Black and Lion mountains, tends to revive the subject of lion control. Some few of us now worry more about the effects of bighorns on lions than of lions on sheep.

The history of lion control for the benefit of bighorn populations does not give such programs strong support. In the San Andres Mountains of New Mexico, for example, a diseased native population of bighorns was captured, treated for scabies, and held away from its original range for a year. During this time lion predation was observed on the few untreated animals remaining on the mountain, and lion control efforts were initiated. After sixty-nine lions were killed in the surrounding area (about two lions for every bighorn being protected), the control effort was stopped. Disease continued to decimate the sheep population. Results of an ongoing lion study in the area show that lions are again abundant but predation on bighorns is negligible.

In a historic range such as the San Andres Mountains, lion control seemed to do no good. Its efficacy in isolated transplant sites surrounded by expanses of lion country is even less likely. In fact, removal of resident lions may actually increase lion densities over time due to an influx of transients vying for empty home areas. Recent research in the San Andres suggests that, if anything, protecting lions and thereby allowing a resident adult population to establish itself has reduced predation on sheep.

But the possibility of lion control to "prepare" sites for sheep transplants leads to another concern. Lion control in isolated transplant sites in good lion country would probably provide only a short-term reduction, if any, in lion numbers. Sheep numbers would ultimately be limited by the availability of suitable escape terrain. Where such terrain does not exist, lions will eventually repopulate and decimate the sheep. Taken to the ridiculous extreme, a potential exists for a cycle of "put-and-take" sheep management, with intervening periods of lion control. Such intensive "management" would ultimately place bighorns in a category with hatchery trout, game-farm pheasants, and shooting-preserve deer. I worry that the helicopter, the dart, and the net may have already begun the process. Sheep are now too easy to catch.

Even the water development activities cannot go completely unquestioned. The effects of such developments on lions and their principal prey, deer, are not clearly understood. It is certain that the water requirements of lions and deer are greater than those of desert sheep. A more readily available water supply could make desert bighorn range more acceptable to lions. Unless carefully placed, water developments might also serve to draw bighorns into situations where they are vulnerable to predation. Man-made water holes could become virtual havens for lions ambushing prey. Under these circumstances, lions could decimate sheep populations, and control of lions could become an issue.

To the credit of sheep societies, the above strategies regarding lion control have not, insofar as I know, been translated into political action. This demonstrates some ecological sophistication among these groups. However, I still worry, for the lion in the Southwest has no similar well-moneyed advocates. Wildlife departments carefully document sheep numbers with expensive helicopter flights to justify issuing sheep permits each year, and these are rigorously based on numbers of mature rams known to be available. These same departments, conversely, have been slow to initiate periodic lion surveys or to manage lions based on population density estimates. As one Arizona employee put it, "We have to justify having seasons on sheep, but we have to justify not having them for lions." The lion may not fare well if saving bighorns continues to be magnified as an issue.

Single-species organizations, while essentially beneficial and deserving of encouragement, carry the potential for creating rival programs to benefit their respective interests. I have already seen, for example, dollars spent for elk habitat management with little regard for effects on wild turkeys or deer. It seems that the group providing the most dollars holds sway.

We live in a society where power is unabashedly pursued. Competition, bullish intimidation, and winning are the buzzwords of those who seek to be leaders. Within the environmental movement, compromise is increasingly seen to be a weakness, and elimination of the opposition—be it environmentalist, hunter, rancher, or logger—from the land is a legitimate mode of operation. Legal or political battles won are viewed as accomplishments in themselves, often with little regard to their real effects on nature. I worry about similar attitudes in advocates of species. Those individuals assertive enough to promote such groups are competitive by nature. Wild species may become stakes in a new contest, but they have no way to understand the games of men. We must therefore beware of this new competition not for food or space, as is the case in classical population biology, but for the right to exist as ordained by the dominant species on earth. As a member of this dominant species and as a lion biologist who once worked briefly on sheep, I am concerned, for I know which species will ultimately lose.

NOTES

1. Valerius Geist's *Mountain Sheep: A Study in Behavior and Evolution* (Chicago: University of Chicago Press, 1971) remains the best place to start any study of sheep interactions with other animals.

2. Ibid.; see also S. Harrison, "Cougar Predation on Bighorn Sheep in the Junction Wildlife Management Area, British Columbia" (Master's thesis, University of British Columbia, 1990).

3. In addition to Geist's work, George B. Schaller's *Stones of Silence* (New York: Viking, 1980) has interesting commentary on sheep evolution and dispersal; see also J. Bailey, "Desert Bighorn, Forage, Competition, and Zoogeography," *Wildlife Society Bulletin* 8 (1980): 208–16.

4. A summary of Terry A. Vaughn's view of the Panama filter and mammalian dispersal can be found in his textbook *Mammalogy* (Philadelphia: W. B. Saunders, 1978).

5. For a recent treatment of the taxonomic history of Arizona cats see D. F. Hoffmeister, *Mammals of Arizona* (Tucson: University of Arizona Press, 1986); see also E. Nelson and E. Goldman, "Three New Pumas," *Journal of the Washington Academy of Sciences* 21 (1931): 209–12.

6. C. Hart Merriam first described the Yuma puma in "Eight New Mammals from the United States," *Proceedings of the Biological Society of Washington* 16 (1903): 73–78. A recent survey is R. Duke, R. Klinger,

R. Hopkins, and M. Kutilek, *Yuma Puma (*Felis concolor browni*): Feasibility Report Population Status Survey* (Alviso, Calif.: Harvey and Stanley Associates, 1987).

7. Merriam's earlier review of mountain lions appeared as "Preliminary Revision of the Pumas (*Felis concolor* Group)," *Proceedings of the Washington Academy of Sciences* 3 (1901): 577–600.

8. Charles Darwin's *The Origin of Species by Means of Natural Selection,* 7th ed. (New York: First Modern Library, 1936), was first published in 1859.

9. Harley Shaw's *Soul Among Lions* (Boulder: Johnson Books, 1989) contains extensive discussions of puma movements; see also Shaw, *Ecology of the Mountain Lion in Arizona* (Phoenix: Arizona Game and Fish Department Final Report, 1980).

10. William T. Hornaday failed to see puma in the desert; see *Camp-Fires on Desert Lava and Sand* (New York: Charles Scribner's Sons, 1908).

11. The Leopold brothers' trip on the Colorado River delta is recounted in Aldo Leopold's classic *A Sand County Almanac and Sketches Here and There* (New York: Oxford University Press, 1949) but was first published as "Green Lagoons" in *American Forests* magazine in 1945, twenty-three years after the trip.

12. L. R. Dice and P. M. Blossom failed to find lions; see *Studies of Mammalian Ecology in Southwestern North America with Special Attention to the Colors of Desert Mammals,* Carnegie Institution of Washington Publication 485 (1937).

13. See publications on disease and mortality listed in P. R. Krausman, J. R. Mogart, and M. E. Chilelli, *Annotated Bibliography of Desert Bighorn Sheep Literature, 1897–1983* (Phoenix: Southwest Natural History Association, 1984).

14. W. E. Kelly discusses the historic distribution of bighorn sheep in "Predator Relationships," in *The Desert Bighorn,* ed. G. Monson and L. Sumner, 186–96 (Tucson: University of Arizona Press, 1980).

15. E. A. Mearns authored *Mammals of the Mexican Boundary of the United States,* U.S. Natural History Museum Bulletin 56 (1907).

16. See R. W. Allen, "Natural Mortality and Disease," in *The Desert Bighorn,* 172–85.

17. Kelly, "Predator Relationships," 14.

18. C. G. Hansen, "Senses and Intelligence," in *The Desert Bighorn*, 113–23.

19. R. E. Welles and F. B. Welles, *The Bighorn of Death Valley*, U.S. National Park Service Faunal Survey Series 6 (1961).

20. M. Hornocker, "An Analysis of Mountain Lion Predation on Mule Deer and Elk in the Idaho Primitive Area," *Wildlife Monograph* 21 (1970): 1–39.

21. S. C. Cunningham, N. Dodd, and R. Olding, "Arizona's Bighorn Sheep Reintroduction Program," in *The Desert Bighorn Sheep in Arizona*, ed. R. Lee (Phoenix: Arizona Game and Fish Department, 1989).

22. *The Personal Narrative of James Ohio Pattie of Kentucky*, ed. T. Flint (New York: J. B. Lippincott, 1831).

23. M. E. Nelson and L. D. Mech, "Deer Social Organization and Wolf Predation in Northwestern Minnesota," *Wildlife Monographs* 77 (1981): 1–53.

PAUL R. KRAUSMAN

The Exit of the Last
Wild Mountain Sheep

While this may be one of Paul Krausman's first attempts at publishing his personal reflections on twenty years of work with large terrestrial mammals, it is not the first time he has addressed the conflicts between humans and other organisms. As his field studies have taken him across the Southwest and into Egypt, India, and Morocco, he has seen the many possible variations of human interactions with wildlife. Closest to home in Tucson, where Krausman is professor of wildlife and fisheries science at the University of Arizona, he has been involved since the late 1970s with controversies surrounding the protection of bighorn sheep in the Pusch Ridge Wilderness adjacent to metropolitan Tucson. There, a small enclave of designated wilderness may not be enough if surrounding land use leaves sheep with little room to move. This theme—that parks and wilderness reserves may not be large enough to maintain viable animal populations over the long run—is a subject of active discussion in the field of conservation biology. Here, Krausman handles it through the use of poignant examples from his own experiences in the field, offering a veracity not found in secondhand journalistic treatments of the same topic.

Krausman is the senior author of a key reference work, *Annotated Bibliography of Desert Bighorn Sheep Literature, 1897–1983* (Southwest Natural History Association, 1984), which highlights six hundred technical and semitechnical articles on this animal. He and his students continue to add new insights to our understanding of the habitat requirements of desert bighorn sheep. From my perspective, this essay has a prophetic

242

ring to it not unlike that of Aldo Leopold's "Thinking Like a Mountain" classic in *A Sand County Almanac* (Oxford University Press, 1949).

When the last mountain sheep disappears, I wonder how humans will explain their exit. Mountain sheep are said to be adaptable when my fellow scientists speak of them. But how much and how far can human activities intrude before these wild critters are pushed to their adaptive limits? I worry that there are but two possible answers; human intrusion will cause their elimination, or the wildness of these animals will be diminished.

As I ponder the limits of their adaptability, I remain struck by just how flexible bighorns are. Mountain sheep habitat ranges from forested slopes in the northern part of their range to barren, rocky crags in the Southwest. Their respective tolerance to temperature is just one indicator of their flexibility. Those in the north withstand temperatures below − 30 degrees Fahrenheit and snow depths of more than fifteen inches for several months, while their southern relatives bask in summer temperatures above 120 degrees. It seems to me that the simplest adaptation of mountain sheep against cold and heat is their insulating coat, a true buffer from the elements. Adaptations in behavior also help sheep conserve or dissipate heat. In cold weather, sheep often rest and bunch their legs underneath, reducing the body's surface area and conserving heat. In warm climates, mountain sheep increase their surface area and thereby dissipate heat by extending their legs while resting.

In my mind, I run through the many adaptive features I've learned about during my fifteen years of sheep research. The remarkable adaptability of mountain sheep is best brought home by the basic feature of their population dynamics: the timing of the lambing period. In the north the lambing period is limited to a few short weeks. In contrast, desert races of mountain sheep drop their lambs from January to June. I am familiar with some desert populations of sheep that drop lambs every month of the year—perhaps in response to an unpredictable climate.

I am also struck by the wide variation in the habitats used by mountain sheep. There are vast differences between the landscapes that sheep occupy in Idaho and those frequented in Arizona. Not too surprisingly, there are even striking differences among the habitats used by the desert races of mountain sheep in the Southwest. At the eastern edge of their range in Texas and New Mexico, mountain sheep share habitat with desert mule deer and mountain lions in much higher abundance than in western Arizona. In the San Andres Mountains, New Mexico, a remnant sheep population exists as a small island surrounded by desert mule deer. In other habitats, mule deer and mountain sheep are segregated both spatially and temporally. Moving westward, the vegetation in sheep habitat varies from extremely densely covered and well-watered ranges such as the Santa Catalina Mountains near Tucson to dry and barren mountains like the Little Harquahala Mountains near the Colorado River valley of Arizona. My point is that the habitats used by mountain sheep are extremely variable across their range. These bovids have an uncanny knack for adapting to a vast array of landscapes.

Wherever freestanding water is available in the desert, mountain sheep rely on such open pools to quench their thirst. At one time I thought freestanding water was a limiting factor to sheep distribution. Now I know better. Lack of water alone does not eliminate mountain sheep from waterless stretches of the desert. Desert races of mountain sheep inhabiting areas without freestanding water are apparently able to meet their moisture requirements by consuming succulent plants such as barrel cacti—which takes some doing, considering their heavy armor of spines. I once watched an older ram crack open the top of a barrel cactus. I couldn't help feeling amused at the ram as he began consuming the succulent interior. He was oblivious to the younger and less dominant members of the herd around him who awkwardly jostled for a place in line, waiting for their turn at the cactus fountain.

Like all animals, mountain sheep can adapt to their varying habitats by altering their behavior, within limits. Their keenly developed sense of sight allows them to survey vast areas. Usually a sentinel member of the group spends additional time on the lookout to alert group members to the presence of predators. In extreme desert climates, mountain sheep shift their bed sites as the day progresses. They move as the shade does. Their horns may also contribute to reducing heat loads.

Both sexes of mountain sheep possess horns that serve several functions (for example, they are both shields and weapons). Females of the desert races of mountain sheep have longer horns than other North American mountain sheep. Their horns are nearly twice as long as those of female Rocky Mountain sheep, and more widely flared. The thermoregulatory function of these horns in the desert may explain their larger size compared with the horns of their northern cousins in cooler climates. Horns may also be used to protect limited resources. When females consume water in small *tinajas* (water holes) or extract the succulent pulp from a barrel cactus, their horns may protect the resource from others eager to consume them. Bigger horns are better protectors of these scarce resources.

Sheep behavior, adaptive or not, is strongly influenced by the activities of humans. Many populations of mountain sheep in deserts have been forced to exist in whatever habitats are available instead of in their historic, now degraded, habitats. Desert races of mountain sheep are especially sensitive to habitat alteration by humans. During their short domination of the arid Southwest, European Americans have pushed sheep back into the remote reaches of their formerly expansive habitats.

I often wonder how future biologists will interpret the relictual distribution and use of habitat by mountain sheep. Today, desert races of mountain sheep are limited to remote mountain areas. Will all habitats formerly part of their historic range be considered for reintroductions? Probably not. Humans have completely destroyed some habitats, making them unsuitable for their previous inhabitants. Once humans have converted a desert area for their own use, restoring it to its natural state is almost impossible. It has never been done in a way that serves mountain sheep, and I do not foresee it being done in the future. How could humans re-create mountain ranges or ancient saguaro forests?

Lacking the capacity for desert habitat restoration, we are left with other options for the future that truly frighten me. Several biologists have proposed genetically engineering wild mountain sheep through transferring DNA from domestic breeds, thus creating Supersheep that can exist on landscapes altered by man. But if we domesticate mountain sheep, what will happen to the wild qualities we treasure in them? Survival on game ranches, another frightening option, has also been proposed. On game ranches, captive sheep would be locked behind fences to allow more intensive management, but their ability to lead a free-ranging life would be lost. A third scenario would allow for a more hands-on approach to managing free-ranging sheep populations so that managers could have a more direct influence on disease, predation, habitat alteration, and other factors. Essentially, free-ranging sheep would be manipulated like domestic livestock.

I offer these bleak scenarios to illustrate my concerns about the future interaction between humans and free-ranging mountain sheep. The biological and aesthetic or moral costs of any degree of domestication can no longer be ignored by biologists, land managers, and the public—especially the public, because they will be ultimately responsible for closing the gate that locks away the last free-ranging mountain sheep. If people continue to diminish the habitat available to mountain sheep, intensive livestock-style management will become inevitable.

Today, mountain sheep still use just about any mountain range they can reach where the necessary habitat mosaic exists and access to the range remains open. Mountains surround Tucson, Arizona, and at one time, so did mountain sheep. A remnant population persists nearby, in the Pusch Ridge Wilderness within the Santa Catalina Mountains. However, sheep have vacated the other ranges surrounding the burgeoning Tucson metropolitan area: the Tortolita, Picacho, Tucson, and Rincon mountains.

Biologists will probably never be able to single out a sole reason for the sheep's departure. Let us just say that a mess of human activities served as the culprit. Through the 1920s, mountain sheep ranged as far east as West Spring; they used more than two hundred square miles of the Santa Catalina Mountains at that time. Today their habitat is limited to less than seventeen square miles in the Santa Catalinas.

My graduate students and I have studied the historic distribution of sheep in the Santa Catalinas and compared it with their current distribution. We have identified two factors that distinguish the abandoned historic habitat from the currently used habitat: human disturbance and fire suppression. Roads, trails, and housing developments are pressing sheep up the mountains, while fire suppression in the upper reaches of the Santa Catalinas provides for taller, denser vegetation that pushes sheep back down the hills.

Early accounts blamed hunters, not habitat loss, for sheep losses. Market hunting or poaching of sheep for food by miners and others certainly depleted some sheep populations directly. Nevertheless, other actions have also curtailed sheep movement between habitats, triggering indirect reductions of populations. I can't drive down the nearest freeway without thinking about this.

Interstate highways such as I-10, with their associated right-of-way fences, create almost insurmountable barriers for mountain sheep. Where sheep could once cross desert flats from one range to another, the land is now littered with all sorts of barriers. Direct competition with livestock, or at least behavioral avoidance of cattle, has also kept bighorns out of their historic range. Livestock and desert mountain sheep do not take well to one another. As humans chopped up the desert, they effectively fragmented the habitat available to sheep in the Tucson area. Once able to roam across a vast expanse of desert, this "metapopulation" of sheep (a metapopulation comprises several populations with free exchange between them) was effectively reduced to several subpopulations, each isolated in its own mountain range. An obvious advantage of free exchange of members between smaller populations is that they breed and exchange genes, a process critical to the maintenance of fitness and variability. As populations become isolated, the likelihood of genetic exchange is reduced and the deleterious effects of inbreeding are more likely to rear their ugly heads.

Had a segment of the metapopulation been reduced due to some natural catastrophe, other members could have come to recolonize from other areas. Not now. Roads and fences have cut off the opportunity for recolonization, and the intervening land between subpopulations has been grazed by livestock. These domesticated cousins of sheep have effectively blocked the flow of genes between subpopulations

These intrusions into the sheep's world surely take their toll. However, I suspect that sheep sometimes find ways to move between ranges and across valleys that have been tamed. The recent reintroduction of mountain sheep into the Galiuros sixty miles east of the Santa Catalina Mountains has given me hope that gene flow can still occur. Radio-collared sheep introduced into that range had a large domain in which to settle, but they crossed the San Pedro Valley and somehow ended up in the Santa Catalinas. This does not surprise me so much when I consider the historic range of sheep. Yet I am still amazed that these sheep found a way to navigate the intervening valleys with their ubiquitous human populations.

I have to accept the fact that metapopulations have already been chopped up. The sheep in the Rincon, Tortolita, and Picacho mountains have become extinct. In my backyard, the Santa Catalinas will have to suffice as habitat for the remnant herd of sheep in the Tucson area. The metropolitan feedlot of Tucson has fenced them in over the past fifteen years—not with wire but with larger and more effective structures. This fencing project actually had its subtle start more than fifty years ago.

Desert races of mountain sheep favor sites where they can see long distances. In the past fifty years the U.S. Forest Service's role has been to squelch fire at all costs. This policy may have allowed vegetation density in some areas of the Santa Catalinas to exceed that suitable for sheep. Clearly, the policy did not mimic nature; it did, however, provide the postholes for the proverbial fence. The proverbial wire was provided in the form of parks, golf courses, resorts, houses, horse trails, and shopping malls.

It is hard to imagine that mountain sheep once roamed the area where the Tucson Mall presently sits. Yet they were commonly seen there twenty years ago; not in large numbers or frequently, but once or twice a year. Of course, Oracle Road was only a two-lane track in those days; now it is a four-lane, shopping center–studded circus.

Since then, the fencing has progressed rapidly. Homesites, resorts, and horse stables prevent movement to the southeast, and westward movement is cut off by Catalina State Park and offices touted for their mountain views. Land developers are now actively promoting plans to encircle the remaining habitat, including Pima Canyon. When they do, mountain sheep in the Santa Catalina Mountains will be destined for certain isolation. Our barrier of urbanity is every bit as effective as barbwire or electric fences.

From there on, the situation may be bleak for "free-ranging" sheep. What happens when disease occurs, when the forage changes through succession, or when the sheep population burgeons because of favorable conditions in its local islandlike pasture? We have built a helluva good barrier around the bighorns, but we have forgotten to give them an ecological gate, a way out.

The human blockade around Pusch Ridge Wilderness Area is not unique. Similar fences elsewhere have caused disastrous results. Consider the population of sheep in the San Andres National Wildlife Refuge in New Mexico. The number of animals in this range has probably always been less than several hundred. The San Andres Mountains are near the eastern edge of the range of mountain sheep in the Southwest, where suitable habitat is patchy. Pervasive human activity has overwhelmed the few remaining sheep in the area. Surrounded by the White Sands Missile Range, the Jornada Experimental Range, and White Sands National Monument, the San Andres Mountains are truly corralled. Not surprisingly, the "captive herd" there has been devastated whenever disease has struck. In the late 1970s there were more than two hundred sheep on the mountain, until a severe outbreak of mites predisposed the population to predation and disease. The herd size had dropped to less than thirty individuals by 1991.

Dealing with such problems today requires cooperation and coordination from at least three agencies that manage the herd in the San Andres Mountains: the U.S. Fish and Wildlife Service, the Department of Defense, and the New Mexico Department of Game and Fish. Their cooperation will have to be immediate and aggressive, because the mites that have infected the sheep have probably precluded the sheep's ability to fend off other pressures such as predation. The herds cannot be naturally replenished from adjacent ranges, so there is no relief valve for the sheep on the mountain. They are not headed for the last roundup; they are in it.

One more thing about the San Andres herd. Land managers may never know how the mites entered the sheep population or why they popped up so suddenly, since there is no historic record of their presence in the region. However, most zoologists have little doubt that the mites were dispersed in one way or another as a result of human activities. Incidental dispersals of pests have occurred many times over the centuries, but too often they are hidden from view until the infestations are out of control.

Both the Pusch Ridge Wilderness and the San Andres National Wildlife Refuge were established to preserve mountain sheep habitat. The irony is that nearby human activities will necessitate severe and sophisticated management of mountain sheep if their needs are to be met in such hemmed-in habitats.

If disease strikes the sheep at Pusch Ridge as it did in New Mexico, land managers can probably count on a similar disaster. We have built our fence all too well. If the barrier is to be breached, it will have to be by the ones who have constructed it.

By now it must seem that I am opposed to the management and manipulation of mountain sheep and their habitats. That's not entirely true.

Overall, I feel that wildlife managers' interventions on behalf of sheep have been truly successful. Those involved with reintroducing sheep to parts of their historic range should be proud of their efforts. Their neighbors present and future should be thankful.

What has been done by my colleagues to this point is well and good. But we are at a threshold now. My deepest doubts are about those who call for further intensification of management. For me, it is but one more indicator of the artificial world being generated by our own activities. How soon before the habitat available for wildlife is so limited that the degree of management intensity becomes identical to farm management? Every bit of domestication takes a little away from the wild side of wildlife.

Is that choice more desirable than extinction? It is a choice between smacking your thumb with a sledgehammer or having your thumbnail pulled out with pliers. Neither alternative avoids pain. This is the threshold that management of desert races of mountain sheep has reached. From here on, protection, coupled with *intensive* management, is only a shade different from domestication. Will we cross that threshold without turning back? Our only hope is that wildlife managers will learn to select and push for actions that have the least impact on the critter, letting natural selection, not cultural selection, take its course.

Counting Sheep

I think the slain
Care little if they sleep or rise again;
And we, the living, wherefore should we ache
With counting our lost ones?

AESCHYLUS, *Prometheus Bound*

Doug Peacock, former geology student and Green Beret, came back from Vietnam in 1968, suffering from wounds of the soul. Over the next quarter century he grew into one of the largest and healthiest of souls and became deeply immersed in the wildness of the intermountain West. Tens of thousands of environmental readers first sensed something about this soul in the guise of Hayduke, hero of Ed Abbey's *The Monkey Wrench Gang* (Dutton, 1975), before most of these readers had ever seen a word written by Peacock himself. Since Abbey's death Peacock has emerged as more than a caricature; he is a fine essayist in his own right and needs no one to speak for him. *Grizzly Years* (Henry Holt, 1990) triggered novelist Jim Harrison to remark, "I cannot imagine that a more worthwhile book will be published this year." Peter Matthiessen recognized that the book is more than just a detailed natural history; it is "a striking metaphor in its impassioned outcry against senseless waste of life on earth, human life included." In my view, *Grizzly Years* and Terry Tempest Williams's *Refuge* (Pantheon, 1991) have pushed nature writing in a new and needed direction, so completely intertwining "inner" psychological growth with a discovery of patterns and behavior in the "outer" world that some critics doubt that they are natural histories at all. Peacock's more recent collaboration with photographer Terrence Moore, *Baja!* (Bullfinch/Little, Brown), celebrates the lower California peninsula, verifying that the powerful style seen in *Grizzly Years* is no fluke. Peacock's magazine pieces in *Esquire, Outside, Wild Earth, Backpacker,* and *Northern Lights* also suggest that his will be a consistently distinctive voice, recognized for many years to come. The short essay included here is an outgrowth of Peacock's oral story-telling skills. When I heard him tell a version of this "legend" at the Dinner Party in Defense of the American West in Wilson, Wyoming, I encouraged him to put pen to paper.

Insomnia has been the central dysfunction of my adult life, and I go into the desert to sleep. I figure I have spent almost two years of my life sleeping under the stars among the cactus of the American Southwest or, on rare stormy nights, in a tent on the desert shores of the Sea of Cortez. My favorite desert for sleeping, however, is the great expanse of country embracing the border of southwestern Arizona and Mexico, the uninhabited desert ranges and valleys of the Cabeza Prieta—one of the best places on earth to get a good night's sleep.

Cabeza Prieta is the name of a block of mountainous hills within an area of the same name now designated as a national wildlife refuge. This refuge is surrounded by similar wastelands managed by the National Park Service or the Bureau of Land Management, or used as a bombing range by the U.S. Marine Corps and U.S. Air Force. It's all great country. The only paved road is Mexican Highway 2 just south of the border, on the northern edge of the Pinacate Protected Zone. I pay no attention whatsoever to these cultural, governmental, and otherwise artificial boundaries and have democratically thrown down my sleeping bag on about 220 different nights in washes on all sides of the fences.

The soporific device of counting sheep in order to fall asleep has never worked for me. Instead, I tend to log the constellations with a star chart or read by a tiny ironwood fire until I'm drowsy. Some nights I just watch the celestial clock unfurl or think about a girl I used to know. Sheep never cross my mind until just around daybreak when, sometimes, the clatter of real desert bighorn sheep startles me fully awake.

This doesn't happen very often, of course; four times, my notebooks say, four mountain sheep on four mornings spread over three decades. Desert bighorns aren't the kind of animals I see in the flesh very often, although

I run across their tracks nearly every time I visit the Cabeza Prieta. The sheep I see I invariably hear first. One of the best times for this is in the morning, from your sleeping bag, though you can also hear them moving about on the scree and rocks toward evening.

The first desert bighorn to cross my path was north of Buck Tank along a low spine of granitic hill running north into the *bajada*. It was daybreak on Christmas Day 1979. I was still in the bag, warming my fingers over the ironwood ashes of the previous night's fire, when the sound of rocks clattering on the ridge startled me. I reached for my field glasses and scanned the ridge for movement. The slope was bare except for a few creosote and elephant trees dotting the hillside. I couldn't see anything moving. Suddenly I heard more racket and caught movement coming over the saddle.

It was then that I saw what looked like a ghostly gray grizzly coming toward me. The animal's head had a curl of corrugated horn. The bear was a sheep, a ram with a full curl. I dropped the glasses, and the bighorn caught the movement; he stopped and looked at me from twenty yards. As sunlight capped the tops of the highest peaks, he turned and ambled back across the crest of the ridge.

The reason I sleep well in the desert is probably because I walk so much out there. Traveling over the land on foot is absolutely the best way to see the country—to scent its fragrance, feel its heat, and get to know its plants and animals; this simple activity is the great instructor of my life. I do my best thinking while walking—saving me countless thousands of dollars in occupational counseling, legal fees, and behavioral therapy. The Cabeza Prieta is my favorite place in the world to walk.

I didn't always do so much walking out on the Cabeza Prieta. My first trips out there, beginning in the late 1960s, were made in the usual fashion, driving a pickup across the Devil's Highway or easing a jeep up the sandy tracks of the spur roads. Most of these trips, and 90 percent of my several dozen nonsolo visits to the Cabeza Prieta, I made with two close friends named Ed: Ed Gage and Ed Abbey.

Later, when truck camping seemed tame and I needed a bit of adventure in my life, I decided to try to walk across the Cabeza Prieta alone. I would cover 120 to 165 miles each trip, depending on the route I took. Taking it easy, I could usually make the trip in about eleven days—ten nights free from insomnia, ten great nights of untroubled sleep.

In all, I've made seven of these trips, solo backpacking the area from Welton, Tacna, or the Tinajas Altas to Ajo, Organ Pipe, or Quitobaquito, and sometimes vice versa; always by different routes, crossing all the big valleys. Adding in my trips by vehicle, this means I've spent more than two hundred nights of my life sleeping out there.

On these desert treks I average from about twelve to twenty miles per day. The mileage I can cover depends on the terrain, on whether I am fasting or low on food, and if I'm walking during daylight or by moonlight. Anything over twenty miles tends to rub raw spots into my aging body or bruise my feet, especially when I'm carrying my full load of water: three and one-half gallons on the longer dry legs of the journey between the Sierra Pinta and Charlie Bell or Papago Well. My exact daily distance is whatever it takes to ensure the fatigue that banishes insomnia. Night walking is more exhausting because you need to brace yourself against injury; for instance, you have to lock your knees and ankles by tensing your quadriceps whenever you break through the honeycombed earth of rodent colonies under the creosote of the bajadas.

I keep crude journal notes of all this and record such things as tracks and sightings of bighorn sheep—a very big deal to me. Actually, on my walks I've seen few bighorn sheep, but then, as everyone knows, the best way to see sheep is to sit quietly, not to walk with your nose at the level of the creosote. I have, however, seen a lot of tracks.

What little I know of desert bighorn sheep is mostly inferred from these tracks and the few sheep sightings I've lucked into: to be exact, thirty-four bighorn sheep scattered throughout the desert ranges of the Cabeza Prieta during the past two decades. Ed Gage saw the first one just north of Cabeza Prieta Tanks back in the winter of 1972, one of our first trips together. He had been sitting on a ridgetop reading Kazantzakis when he heard rocks clattering on the slope above him. Gage looked up and saw a magnificent ram with a full curl amble down the ridge away from him, big scrotum swinging from side to side, he said, so he knew it was a ram (he had never seen a sheep before). The bighorn passed down the slope and disappeared below him.

My sheep count began in 1972 (I didn't see any the first three years) and ended in March 1992. Except for the ones I glimpsed from my sleeping bag, I saw all these sheep in precipitous terrain much like that of Gage's ram. My biggest count was a mixed herd of seven ewes and younger sheep one mile east of Half Way Tank in the Cabeza Prieta Mountains. Once I saw four rams bedded together and facing out in the four directions on a spur ridge running off the Sierra Pinta into the Tule Desert north of Sunday Pass. I've seen pairs of desert bighorns three times—in the Growlers, the Agua Dulce, and the Cabeza Prieta Mountains—and once I startled a group of three ewes near an outlier hill south of the Aguila Mountains. The rest of my sightings have all been of single animals.

The tracks are a different story. My field notes indicate behavior I have never witnessed: sheep crossing the big valleys and using the creosote-covered bajadas. I found sheep tracks crossing and recrossing the Tule Desert using the same route, from the mouth of Smoke Tree Wash east to Isla Pinta, during three different years. One of these crossings was made by a mixed herd of four or five ewes and two young ones. Other odd crossings include a ram from just south of Bean Pass trekking nonstop west along the Devil Hills to the north end of the Cabeza Prieta, a single sheep from the Agua Dulce by way of O'Neill Hills into the Pinta Sands, and two sets of bighorns tracks starting from an old, man-made pile of rocks, perhaps marking a very large grave, on the mideastern flank of the Granite Mountains across the Growler Valley and disappearing in the basaltic cobbles of the Growlers just north of Charlie Bell.

You would think bighorn sheep would be nervous out in these flats and open areas where they are vulnerable to predators. I've seen circumstantial sign of sheep predation only twice, and both times it involved mountain lions. Lions are not common in this low desert because their preferred prey, deer, come down here only infrequently. The first time I saw lion sign was on a trip with Ed Gage back in 1973 near one of the higher tanks of the Tinajas Altas; it consisted only of a recent lion track near a much older disarticulated bighorn skeleton. The other, seen while I was visiting Ed Abbey in 1990, was a dismembered carcass of a young sheep; there was indirect evidence that the bighorn had been cached, and I found lion scat and scrapings nearby.

The only times I've run into—actually I heard them—desert bighorns at night has been when the moon was big. Twice I was sitting quietly, and the other time I was backpacking by the light of the nearly full moon. I like to walk at night in the desert, especially when I'm having trouble sleeping. One such night, at the southern tip of the Copper Mountains, I heard the clatter of rolling rocks and the dull clank of hooves high on the slope. This racket had to be sheep moving on the hillside. What else could it be?

Sometimes I wonder how anybody ever manages to study desert sheep; I have enough trouble just seeing them. When I'm up north—in Montana, British Columbia, or Alaska—I see bighorn sheep all the time. I see them in the spring down low in the valleys when snow still clogs the passes and slopes. Later in the year I watch them feeding and bedding on grassy ridges and avalanche chutes above the timberline. Twice I've found sheep carcasses buried by grizzlies, and, though I have never seen a grizzly bear successfully chase and kill a bighorn, I once followed a big male grizzly in Glacier National Park who charged a herd of rams, scattering them up the scree and on up the cliffs behind Haystack Butte, where the bear turned back. Even as late as November, I sometimes linger in grizzly country and watch the big rams clash, the clank of their hollow horns resounding through the absorbent air of the snow-filled basins of the Rocky Mountain Front near Many Glacier.

I've never seen that sort of thing in the desert. One March, from a great distance, I watched a three-quarter-curl ram south of Growler Peak, probably browsing on lupine brush. At any rate, he was feeding; I couldn't be sure on what. During the spring of 1973 Ed Abbey and I found agave flowers in the Agua Dulce chewed off by sheep and the remains of smashed barrel cactus near Sunday Pass with sheep tracks all around. But what desert bighorns eat from day to day remains a mystery to me.

All this sheep lore doesn't add up to much when it's spread over thirty years. To me, the sudden appearance of desert bighorn sheep has always been a mystery, a blessing, sometimes a specter bearing just the edge of fear. Despite my cryptic field notes, my memory of sheep over the last three decades shrivels to those who roused me from my sleeping bag and startled me on the brilliant nights of the full moon. Those sheep, it seems, I had to earn. Even sheep sign can be a gift. It has been more than twenty years since Ed Gage and I found a sheep track outside a mine shaft southeast of Papago Well. Inside the fifty-year-old hole was an old case of dynamite, the nitroglycerin all sweated out and dangerously unstable. Nearby, at Bassarisc Tank, we found more sheep tracks and the paw print of a lion; suddenly, the entire desert was imbued with unseen power and danger.

During December 1974, Ed Abbey and I drove my pickup into the

Cabeza Prieta. Ed and I were unattached and without families at the time. We had spent a sniffling, lonely Christmas Eve at a topless bar in Tucson drinking whiskey. Thinking we could improve on that, we packed up and drove 150 miles west over Charlie Bell Pass into the Cabeza Prieta. We sipped beer all the way from Three Forks and were a tad plastered by the time we hit Charlie Bell Pass. We got my 1966 Ford truck stuck several times creeping down the dark, treacherous road to the well, hanging up the ass end of the truck, jacking it up in the dark, rocking it free, and then dropping down into the Growler Valley. We continued on for one more six-pack around the north end of the Granite Mountains, where we got stuck in the sand one last time, finally crawling into our sleeping bags shortly after midnight. At six in the morning a sheriff's search-and-rescue team roared up, looking for some high school kids that some criminal son of a bitch had hired to collect 20- and 40-mm brass military cartridges. When a helicopter flew over, this bastard drove off, ditching the kids. One of the kids, we later learned, died of thirst and exposure. The search team pulled us out of the sand and went on. Ed and I drove through Montrose Well west into the Mohawk Valley. At the low pass we found bighorn sheep tracks. Later, on New Year's Eve at Eagle Tank, it sleeted and snowed on us—an unusual occurrence. We stayed three days in the Sierra Pinta, then dropped south onto the black basalt of the Pinacate lava fields.

Years later, I followed the tracks of a desert sheep from the bottom of Temporal Pass in the Growler Mountains to the center of the Growler Wash, where I lost the trail. I had gotten out there by walking southwest from Ajo after I had taken the bus from Tucson. I had come on a one-way ticket purchased for me by Lisa, the woman I later married. The Greyhound Bus clerk had been reluctant to even sell her the ticket for me.

"Lady," the clerk had said to Lisa, "nobody buys a one-way ticket to Ajo."

From Ajo I shouldered my backpack and disappeared over the mine tailings, passing the camp of the O'odham hermit, Chico Shunie, just before daylight. It was dark again the next night when I reached the bottom of the Growler Valley. Even by the dim light of the moon I could see big pieces of Hohokam pottery and *Glycymeris* clamshells lying on the desert pavement—it was the "Lost City" of the Hohokam shell trekkers. From here in the Growler Valley, an ancient shell trail ran south to Bahia Adair on the Sea of Cortez and north to the Gila River near Picture Rocks, where desert sheep are the most common animal petroglyph motif. I lost the trail of the bighorn because of the darkness and because a rattlesnake nailed me in the calf that night, though the bite turned out to be a dry one. The next day, with a story to tell, I walked twenty miles to Papago Well, where Clarke and Ed Abbey were waiting for me.

Shortly after Gage's death, a mutual friend of ours contacted me. He was one of the cofounders of the Sanctuary Movement for Central American refugees, and he asked me to consider "taking over the Southwest Sector." This meant that I might illegally lead small groups of refugees, mostly from El Salvador, from Highway 2 in Mexico, north through the Cabeza Prieta, and up toward Interstate 8 or some other point where they could be picked up by vehicle.

I agonized long and hard over this decision. I had already begun my work with grizzly bears and was immersed in it. I also knew a lot about myself from my exposure to the radical politics of the 1960s and my time in Vietnam. It was clear that this kind of effort was one where my talents did not lie. There was also the danger of overcommitting and exhausting myself. Nevertheless, this was something I could do, and it needed doing.

The dilemma tore at me and I couldn't sleep. Once again, I went into the Cabeza Prieta to slumber and to track the sign that would show me what to do. The bus dropped me on the Tacna off-ramp. I shouldered my backpack draped with three-gallon canteens and staggered into the creosote, headed toward Mexico. I skirted the Copper Mountains, passed Buck Mountain, and, at the mouth of A-1 Wash, I found the corrugated remains of a giant set of ram's horns. The next morning I followed another sheep's tracks south up the wash until I passed over the tiny divide into the inner valley north of the tanks where Gage had seen his ram.

Sooner or later everyone runs into death, and I ran into a lot of it early on. And so I have used this great desert to bargain with the departed and get a handle on my insomnia. It's true, I invent ceremonies when necessary, especially when my own culture provides none; I erect my own memorials and celebrate my own Day of the Dead. But mostly I just shoulder a backpack and walk beyond fatigue across the bajadas, maybe crossing a set of sheep tracks and following them up a wash, finding a perfect campsite. The story of this place is not of loss but renewal.

The Cabeza Prieta desert is the most important thing Ed Abbey, Ed

Gage, and I ever shared, and it is no coincidence that these two closest desert friends from the past two decades are out there now. Gage's death was a tough one because he was a suicide. I maintain a secret and no doubt illegal memorial for him on a hilltop in one of these desert valleys. Each year for the past seven years I have hiked to this monument and held a private ceremony.

The last time Ed Abbey smiled was when I told him where he was going to be buried. I smile too when I think of this small favor, this last simple task friends can do for one another—the rudimentary shovel work, the sweaty labor consummating trust, and finally testing the exact confirmation by lying down in the freshly dug grave to check out the view: the bronze patina of boulder behind limb of palo verde and turquoise sky, beyond branch of torote. It was then that I received a sign: seven buzzards soaring above, who were soon joined by three others, all ten banking over the volcanic rubble and riding the thermal up the flank of the mountain, gliding out and over the distant valley.

Even now, years after his death, I grin when I crest the ridge above his grave. The earth falls away and mountain ranges stretch off into the gray distance as far as the eye can see; there is not a human sign or sound, only a faint desert breeze stirring the blossoms of brittle-bush. We should all be so lucky.

On the eve of March 16, I journeyed to the edge of this desert place. March 16 is a "Day of the Dead" for me, the anniversary of the My Lai massacre (I was twenty miles away in Vietnam that day) and also the day in 1989 that three friends and I buried Ed Abbey here, illegally, in accordance with his last wishes.

I had traveled out here alone to Ed's grave, bearing little gifts, including a bottle of mescal and a bowl of pozole verde I had made myself. I sat quietly on the black volcanic rocks listening to the desert silence, pouring mescal over the grave and down my throat until the moon came up an hour or so before midnight. Suddenly I heard a commotion to the south, the roar of basaltic scree thundering down the slope opposite me. A large solitary animal was headed my way.

I got the hell out of there.

Two days later I told my story of the desert bighorn ram I heard but never saw to my poet friend Jim Harrison.

"Well, Doug," Jim said, "maybe it was old Ed."

ABOUT THE EDITOR

GARY PAUL NABHAN is a cofounder and Research Director of Native Seeds/ SEARCH, a grass-roots conservation organization which works with traditional agriculture and wild plant conservation efforts throughout the binational Southwest. He currently serves as writer-in-residence at the Arizona–Sonora Desert Museum and as research associate in plant conservation for Conservation International. Nabhan received his undergraduate degree from Prescott College and his master of science and Ph.D. degrees from the University of Arizona, where he studied the ethnobiology of desert peoples. He has received numerous honors, including the John Burroughs Medal for nature writing, the Premio Gaia Award toward a culture of the environment, a MacArthur Fellowship, and a Pew Scholarship on Conservation and Environment. The father of two young naturalists, he currently lives with his wife, Caroline Wilson, in Stinking Hot Desert National Monument, a mirage somewhere in the desert borderlands between the United States and Mexico.